TERRORISM AND DEMOCRACY

Terrorism and Democracy

Some Contemporary Cases

**Report of a Study Group of
the David Davies Memorial Institute
of International Studies**

Edited by
Peter Janke

Introduction by
Sir Anthony Parsons

St. Martin's Press   New York

© The David Davies Memorial Institute of International Studies 1992

All rights reserved. For information, write:
Scholarly and Reference Division,
St. Martin's Press, Inc., 175 Fifth Avenue,
New York, N.Y. 10010

First published in the United States of America in 1992

Printed in Great Britain

ISBN 0–312–06822–0

Library of Congress Cataloging-in-Publication Data
Terrorism and democracy:some contemporary cases:report of a study
group of the David Davies Memorial Institute of International
Studies/edited by Peter Janke;introduction by Sir Anthony
Parsons.
p.   cm.
Includes index.
ISBN 0–312–06822–0
1. Terrorism—Case studies.   I. Janke, Peter.   II. David Davies
Memorial Institute of International Studies.
HV6431.T4613   1992
363.3'2—dc20   91–31619
                                                  CIP

Contents

Members of the Study Group

CHAIRMAN

Sir Anthony Parsons GCMG, LVO, MC   Retired from the Diplomatic Service in 1982, he is now an Honorary Research Fellow in the Centre for Arab Gulf Studies at Exeter University. His diplomatic career was spent largely in the Middle East and the United Nations. He was Under-Secretary at the Foreign Office with responsibility for the Middle East from 1971 to 1974 at a time when terrorist activity in the region was at its height, and he was Ambassador to Iran from 1974 to 1979. His last posting was as UK Permanent Representative to the United Nations from 1979 to 1982. After retirement he became special adviser to the Prime Minister on foreign affairs until 1984 when he took up, until 1987, the post of Lecturer in Modern Middle East History at Exeter University and Research Fellow in its Gulf Centre. He has written two books on the Middle East, and is a frequent contributor to newspapers and television on events in that region and elsewhere.

RAPPORTEUR

Dr Peter Janke   Received his doctorate in history at Oxford in 1973 for research into the growth of constitutional government in Spain and Portugal. After a period working with the BBC external services he joined the Institute for the Study of Conflict, London, where he became Head of Research (1975–80). In 1981 he joined Control Risks Ltd, London, where he is Research and Projects Director. In that capacity he leads a team of regional experts whose task is to analyse political stability and the security risk to corporate personnel, fixed assets and investments in countries all over the world. He was the co-ordinator and British participant in the International Commission on Violence in the Basque country, which reported to the Basque government in Spain in 1986. He lectures at the Royal College of Defence Studies and is the author of *Guerrilla and Terrorist Organizations: A World Directory and Bibliography* (1983).

Peter Calvocoressi   Called to the Bar in 1935, he worked for British Intelligence on Ultra Intelligence during the Second World War and attended the Nuremberg Trials (1945–6). He was on the staff of the Royal Institute of International Affairs from 1949 to 1954 and wrote many of their *Annual Surveys*. He was Reader in International Relations at Sussex University from 1965 to 1971 and a member of the Council of the International Institute for Strategic Studies from 1961 to 1971. From 1962 to 1971 he was a member of the UN Sub-Commission on the Prevention of Discrimination and the Protection of Minorities, Chairman of the Africa Bureau from 1963 to 1971 and a member of the International Executive of Amnesty International from 1969 to 1971. He has been a partner in Chatto and Windus and the Hogarth Press (1954–65), Editorial Director and Chief Executive of Penguin Books (1972–6), and Chairman of Open University's Educational Enterprises (1980–9). He has written many books on recent history.

Major-General Richard Clutterbuck CB, OBE, PhD   Served in the British Army for 35 years, retiring in 1972. During this time he was involved in four anti-terrorist operations including those in Palestine and Malaya. He took his MA at Cambridge University in 1939 and his PhD at London University in 1971, whilst still in the army. He taught International Politics and Political Violence at Exeter University from 1972 to 1983. He was a member of the BBC General Advisory Council from 1975 to 1981. He has advised, and continues to advise, a number of governments and multinational corporations on political risks and combating terrorism, and gives lectures all over the world. He has written fifteen books including *The Media and Political Violence* (1983), *Conflict and Violence in Singapore and Malaysia* (1985), *Kidnap, Hijack and Extortion* (1987), *Terrorism and Guerrilla Warfare: Forecasts and Remedies* (1990) and *Terrorism, Drugs and Crime in Europe after 1992* (1990).

Sheila Harden   Director of the David Davies Memorial Institute of International Studies since January 1984. Worked in Naval Office Trincomalee from 1939 to 1942 and in the Admiralty from 1943 to 1946. She joined the staff of the Royal Institute of International Affairs in 1947 working first in the Asian section and then as assistant to Peter Calvocoressi on the 1947–8 and 1949–50 *Annual Surveys*. Joined the diplomatic service in 1952 and retired in 1981. Most of her diplomatic career was spent in the UK Mission to the United Nations. She served on five visiting Missions to the Trust Territory of the Pacific Islands, chairing two, and was President of the Trusteeship Council 1979–80.

Dr Dirk Mulder After studying medicine at the Municipal University, Amsterdam, he joined the army. After leaving the army, with the rank of colonel, he specialized in neurology and psychiatry and rose to become the psychiatric adviser to the Dutch Department of Justice. He was negotiator and adviser in seven well-publicized terrorist and criminal cases. He was president of the Dutch government's council 'Victims of Violence', and president of the Government committee on 'Psychiatric/Therapeutic Treatment in the Penitentiary System'. He has recently been a consultant to the Council of Europe's 'Committee of Present Day Violence'. He is the co-author of a book *People at Hostage-Takings*. Since July 1984 he has been a private counsellor and adviser, based in Spain.

Desmond O'Brien OBE, FBIM Chief Constable of the British Transport Police. He began his police service in the Royal Ulster Constabulary (RUC), becoming Chief Superintendent in 1974. He was subsequently appointed to the teaching staff of the National Police Staff College, Bramshill, where he ran exercises on multi-agency contingency planning to manage major terrorist incidents for police forces world-wide. From 1975 to 1978 he was in charge of the Anti-Sectarian Murder Squad and Special Patrol Group in Northern Ireland. In 1978 he became Assistant Chief Constable in the Greater Manchester Police. In 1982 he was a member of the National Working Group at New Scotland Yard which produced the *Tactical Options Manual* which is the standard reference book of its kind for police in England and Wales. From 1983 to 1989 he was Deputy Chief Constable of Kent County Constabulary.

Dr Claire Palley The Principal of St Anne's College, Oxford, since 1984. Born in South Africa, she took Law degrees at the University of Cape Town and a London PhD in 1965. She lectured at the University of Cape Town and the University College of Rhodesia and Nyasaland, becoming Professor of Public Law at the Queen's University of Belfast and later at the University of Kent, Canterbury. She advised the African National Council of Rhodesia in 1975–6 in Salisbury and at Geneva and has been adviser to the Republic of Cyprus since 1979. A Council member of the Minority Rights Group since 1976, in 1988 she became a member of the UN Sub-Commission on the Prevention of Discrimination and the Protection of Minorities. She has acted as consultant on minorities, human rights and public order law questions to international organizations and has written books on Rhodesia and Northern Ireland.

The Rt Hon. Merlyn Rees MP   Member of Parliament (Labour Party) since 1963, having previously been a teacher of economics. From 1964 to 1970 he was Minister for the Army, Minister for the Royal Air Force and Under-Secretary of State at the Home Office. From 1974 to 1976 he was the Secretary of State for Northern Ireland and became Home Secretary in 1976. Since the Conservative Party came to power in 1979, he has been the Shadow Home Secretary, Shadow Energy Secretary and Co-ordinator of Economic Affairs. He was a member of the Franks Select Committee on the Official Secrets Act in 1972 and in 1982 served on the Franks Select Committee on the Origins of the Falklands War. He is Chairman of the All Party Group on War Crimes.

Abbreviations

AD	Action Directe – Direct Action (France)
ALQ	Armée de Libération du Québec–Quebec Liberation Army
API	Alliance of Ambonese Youth for the Republic of Indonesia
BAS	Befreiungsausschuss Südtirol – South Tyrol Freedom Committee
BBE	Bijzondere Bijstands Eenheden – Special Assistance Units (Netherlands)
BfV	Bundesampt für Verfassungsschutz – Federal Office for the Protection of the Constitution (FRG)
BKA	Bundeskriminalampt – Federal Criminal Agency (FRG)
BR	Brigate Rosse – Red Brigades (Italy)
BVD	Binnenlandse Veiligheidsdienst – Department of Internal Security (Netherlands)
CATS	Combined Anti-Terrorist Squad (Canada)
CBC	Canadian Broadcasting Corporation
CDU	Christliche Demokratische Union – Christian Democratic Union (FRG)
CESIS	Comitato Esecutivo per i Servizi di Informazione e di Sicurezza – Executive Committee for the Intelligence and Security Services (Italy)
CIS	Comitato sulle Informazioni e la Sicurezza – Inter-ministerial Committee for Security (Italy)
CP	Command Post (Netherlands)
CRI	Centrale Recherche Informatsiedienst – Central Investigation Information Service (Netherlands)
CSN	Central des Syndicats Nationaux (Quebec)
DC	Democratici Cristiani – Christian Democratic Party (Italy)
DIGOS	Divisione Indagini Generali e Operazioni Speciali – Division for General Investigations and Special Operations (Italy)
ETA	Euskadi ta Askatasuna – Freedom for the Basque Homeland (Spain)

FLN	Front de Libération Nationale – National Liberation Front (Algeria)
FLP	Front de Libération Populaire – Popular Liberation Front (Canada)
FLQ	Front de Libération du Québec – Quebec Liberation Front
GIS	Gruppi di Intervento Speciali – Special Intervention Groups (Italy)
ICBZ	Informatsie Centrum Bijzondere Zaken – Information Centre for Special Affairs (Netherlands)
IRA	Irish Republican Army
JRA	Japanese Red Army
KNIL	Kaninklijk Nederlands Indisch Leger – Royal Dutch Indian Army
KPK	Korps Penjagaan Keamanaan – Corps for the Maintenance of Order (South Moluccans)
LBT	Landelijk Bijstandsteam Terreurbestrijding – National Support Group against Terrorism (Netherlands)
MSI	Movimento Sociale Italiano – Italian Social Movement
NAP	Nuclei Armati Proletari – Armed Proletarian Nuclei (Italy)
NAPAP	Noyaux Armés pour l'Autonomie Populaire – Armed Nuclei for Popular Autonomy (France)
NOCS	Nucleo Operativo Centrale Sicurezza – Central Operative Nuclei for Security (Italy)
OAS	Organisation de l'Armée Secrète (Algeria)
OVP	Oesterreichische Volkspartei – Austrian People's Party
P2	Propaganda 2 (Masonic Lodge) (Italy)
PC	Policy Centre (Netherlands)
PCI	Partito Communista Italiano – Italian Communist Party
PFLP	Popular Front for the Liberation of Palestine
PL	Prima Linea – Front Line (Italy)
PLO	Palestine Liberation Organization
PMO	Prime Minister's Office
PQ	Parti Québécois – Quebec Party
PSI	Partito Socialista Italiano – Italian Socialist Party
RAF	Rote Armee Fraktion – Red Army Faction (FRG)
RCMP	Royal Canadian Mounted Police
RIN	Rassemblement pour l'Indépendance Nationale – Assembly for National Independence (Quebec)

RMS	Republika Moluku Selatan – Independent Republic of South Molucca
SID	Servizio Informazioni Difesa – Defence Information Service (Italy)
SIFAR	Servizio Informazioni Forze Armati – Armed Forces Information Service (Italy)
SISDE	Servizio Informazioni Sicurezza Democratica – Service for Intelligence and Democratic Security (Italy)
SISMI	Servizio Informazioni Sicurezza Militare – Service for Military Intelligence and Security (Italy)
SOC	Strategic Operations Centre (Canada)
SPD	Sozialistische Partei Deutschlands – German Socialist Party
SPO	Sozialistische Partei Oesterreichs – Austrian Socialist Party
SVP	Südtiroler Volkspartei – South Tyrol People's Party
UCIGOS	Ufficio Centrale Indagini Generale e Operazioni Special – Central Office for General Investigations and Special Operations (Italy)
VOC	Verenigde Oostindische Compagny – United East India Trade Company
WMA	War Measures Act (Canada)

Introduction

The David Davies Memorial Institute decided that it would be timely and useful for policy makers and others concerned with the subject to commission a study of instances in which politically motivated violence – terrorism – had been successfully combated in First World democracies in the post-1945 period by political, legislative, judicial and police action. The study was deliberately confined to democracies since the methods used to suppress alleged terrorist revolts in totalitarian countries would be unacceptable to democratic states.

The purpose was to consider in each case studied the short-term steps taken to stop the violence and protect those at risk, and the longer-term policies which contributed to the subsequent loss of support for the terrorist movements under consideration. It was hoped that lessons would emerge which might help governments to recognize potential terrorist situations and tackle the underlying causes at an early stage.

Accordingly, the Institute assembled an interdisciplinary group (composition on pp. vii–x) to carry out this study, the results to be published. The Study Group held seven meetings. This book is the outcome of those deliberations.

The book comprises six case studies, one on each of the following subjects: terrorism in the South Tyrol (Alto Adige), Canada and the Quebec Liberation Front (FLQ), South Moluccan terrorism in the Netherlands, the German Red Army Faction (RAF), the Italian Red Brigades (BR), and the Japanese Red Army (JRA). These chapters are based on original reports written for the Group by specialists, namely Professor Anthony Alcock, Dr Randall Heather, Dr Dirk Mulder (who was also a member of the Study Group), Dr Hans Horchem, Alison Jamieson and Professor Nobuhiko Suto. The Group wishes to express its thanks to them for their valuable contributions to the study. The case studies are followed by a chapter on social and psychological aspects of certain terrorists, on the basis of concepts developed by Study Group member Dr Mulder, and the study concludes with a chapter drawing lessons for the future from the incidents reviewed in the case studies.

At the outset it was agreed that the study would exclude political violence experienced by First World democracies in dependent territories in the process of decolonization. The case studies eventually chosen

by the Group were selected as being representative of the main types
of terrorism experienced today in the democratic world including, as
they do, three cases of ideologically inspired terrorism (Japan, Italy
and Germany); one case of recent Third World immigrants (the South
Moluccans); and two that are the consequence of earlier territorial
settlements which left substantial minorities under the domination of
ethnically and culturally distinct majorities (Canada and the South
Tyrol).

We decided not to include a case study from the largest Western
democracy, namely the United States of America. There have been
a number of instances of political terrorism in that country during
the post-1945 period, notably the Black Power Movement, Puerto
Rican separatists, and ideologically motivated groups such as the
Weathermen. However, possibly due to the vast size and disparate
nature of the United States, possibly due also to the lack of ideological
polarization in the mainstream political culture, none of the movements
mentioned, or any others, even though they achieved nation-wide prominence through the media, caused the state to galvanize its own
democratic defence in quite the same way as did their counterparts
in the other First World democracies considered by the Group.

The Group provided the authors of the case studies with comprehensive guidelines on which to base their reports, which were subsequently
discussed and edited. The two final chapters were prepared and agreed
within the Group itself.

When the final chapter was first conceived, the Group was thinking
in terms of possible lessons to be learnt in Western democracies and
Japan. However, the astonishing developments in the Soviet Union
and Eastern Europe since late 1989 have greatly widened the relevance
of the study. It is certain that the number of democracies – in Europe
and perhaps elsewhere too – is set to increase. These new democracies
will be no more immune than the old to terrorism. They contain similar
ethnic, social and other tensions, which will nourish violent as well
as non-violent protest, so that the analysis and criticism present in
this book will be broadly relevant over more and more of the world,
particularly in parts of the world where hitherto protest has been met
only by brute force and the counter-terrorism of the state. Our studies,
therefore, could prove to be of singular use to these emerging democratic countries.

Over the past 40 years or so, centralized, totalitarian control has
insulated the communist world from the currents which led to outbreaks of indigenous terrorism in the West, namely the student and

radical left- and right-wing movements, as well as ethnic unrest.

Now that the glacier is melting, a new landscape is emerging. In the established nation states of Eastern Europe, there are latent problems analogous to those considered in the case studies. The changes in the map of Europe following the Second World War in many cases separated ethnic minorities from their natural homelands, as happened with the South Tyrol after the First World War. There are distinct ethnic and linguistic, also religious, communities within many East European states which can be compared to the French Canadians or the Spanish Basques. In certain states, there could be militant left- and right-wing ideological outbreaks similar to those which have bedevilled Italy.

In the Soviet Union itself, the nationalities problem is closer to the classic drive for decolonization, with many of the republics aiming at full independence, as was the case with the Hapsburg, Ottoman and West European empires. However, some of the Soviet territories are contiguous with ethnically homogenous independent states, a situation which could stimulate terrorism on the Northern Ireland pattern. The displacement of communities which occurred in the Stalinist era could also generate violence. Some of these undercurrents have already manifested themselves, short of terrorism, in the form of demonstrations, mob violence and the emergence of Popular Fronts.

All the factors which gave rise to this study are thus present below the surface in Eastern Europe and the Soviet Union. Assuming that the flight from communist totalitarianism to genuine democracy continues, it is reasonable to suppose that the authorities in question will be both disposed, and under popular pressure, to deal with such problems, if they arise, within the framework of democratic constraints rather than by ruthless repression. However, both they and the forces of law and order at their disposal are likely to be unfamiliar with the various democratic policies and procedures which have been successfully used elsewhere.

SIR ANTHONY PARSONS

1 Terrorism in South Tyrol

Before the 1914–18 war, Italy had long coveted the part of the Austrian Crown Land of Tyrol lying to the south of the Brenner Pass, comprising today's Italian provinces of South Tyrol and Trento. It wished to unite the almost entirely Italian-speaking population of Trento with the rest of Italy, and to gain the strong military barrier against the German-speaking world that the Brenner frontier would provide. Having entered the war on the winning side, Italian troops took over not only Trento but also South Tyrol, where 86 per cent of the population of 250,000 were German-speaking and only 4 per cent Ladin and 8 per cent Italian.[1] In 1920, South Tyrol was formally incorporated into Italy, without a plebiscite to obtain the consent of the population.

The Italians argued that the South Tyrol belonged to Italy since it was on the Mediterranean side of the Alpine watershed, and that South Tyrol and Trento were one geographically. Moreover, since most of the people in the area as a whole were Italians (there being more Italians in Trento than South Tyrolese in South Tyrol), they claimed that there were democratic grounds for saying that the territory should go to Italy. Nevertheless, some South Tyrolese still feel that the failure to hold a plebiscite to let the people decide their own destiny was a flagrant act of political injustice, and that this justifies terrorism.

UNDER THE FASCISTS

When the Fascists governed Italy their policy towards the South Tyrolese was to de-Germanize them and turn them into Italians. The German language was forbidden in schools, public offices and courts. Those officials not knowing Italian were dismissed, and their places were taken by Italians from other parts of Italy. Place-names and public inscriptions could only be in Italian.

In addition, Mussolini set up an Industrial Zone in Bolzano, the capital of South Tyrol, and thousands of new Italian workers and their families arrived. By 1939 the population of the province had risen to 335000 of which 72 per cent were German, 24 per cent Italian and 3 per cent Ladin.[2] Four years later, following the departure of some South Tyrolese to Germany as a result of a German–Italian agreement, and their replacement by more Italians, the proportions

1

had become 64 per cent German and Ladin and 36 per cent Italian.[3]

As a result of the fascist policy, an entire generation of South Tyrolese political, administrative and intellectual leaders were eliminated, and South Tyrolese and Italians became sharply divided economically and socially. Italians lived almost exclusively in the big cities like Bolzano and Merano. They had a higher standard of living, better-paid jobs and full employment, while the South Tyrolese stayed huddled on the land, with its poor alpine economy. Some of the South Tyrolese took their revenge on the Italians when the Germans took over the province in the period between the fall of Fascism in 1943 and the end of the 1939–45 war. This led to their being labelled nazis after the war.

THE PEACE SETTLEMENT

When peace came, the South Tyrolese were bitterly disappointed to learn that the Allies were not going to grant them self-determination. However, the new democratic Italian government announced that it would give South Tyrol an autonomy which would safeguard its ethnic character and cultural and economic development. The Allies were delighted by this solution and promoted the De Gasperi–Gruber Agreement, signed in September 1946 by the Foreign Ministers of Italy and Austria. Almost everything that has occurred in South Tyrol since then has had its origins in this Agreement.

The South Tyrolese were granted primary and secondary school education in German; 'parification' of the German and Italian languages in public offices, official documents and place names; and 'equality of rights' in public service recruitment to produce a balance of employment between the two ethnic groups. They were further promised autonomous legislative and executive 'regional' power, and that the 'framework' for autonomy would be drafted in consultation with the South Tyrolese. This vague wording meant that implementation would lie in the hands of the stronger party – Italy.

The Austrians did not renounce South Tyrol in return. There was a tremendous outcry in Austria and South Tyrol against the Agreement, and it was made clear that, in spite of the Agreement, self-determination was still on the agenda. It was another 18 months before the autonomy statute resulting from the De Gasperi–Gruber Agreement was promulgated.

According to the Italian system of regional government, regions have primary, secondary and tertiary legislative powers. Under primary legislative power, with certain limitations including the need to observe national interests, the region may issue laws in fields stated explicitly in the autonomy statute. Under secondary legislative power, the region may issue laws in fields stated in the statute which, in addition to having to observe the limitations mentioned, must also observe the fundamental principles of state laws already enacted in those fields. Tertiary legislative power merely gives the regions the right to adopt or integrate the provisions of existing state laws into the regional or provincial statute book.

Part of the background to the 1948 autonomy statute was that, although the state and the regions normally exercised their executive functions by delegating them to the provinces, municipal authorities or other local public bodies, there were no limits to the ability of the state to decide what were 'national interests', or to adopt programmes of economic and social reform which might invalidate regional legislation. In addition, the validity of laws passed by the regions had first to be checked by the government commissioner of the territory concerned and then sent to Rome, where they would be checked again to ensure that they did not need Cabinet decrees. And although the regions had some small sources of revenue, when it came to big programmes of economic and social development there was only one body which had the financial means: the state.

The Austrian and South Tyrolese support for self-determination alarmed all Italian political, governmental and administrative circles, so the autonomy statute specifically aimed at ensuring that South Tyrol remained not only with Italy, but as Italian as possible. In particular, it was intended that the economic and social development of the South Tyrolese should remain in the hands of Italians, and that any developments should not be at the expense of the Italian community. In December 1946 the population of South Tyrol was 311,000 – 63.3 per cent German, 3.9 per cent Ladin and 32.8 per cent Italian – but 80 per cent of the Italian population lived in the provincial capital Bolzano and its neighbouring communes.[4]

Under the autonomy statute the province of South Tyrol received its autonomous legislative and executive powers within the framework of a region, Trentino–Alto Adige, which consisted of the two provinces of Trento and Bolzano (South Tyrol). Since Trento had, as in 1920, the larger population, which was practically 100 per cent Italian, and since a third of South Tyrol's population was Italian, the ethnic composition of the region was two-thirds Italian and a third German and Ladin.

A second and decisive feature was that it was the region and not the provinces which exercised primary legislative power over agriculture and forestry, tourism and the hotel trade; it had secondary legislative power over industry and commerce. The two provinces had primary legislative power only over housing and matters such as place-names, handicrafts, fairs and markets, first aid and accident services. When the state rejected regional or provincial laws there could be an appeal to the Constitutional Court, though provinces had to obtain the permission of their region to impugn state laws.

The South Tyrolese leaders accepted the statute after minimum consultation, but nevertheless signed a letter saying that with the statute '... the De Gasperi–Gruber Agreement ... has been translated into reality in so far as the fundamental problem of the autonomy is concerned'.[5]

THE BOMBINGS BEGIN

The first bombs thrown in September 1956 caught the Italian public and government completely by surprise, because the South Tyrolese representatives in the national parliament – only three deputies and two senators – were disregarded. Also, within the province language was a barrier. Among the Italians who lived there, very few indeed spoke German. It was the 1961 bombs that made Italians generally aware of the existence of a problem.

Italians were still massively concentrated in the big urban centres of Bolzano, Merano and Bressonone (Brixen), and involved in the administration and in the Industrial Zone. Of the 16 communes in South Tyrol only five had Italian majorities, and most of the Italians who lived outside these five were in the panhandle of South Tyrol linking Bolzano with the province of Trento. In the great valleys of Val Venosta (Vinschgau) and Val Pusteria (Pustertal), the only Italians were the *carabinieri*. A further factor in the lack of understanding was the very negative view that the groups in South Tyrol had of each other.

South Tyrolese representation and leadership were concentrated in one political party, the *Südtiroler Volkspartei* (SVP). In 1980 the party had 70,000 members, 35 per cent of the South Tyrolese ethnic electorate of 200,000 and more than 23 per cent of the entire provincial electorate.[6] In 1988 the number had risen to 80,000. Small splinter groups have frequently appeared, but the SVP has always enjoyed the confidence of the South Tyrolese people.

The South Tyrolese, who still lived overwhelmingly on the land, wanted to correct the imbalance and develop with their homeland, finding jobs in the towns, in commerce and industry and in the administration. The three key points were vocational training and housing, which were within the primary legislative competence of the province, and the administration which seemed to have been covered by the De Gasperi–Gruber Agreement.

Vocational training was important to enable the South Tyrolese to compete for jobs. Italy in the 1950s was enjoying a boom, and the jobs were going not so much to Italians already in the province as to top Italians immigrating from elsewhere in Italy; this upset the existing two-thirds/one-third ethnic balance. And if South Tyrolese were to take jobs in industry, commerce and the administration, there would be a need for housing programmes capable of providing many units. When it came to financing the programmes, however, it was not the province but the state that found the money.

As for the administration, there were three types of public employment: the provincial administration; institutions of the state operating in the province, such as the post and the state railways; and semi-state bodies, such as social security and insurance companies. Posts in these areas were almost entirely filled by non-German-speaking Italians; although the De Gasperi–Gruber Agreement had spoken of 'equality of rights' in public service, German-speakers had little hope against competition from all over Italy. If South Tyrolese did not get these posts, their homeland would continue to be administered by non-German-speakers, and as incomers arrived the ethnic balance would change. On the other hand, the reverse discrimination needed to maintain the ethnic balance would offend against merit and 'equality of rights'.

HOW THE AUTONOMY STATUTE WORKED

The statute laid down that the region and the province of Bolzano (South Tyrol) had to be governed by institutionalized power-sharing between the two main language groups. The Cabinet which governed the region was two-thirds Italian and a third German. The ratio was reversed in the provincial Cabinet, which in the 1950s had six members, four South Tyrolese and two Italians; in the 1970s the total number of members rose to ten (with a ratio of 7:3), and in 1989 there were

15 (10:5). The increase has reflected not only the increase in seats in the provincial parliament, but also the increased autonomy of the province after 1970.[7]

Cabinet members had to agree on a joint programme, and since 1948 the province has been governed by a coalition of the SVP and, mainly, the Christian Democratic Party (DC), representing the Italian-speakers. The SVP has had an absolute majority in all the provincial parliaments since 1948, but its particular fear is that the Italian-speaking vote will bring to power either the Communists or the ultra-right Italian Social Movement (MSI). In the 1985 communal elections the MSI polled 22.6 per cent in Bolzano, and became the largest party in the city council; those results caused a sensation throughout the country and particularly shocked the South Tyrolese.

It was frustration with the narrow implementation of the autonomy statute that led the South Tyrolese to resort to violence in 1956. There were four chief grievances:

i) The ethnic imbalance in state and semi-state bodies. The Italian position was upheld by the Constitutional Court, so that the province continued to be largely administered by non-German-speakers.

ii) The government dragged its feet in enabling the province to legislate in matters on which it had primary legislative power. Attempts to go ahead and adopt laws regardless were rejected by Rome.

iii) The state did not sufficiently delegate the administrative powers relating to matters on which the province could legislate. Again, the government in Rome rejected attempts to pass provincial laws to govern administrative functions. When challenged, the failure by either the state or the region to delegate these powers was upheld by the Constitutional Court.

iv) The South Tyrolese believed that they had primary legislative power over housing, and therefore looked to the state to provide money for housing programmes agreed by the province. But the state went ahead with its own programmes, and assigned housing to Italians.

In 1954 the SVP leaders sent to Rome a detailed memorandum setting out their complaints about the fulfilment of the autonomy statute. Two extracts reveal how the South Tyrolese felt about the meaning of protection of minorities, and about their treatment at the hands of the Italians:

> For the protection of minorities one needs equality, but this equality must be more than formal ... it must also be effective, and this means that the minority should have the faculty and possibility of satisfying its own interests and spiritual, cultural, economic, administrative and political needs with means as effective as those used by the majority. There is no greater inequality than to treat unequal things equally. Therefore special laws to protect a minority are not privileges but measures to create this material equality between majority and minority.

and

> Every time we affirm the existence of a particular   interest or request ... there is a search to find if there is a law that grants a right to what we ask; if one is not found, the request is refused.

Rome sent no official reply to the SVP memorandum. Instead, an indirect reply appeared in the province's leading Italian daily newspaper, *Alto Adige*. After pouring scorn on the fears of the South Tyrolese and their interpretation of minority protection, as well as refuting the various claims made in the memorandum, the author accused the South Tyrolese of wanting to clear the Italians out of South Tyrol and turn it into a South Tyrolese national park.

THE SEARCH FOR SUPPORT ABROAD

Considering that nothing further was to be gained, Canon Gamper, editor of the South Tyrolese daily *Dolomiten*, travelled to North Tyrol in Austria and set up the *Berg–Isel Bund* in Innsbruck. The Bund was to act as an umbrella organization for the protection of South Tyrolese interests. It included members of both of Austria's largest political parties, the Austrian People's Party (OVP) and the Austrian Socialist Party (SPO), academics, journalists and civil servants, and its first chairman was the North Tyroler Dr Franz Gschnitzer, the Austrian Secretary of State for Foreign Affairs.

In 1956 Gamper travelled to Munich, and there set up another organization, *Kulturwerk für Südtirol*, to co-ordinate help for South Tyrol in West Germany. This organization became prominent in sending money to South Tyrol to help social and cultural causes among the

South Tyrolese. Later, the Italians were convinced that it provided money for terrorist activities as well. Their suspicions were founded on the fact that the organization soon became closely linked to extreme right-wing groups, particularly *Sudeten* German. Many such groups had emerged in Austria and West Germany with the objectives of supporting ethnic Germans still in Eastern Europe and reclaiming lands considered to be ethnically German. Sudetenland was the chief target and the *Sudeten* Germans in exile were the best organized, the most vocal, and the best off in terms of funds.

South Tyrol became caught up in the whole issue of German homelands. *Sudeten* groups began to hold school, youth and holiday camps in South Tyrol to make contact with their German kin, and so did other groups, Austrian as well as German, with a pan-German or neo-nazi orientation. They believed that Italians could be terrorized out of South Tyrol and that this would create the conditions for a successful appeal for self-determination which would be a precedent for all former German lands.

On 15 September 1956 the Italian President and the Minister of the Interior visited Bolzano. The latter declared that there was no South Tyrol problem and that the Bolzano Industrial Zone should be encouraged to develop. Less than a week later bombs blew up electric pylons on the Bolzano – Merano railway line.

Further attacks, against electric pylons and railway lines, occurred intermittently in the period up to January 1957. The perpetrators, arrested later that month, were a group of 14 South Tyrolese led by Hans Stieler, today chairman of the politically-extreme Heimat Bund (Homeland Association). Their bombings were in protest at the lack of progress towards autonomy, and were aimed at drawing the attention of the international press to South Tyrol. The group had approached the *Berg–Isel Bund* for money for explosives, but the Bund's leaders were divided: the politicians were against helping in this way, while the others favoured it as long as the attacks did not involve loss of life. It was agreed that there should be demonstrations which would give Dr Gschnitzer the opportunity to raise the matter with the Italian government, and in October 1956 the Austrian government intervened officially, sending a memorandum to Rome giving its reasons for dissatisfaction with implementation of the De Gasperi–Gruber Agreement. In February 1957 the Italian government rejected the Austrian claims.

Eight months later, the political situation in South Tyrol deteriorated sharply, and not long afterwards terrorism began in earnest in 1959.

TERRORISM SPREADS

By 1956 much of the SVP leadership that had 'negotiated' the autonomy statute had been ousted, and the new leader was Silvius Magnago. In February 1956 he presented to the Italian government a draft statute for a new autonomy. It called for South Tyrol to be a region in its own right with exclusive legislative power over all sectors of the economy including residence regulations and automatic administrative powers in all fields where the province was to have legislative powers; it also stipulated that only those with five years' residence should be able to vote in regional and communal elections. The draft was supported in Austria but the Italians saw it as creating a state within a state prior to the closing down of the Industrial Zone and the ejection of the Italian population.

The issue that brought matters to a head was housing. In October 1957 the Italian government announced its intention of building a new quarter in Bolzano with 5000 housing units, as well as public buildings. The South Tyrolese condemned this project because it was expected that the housing would be filled by Italians from the south coming to take work in an expanded Industrial Zone. The South Tyrolese held an enormous demonstration outside Bolzano, and repeated calls by SVP politicians for the separation of South Tyrol from the region and its conversion into a region in its own right.

In January 1959 the South Tyrolese withdrew from the regional government, so ending power-sharing at regional level, and in February 1959 the bombing recommenced. The targets were monuments and public housing occupied by Italians, and leaflets made clear that the object of the attacks was to stop Italian immigration and get Italians to leave South Tyrol. Care was taken to preserve life.

This new bombing was the work of the *Befreiungsausschuss Südtirol* (BAS – South Tyrol Freedom Committee), set up in 1958 by an ex-branch chairman of the SVP, Sepp *Kerschaumber*. At most 200 people appear to have been involved, more than four-fifths of them South Tyrolese resident in Italy and the rest Austrians or South Tyrolese resident permanently abroad. The long-term dream of most of them may have included reunification of Tyrol and self-determination, but their immediate aim was greater autonomy. However, Kerschbaumer himself had resigned from the SVP and set up the BAS to liberate South Tyrol from the Italians. He approached the *Berg–Isel Bund* for help. The Bund now had to face up to the issues, and had to choose between three objectives:

- The first, espoused by the politicians and based on the facts of international politics, was a 'South Tyrol' region.
- The second, put forward by the South Tyrolese and some of the Austrians together led by Dr Widmoser, archivist of the North Tyrol regional government, was an 'Austrian' solution – full self-determination with the aim of reuniting South Tyrol with Austria.
- The third, advanced by the rest of the Austrians and particularly those connected with pan-German and neo-nazi circles in West Germany, was a 'German' solution. This group saw the Bund's activities in the context of German ethnic revanchism, and so saw self-determination for South Tyrol as a first step in a process that would lead to the inclusion of Austria itself in a Greater Germany.

In the meantime, probably without the knowledge of the politicians, it was agreed to instigate guerrilla warfare and set up 12 operational groups in various parts of South Tyrol.

Whatever the Bund thought or did, however, it would clearly find it difficult to act effectively without the support of those who led the South Tyrolese; that raised the question of the relationship between the Bund and the SVP, particularly on the issue of self-determination. It was difficult for those who had campaigned for self-determination in 1919 and 1945 to renounce it, but the party programme adopted in 1947 aimed at protecting the South Tyrolese ethnic group by autonomy within the Italian state.

The problem was that in the 1950s self-determination was the slogan being preached everywhere to end colonialism, but for the party to call publicly for self-determination in circumstances that made it clear that self-determination meant separation could be politically counter-productive. The SVP could hardly seek greater autonomy from Rome while at the same time calling for separation from Italy; a campaign for separation could provoke the Italians into taking anti-South Tyrolese measures; and, although Austria might agree that separation would be the ideal solution, its frontiers had been laid down by the superpowers and great European powers and no other European country was likely to support a move to regain South Tyrol.

THE UN RESOLUTION

The Bund, led by Widmoser, now began to put pressure on the SVP, criticizing the leadership and inciting party members to call for self-determination. The SVP's leader Magnago protested: he did not wish to split his party over the issue. In the meantime, while relations between the Bund and the SVP, and within the SVP itself, were deteriorating, Austria had succeeded in having the South Tyrol question put on the agenda of the 15th General Assembly of the United Nations.

The Resolution that the General Assembly adopted on 31 October 1960 could be considered to be in Austria's favour. The Assembly did not agree to Austria's request that the province of South Tyrol should be raised to the rank of a region, but it rejected the Italian objective of having the matter referred at once to the International Court. And it did call for negotiations to be resumed between Austria and Italy on all matters relating to the implementation of the De Gasperi–Gruber Agreement, so seeming to rebut Italian protestations that the implementation of South Tyrolese autonomy was a purely internal affair.

The subsequent Austro-Italian negotiations took place in Milan and later in Klagenfurt during the first five months of 1961. In Milan the Italians offered to improve the administration of autonomy but refused to change the structure of the region, and in return wanted Austria to agree that the South Tyrol question should be declared closed. In Klagenfurt the Austrians proposed to withdraw the claim for separate regional status for South Tyrol if Italy granted the province the legislative and executive powers demanded by the SVP.

Although 1961 brought the opening of serious Austro-Italian negotiations, it also ushered in a period of prolonged and violent terrorism. There were six incidents between February and April, and as before the targets were facilities rather than people. The aim was to put pressure on the negotiations.

The Austrians and Italians had agreed to hold a third round of negotiations in Zurich, Switzerland, in mid-June. On the night of 11–12 June, just before their negotiations were due to begin, a terrorist attack was launched on the provincial electric pylon system: 47 separate attacks were recorded, and Bolzano and the Industrial Zone were blacked out for a time. Leaflets were found urging the South Tyrolese to rise up in revolt, and there were further explosions in the following week. Clearly the terrorism had advanced from the improvised uncoordinated episodes of the early days to a coherent programme organized across the province. These attacks also brought about the first death, though it was accidental: an Italian road worker was killed while trying to remove a time bomb placed against a tree. A few days later the *carabinieri* shot dead two South Tyrolese loitering near presumed terrorist targets. July saw continuing terrorist activity. There were 10 more incidents, and in addition to further attacks on electric pylons in South Tyrol there were attacks on railway facilities in Italian provinces outside South Tyrol as well as an attempt to kill. The target was Benno Steiner, the editor of the German-language pages of the Italian-language provincial newspaper *Alto Adige.*

THE COMMISSION OF NINETEEN

The immediate result of these attacks was that, at last, the Italian government agreed to open talks with the South Tyrolese. To that extent at least, terrorism had paid off. On 1 September 1961 a Commission of Nineteen was appointed 'to study the problems [of South Tyrol] and report to the government on the results of its work'. The Nineteen were made up of 11 Italians from the five political parties forming or supporting the government, seven South Tyrolese, six of them members of the SVP, and one Ladin. A new Italian government, led for the first time by Christian Democrat Aldo Moro and Socialist Giuseppe Saragat, was formed in October 1961. This government declared that the conclusions of the Commission of Nineteen would be used 'to restore tranquility and confidence in the region'.[9] This was the first time that the question had found an explicit place in a government programme.

The Commission met more than 200 times, and submitted its report in April 1964. What was of great significance in its deliberations was a memorandum from the SVP in August 1962, to the effect that if the province was given legislative and administrative powers over a large number of economic, social and cultural matters, the SVP would no longer call for the creation of a separate South Tyrol region. The Commission's report formed the basis for negotiations between the Austrian and Italian governments, and for further negotiations between Rome and the South Tyrolese which would end in the famous Package Agreement of 1969 that completely changed the South Tyrol question.

PROBLEMS FOR THE BERG-ISEL BUND

The adoption of the UN Resolution and the opening of negotiations between Austria and Italy and between Rome and the South Tyrolese meant that the *Berg–Isel Bund* had to consider what to do next. Bombs had brought Italy to the negotiating table to improve autonomy, but now this had been achieved should the campaign continue in an effort to get self-determination and separation, even though this was against Austrian and SVP policy, or should matters be left as they were? And if the campaign were to continue, should it employ the same tactics, targeting facilities rather than people, or should it be stepped up and turned against people? As it happened, it was the success of the Italian security forces in the second half of July 1961 that provided the Bund with the answer.

The security forces were lucky, considering the problems they had to face. After an attempt on his life, Benno Steiner gave the *carabinieri* the name of one of the terrorist leaders. The leader was arrested, and gave the names of his accomplices. All in all, the *carabinieri* arrested 90 people, almost all of them South Tyrolese, including Kerschbaumer; the rest fled to Austria. These arrests had immediate results:

- Because the South Tyrolese terrorist element was decimated, the Bund fell into the hands of Austrians whose aim, whether for pan-German, neo-nazi or greater Tyrol reasons, was separation of the province from Italy.
- As a result of these changes in the Bund, and because of the large numbers of security forces moved into South Tyrol, North Tyrol (and particularly Innsbruck) now became the centre of anti-Italian activity in both the preparation of terrorist acts and the dissemination of anti-Italian propaganda. Since there were now few, if any, South Tyrolese activists in South Tyrol, action was taken by groups slipping across the border and, if necessary, guided to their targets by sympathizers.
- There was now no room for moderates in the organization. In February 1962, when the Austrian government had arrested leading members of the Bund for possession of arms and explosives, the moderates tried to push through a motion on the incompatibility of membership with illegal activities and national socialism. The motion was defeated, and Gschnitzer, together with a number of politicians, academics, journalists and North Tyrolese civil servants, left the Bund.

Now there would be no restraining the extremists in the Bund. The arrested Kerschbaumer's place was taken by Dr Norbert Burger, a former lecturer in Innsbruck and closely involved in extreme right-wing pan-German and neo-nazi youth groups and associations in both Aus-

tria and Germany. These organizations had contacts with similar Western European groups, many of them clandestine, such as the French
Algerian OAS. With the arrest of South Tyrolese and the consequent
difficulties in re-establishing locally-based terrorist groups, Burger was
obliged to use 'foreigners'. The Italian authorities were aware of contacts between Burger and the Algerian OAS aimed at providing help
and materials for 'liberating' South Tyrol.

Soon afterwards, the pattern of outrages showed that targets had
been switched from facilities to human beings and were no longer
confined to South Tyrol. From July 1962 to September 1963 Italian
police and troops were fired on, and bombs were left in railway stations
in Trento, Verona, Milan and Genoa. In Verona one person was killed
and 19 injured; in Trento and Milan six people were injured. Then,
from the autumn of 1964 to June 1967, 10 members of the security
forces (3 *carabinieri*, 3 financial police and 4 soldiers) were killed in
South Tyrol. Some were ambushed, some blown up by mines and some
killed when their small commune police station was raked by automatic
weapons.

Since the policy of the Bund was no longer greater autonomy for
South Tyrol but separation from Italy, the terrorists' objective was
no longer to get negotiations going but rather to exacerbate the situation so much that an agreement between the parties would be impossible. Terrorist outrages were therefore undertaken with an eye to
crucial stages in the negotiations.

ITALIAN GOVERNMENT POLICIES

With the outbreak of widespread co-ordinated terrorism in 1961, the
Italian government adopted two policies. The first was to diffuse the
crisis by taking political measures to reduce support for the terrorists
amongst the German-speaking population, and the second was to
uproot the terrorism itself. The extent to which the first was successful
would affect the chances of achieving the second, and it was in the
political conduct of affairs that the Italian government had the greatest
room for manoeuvre.

One point of undoubted concern was that the clear majority of the
population of South Tyrol was not Italian, and there might have been
sympathy in the rest of Italy for a group thrust unwillingly into another
state and then subjected to cultural genocide; such sympathy did of
course exist everywhere in the German-speaking world. But the ignor-

ance of the Italian population about South Tyrol, as well as the tendency to associate the South Tyrolese with nazism, meant that as long as fundamental principles of state security and integrity were maintained, the public would probably go along with any measures that the government cared to adopt. No one would really care if a hard line was taken; concessions might arouse the hostility of the extreme right, but for a long time the MSI were political lepers. Nevertheless, the threat that the issue might present to the management of the crisis was one that could be underrated.

There was no chance that publicity in the media would be allowed to work to the advantage of the terrorists. Radio broadcasting and television in the 1960s were in the hands of the Italian state television and broadcasting company, and in South Tyrol itself the few German-language programmes were carefully vetted. The danger was rather the other way round – that the Italian public might be inflamed to such a degree that concessions would be difficult – and here the problem was not radio and television, but the press. Even today Italy does not have a truly 'national' newspaper. Each of the great Italian regions has its own traditional leading paper, and news from other parts of the country comes from contacts or correspondents in the areas concerned. When something happened in South Tyrol, these regional papers would refer to the leading South Tyrolese or Trento Italian papers – precisely the papers that saw themselves as the watchdogs of the Italian state and defenders of the Italian community against South Tyrolese 'intransigence', 'revanchism' and 'nazism'. Few Italian journalists bothered to find out what the situation was really like in South Tyrol, let alone explain the South Tyrolese point of view. The result was that not only was the Italian public not informed on the issues on both sides of the dispute, but there was scope for the wildest exaggerations and the most sensational and alarmist claims, sometimes perhaps intended to inflame feeling against the South Tyrolese.

On the other hand, the Italian government itself would be in no danger if it was seen to uphold the integrity of the state. It repeatedly made clear the principles on which it intended to act, and it never changed its stance. This involved:

- the maintenance, at whatever cost, of South Tyrol as part of Italy
- insistence that the autonomy statute fulfilled the De Gasperi–Gruber Agreement, as accepted by the South Tyrolese in 1948, and that therefore any improvements on it would be an act of generosity which Italy was not obliged to perform

- insistence that the implementation of the autonomy statute, and amendments to it, were a purely internal Italian affair
- the maintenance of the Trentino-South Tyrol region as a political structure
- the treatment of the South Tyrolese people as German-speaking Italian citizens with all the rights and duties, including loyalty, that went with Italian citizenship
- the requirement that disputes with Austria over the implementation of the De Gasperi–Gruber Agreement should be solved before the International Court.

These principles, which removed any doubts about the political destiny of South Tyrol, were well known and had the support of almost the entire Italian political spectrum.

It was perhaps fortunate that the Italian governments which negotiated the Package Agreement with the Austrians and South Tyrolese were centre–left coalitions with an understanding of the effects of social and economic developments on policies. They were disposed to make concessions that the right-wing governments of the 1950s, tacitly supported by the MSI, would have been unlikely to make. Management of the crisis was aided by the determination of Italy's leading political personality, Aldo Moro, whether as Prime Minister or Foreign Minister, to achieve a successful conclusion.

The ministry in charge of the crisis was the Prime Minister's own office, the Presidency of the Council of Ministers. It was to the Presidency that the Commission of Nineteen submitted its proposals, though decisions were adopted by the Cabinet. And it was through the Commission of Nineteen that for the first time the isolation of the South Tyrolese was ended, and that continuous contacts between the SVP and the Italian political parties forming the national and regional governments were introduced in circumstances which ensured that the South Tyrolese would be heeded.

Relations between the SVP and political parties at provincial and regional level had so far been a dialogue of the deaf, with the Italians prepared only to act as watchdogs over the security of the province. The SVP had little to say, except with reference to South Tyrol, about the national affairs discussed in the national parliament; and it was very rare indeed for a minister from Rome to make the long journey to the distant borders of the country. Rome preferred to use Trento to do its work for it.

It was fortunate, too, that the South Tyrolese did not have a tradition of violence. The Italian government could take much comfort from the fact that, although there was obviously sympathy for the terrorists, particularly in the early stages, it was quite another matter in June 1961 when the terrorist onslaught was so violent that tourism, the province's main source of wealth, was badly hit as a result of cancellations by foreign holiday-makers. Indeed, in September 1961 a number of politicians and businessmen set up a not insignificant movement called *Aufbau* (Reconstruction), with a programme based on loyalty to the Italian state, co-operation with the local Italian population and the rejection of irredentism and terror, as well as improved autonomy. As the terrorism increased, South Tyrolese support for the perpetrators declined: killing and wounding innocent people in railway stations or killing members of the security forces damaged the South Tyrolese and their case, particularly when greater autonomy was a feasible goal and separation was not.

Politically speaking, therefore, the Italian state had a relatively easy ride. On the other front, ending terrorism meant combating both terrorism in South Tyrol itself and its preparation and support in Austria.

Within South Tyrol, the main problems were the silence of the South Tyrolese population – at least as long as the perpetrators were South Tyrolese; the lack of German-speaking police and security forces; the lack of South Tyrolese in the police and security forces; and the need to control a long and difficult mountainous frontier.

THE SECURITY FORCES

The Italians relied upon the *carabinieri* for maintaining law and order, and on the financial and customs police for frontier security. In the front line against terrorism were the criminal police, with co-ordination of information at the centre in Rome (UCIGOS) dealing through the *questura* (the headquarters of the police) in Bolzano (DIGOS). In addition the state called upon the the state police's special action squads, the *celere*, as well as the secret service. South Tyrol was also the home base of two brigades of Italy's famous mountain troops, the *alpini*, stationed in Merano and Brunico (Bruneck). The monument to the *alpini* in Brunico was a favourite target of South Tyrolese terrorists.

It was the local criminal police who carried out investigations into terrorist activity. When this activity was at its height and manpower was needed to surround areas or villages and carry out intensive

searches, the *celere* would be brought in from outside the province.
The *carabinieri* maintained a presence in every commune in the province. The role of the army was to guard key installations that were
potential terrorist targets, as well as to patrol the difficult frontier
and provide bomb-disposal squads.

The ministries involved in combating terrorism were those of the
Interior, Defence and Finance and the Presidency of the Council of
Ministers, with the Ministry of the Interior playing the most prominent
role since it controlled the criminal and state police. The *carabinieri*
and the secret service depended on several ministries, though the Prime
Minister received all security reports as the person ultimately responsible for state security. The financial police reported to the Ministry
of Finance, and their responsibilities included investigations of suspicious bank accounts, which in at least one case gave them leads.

In an ethnically sharply divided area the security forces' main problems were their relations with the South Tyrolese. Apart from Steiner,
no South Tyrolese voluntarily offered information to the security
forces. *Omertà* (silence) was as respected in South Tyrol as it was
in Sicily; and since there has been no evidence to suggest that pressure
was applied to maintain that silence, the presumption must be that
the terrorists enjoyed a considerable degree of public sympathy, particularly as long as they targeted facilities rather than people.

It has already been pointed out that few police spoke German. The
South Tyrolese spoke Italian since it was taught in school, but most
of the community, living in the valleys, hardly used it. This led to
terrorist suspects being interrogated in Italian and admitting everything
but then retracting their statements on the grounds that they did not
fully understand what was being asked. Indeed, the terrorism of the
1950s led to bilingualism in police procedure, legal proceedings and
competitions for public appointments generally. Things might have
been better if South Tyrolese had been willing to join the South Tyrol
police, but very few did so. Even today only about six per cent are
South Tyrolese, though the SVP would like police numbers to reflect
ethnic proportions.[10] The police are too closely associated with a heavy-
handed Italian state for the South Tyrolese to be attracted.

A recent exception to this has been recruitment into the *carabinieri*.
As a paramilitary force, it has been possible to do military service
with them and the pay is better than in the army. South Tyrolese
are often posted in the province's villages, thus providing a German-
speaking representative of the forces of law and order.

Some of those accused of terrorism in 1961–2 fell victim to torture and ill-treatment at the hands of the *carabinieri*, and several died in prison. Proceedings against 21 *carabinieri* were instituted, but the Court decided that it was impossible to identify all the culprits and only 10 were actually charged. In the end eight were acquitted, but the two found guilty were not sentenced since their activities came under an amnesty.

IMPORTANCE OF THE STEINER CASE

In the event, police luck in the Steiner case meant that terrorism in South Tyrol was largely defused. Since there was no general South Tyrolese uprising and many were against such a course, the problems proved less serious than at first thought. The silence of the population could not shield names already known from the Steiner case; language barriers were no impediment once the names were known; and problems inherent in rival security forces and overlapping responsibilities did not weigh heavily.

The state did not therefore need to introduce special laws, rules or regulations covering the criminal justice system or law and order in South Tyrol, measures which in any case, would have been unconstitutional in one region only. The only unusual aspect was the holding of trials of South Tyrolese outside the province. Through fear of sympathetic demonstrations, the Stieler group were tried in Bologna and there were two BAS trials in Milan. Once it was suggested that South Tyrolese involved in terrorism should be stripped of their Italian citizenship, particularly if they had opted for Germany in 1939, but the proposal was not taken up.

THE AUSTRIAN FACTOR

The most serious aspect of South Tyrolese terrorism was the fact that outrages were planned and prepared in Austria. From 1956 to 1970 the South Tyrol question was high on Austria's foreign policy agenda, with Austrian public opinion deeply concerned by and involved in the fate of their kin over the border. Austrians were generally well better informed about South Tyrol, and sympathy for the South Tyrolese was reflected in strong anti-Italian sentiment.

Another factor was the relationship between Vienna and North

Tyrol, where anti-Italian feeling and emotional commitment to the South Tyrolese were strongest. The North Tyrolese saw the question as one of Tyrolese unification rather than South Tyrol's return to Austria. Indeed, during the Austro-Italian negotiations the North Tyrolese felt that Vienna was only lukewarm in its defence of the South Tyrolese, and on one occasion North Tyrolese members of the Austrian delegation put pressure on Vienna by leaking information to the press. Some North Tyrolese politicians had long had links with the *Berg–Isel Bund*, and evidence suggests that close contacts existed between individual policemen (federal as well as state) in Innsbruck and the BAS. Under these circumstances, BAS members prepared outrages in North Tyrol and their extremist views on South Tyrol were aired, unchallenged, in the media.

The organizers and perpetrators of the South Tyrol outrages who lived in North Tyrol were of course well known to the Italian authorities, but it was difficult to get convictions for their crimes. To begin with, there was the question of extradition. Often South Tyrolese (i.e. Italian citizens) were warned in advance of Italian requests for their extradition and would disappear for as long as was necessary. As for Austrian citizens, the 1957 European Convention on Extradition allowed citizens of one country to be extradited to another to face charges, and if a country refrained from extraditing its citizens under Article 6 of the Convention the other country involved could submit evidence to have the persons concerned tried and sentenced in their own country. Austria signed the Convention on the day it appeared, and although she did not ratify it until April 1969 she was sensitive to the possible damage of being charged with allowing her territory to be used for outrages abroad. On a number of occasions, therefore, Austria brought members of the *Berg–Isel Bund* and the BAS to court.

Several members of the Bund who were arrested in December 1961 for illegal possession of arms and explosives were tried in Graz but received light sentences on the legal grounds that they could be held responsible only for the preparation of outrages abroad and not for the outrages themselves. And as the situation in South Tyrol deteriorated, Austrian juries simply would not convict Austrians helping to 'free' the province from Italy. When Wolfgang Pfaundler, a leading Austrian Bund member, was tried in Graz in June 1962 for possessing rifles, machine-guns, pistols, ammunition and explosives, he was acquitted unanimously, the theme of the trial being that it was no business of an Austrian jury to keep the peace in Italy. At further trials in

Graz in 1965 and in Linz in 1967 the accused, amid scenes of tumultuous enthusiasm, were either acquitted or received sentences so light that they were almost immediately set free. At the Linz trial two of the most notorious terrorists involved in South Tyrol, Dr Norbert Burger and Peter Kienesberger, were acquitted after openly confessing to stealing dynamite for outrages in South Tyrol.

At this the patience of the Italian government snapped. It vetoed Austrian talks on economic relations with the European Community on the ground that Vienna's action against the preparation of terrorism on Austrian soil was inadequate, and within a year Austrian terrorism and the South Tyrolese terrorism which had found a refuge in Austria faded away. The veto lasted until the signature of the Package Agreement in November 1969. Significantly, that was also the year in which Austria ratified the European Convention on Extradition.

THE PACKAGE AGREEMENT

In the autumn of 1969, Aldo Moro for Italy and Kurt Waldheim for Austria agreed on a package of measures and a timetable to give South Tyrol improved autonomy. This package required the approval of the South Tyrolese and was submitted to an extraordinary congress of the SVP. The congress only narrowly accepted it – by 52.9 per cent, with 2.6 per cent abstentions.

Apart from perceived shortcomings arising from guarantees for the Italian presence in the province, and in particular the absence of effective measures to stop Italian immigration, the main reason for the SVP's hesitation was the continuing Italian claim that the 1948 autonomy statute fulfilled the De Gasperi–Gruber Agreement, and the package was therefore a freely granted additional offering which Italy was in no way obliged to make. The SVP and Austria, mindful of the way in which Italy had implemented the De Gasperi–Gruber Agreement and the 1948 Autonomy Statute, had sought an international guarantee to ensure that Italy did not later revoke any of the measures of the package. If it was accepted that the package was part of the De Gasperi–Gruber Agreement, the revocation of all or part of it could be brought before the International Court at The Hague as a failure to fulfil an international obligation. But if Italy did not accept this view, there was no guarantee that it would keep its word and it would be up to the court to decide whether the package was part of the Agreement or additional to it.

Another controversy surrounded the declaration that Austria was supposed to make after Italy had implemented the package proposals. The Italian interpretation was that Austria should declare the South Tyrol question closed. The SVP and the Austrians maintained that the declaration merely referred to the closing of the dispute on whether the De Gasperi–Gruber Agreement had been fulfilled.

Those of the SVP in favour of accepting the package argued that it would give South Tyrol greater autonomy; that to reject it would mean going to the International Court; and that if the court ruled that the 1948 autonomy statute fulfilled the Agreement, Italy would be under no obligation to do any more and would have international opinion on its side if terrorism broke out again.

The package did indeed provide immensely wider autonomy, and worked greatly to the advantage of the South Tyrolese. Its chief features were:

i) The maintenance of the regional structure, but with a massive transfer of legislative power from the region to the two provinces of South Tyrol and Trento. Instead of 14, South Tyrol now had 29 areas of primary legislative competence, the new ones including agriculture, forestry and tourism, mines, environmental protection and vocational training. Areas of secondary legislative competence were increased from eight to 11.

ii) In all areas where the province had legislative competence, it also received the appropriate administrative powers.

iii) The principle of ethnic proportions which had so far applied only in offices of the provincial administration was extended to all state and semi-state bodies operating in the province, with the exception of the Ministry of Defence and the various police forces. This had to be achieved by the year 2002. However, no compulsory redundancies were expected to be necessary to bring this about.

iv) The clause relating to finance was interpreted to mean that the province would automatically receive 1.61 per cent of any state expenditure in all the important and relevant sectors of the economy and social welfare.

v) Through executive measures, occupants of posts in public employment had to be bilingual, and grade, promotion or transfer to another administration would also depend on language skills, to be established by public examination.

vi) Everyone in the province was now required to declare his or her ethnic group, i.e. German, Italian or Ladin, at the time of the national census. Parents were to make declarations on behalf of their children, and declarations could not be verified or disputed by the authorities.

Within 15 years the political, economic and social situation in the province was transformed. For the South Tyrolese, the new autonomy statute of 1972 enabled them to be very much masters of their own destiny in their homeland. Most of the province's economy could now be regulated by provincial laws, which were adopted in the provincial parliament on the basis of the wishes of the SVP majority. Administration – in ethnic proportions and bilingual – expanded rapidly as the province took over legislative powers from the region. And the province received from the state considerable amounts of money to carry out policy – economic, social or infrastructural.

In addition, the 1970s saw tourists flocking to the province, attracted on the one hand by the falling lira and the rising German mark and Austrian schilling, and on the other by the completion of the Innsbruck–Brenner–Bolzano motorway. Tourism in South Tyrol now became an all-year-round activity, and the money coming from tourism and the Italian state was augmented by sums from the European Community's Common Agricultural Policy. By 1980, unemployment in the province had fallen to less than one per cent.

ITALIAN MISGIVINGS

However, it was the South Tyrolese who were benefiting from these developments. By contrast the Italian group, previously the masters of the province, were about to become the underdogs. Agriculture and tourism had been South Tyrolese bastions, but theirs had been the administration and industry. Now Italians found it very difficult to be taken on in state and semi-state employment where room had to be made for incoming South Tyrolese, and in any case there was the additional obligation to be able to speak German. As for industry, the 1970s brought a crisis in Italian industry as oil prices rose, resulting in stagnation, rampant inflation, rising unemployment and frequent bankruptcies. Industry had become a declining sector, and the Bolzano Industrial Zone suffered. What is more, the Italian community in South Tyrol found cause for concern in two of the ways in which the autonomy statute had to be implemented.

First, not enough South Tyrolese were applying for posts in state and semi-state bodies. Competition from the expanding provincial administration and the expanding tourist sector, and housing shortages in Bolzano, played their part. The result was a crisis in some organizations, particularly the railways and postal services. Yet the package allowed the shortfall to be made up only by importing staff from elsewhere in Italy on temporary non-renewable contracts.

Secondly, some children of mixed marriages were genuinely unable to decide which group they belonged to and therefore felt unable to make the declaration required in the census. Others, alarmed by the possibility that rights might be lost if no declaration was made, argued that it was unconstitutional to have to make such a declaration because the system that called for it violated Article 3 of the Italian Constitution, providing for equality of rights for all citizens without distinction as to sex, race, language, religion or political belief. And there were reported cases of Italians declaring themselves German in order to obtain jobs. In fact, in 1984 the Council of State declared the ethnic declaration illegal because it did not provide for citizens to declare themselves as 'other language' or 'mixed language'. In any case the proportion of Italian-speakers fell from 34.3 per cent in 1961 to 29.4 per cent by 1981, and is expected to fall below 25 per cent by 1991.

In recent years the SVP has been taking the attitude that, although no one would be dismissed, the new ethnic proportions should now be applied when filling posts in the public administration. The screw is thus being turned on the Italian community and this gives Italian nationalists, particularly the MSI, the opportunity to attack Rome for handing over the province to the South Tyrolese. The MSI continually insists that SVP policy is to eliminate the Italian presence, and that the package is a means to that end.

EXTREMIST ACTIVITY

In the 1985 commune elections, the MSI capitalized on the fears of the Italian community in Bolzano to take 22.6 per cent of the vote and emerge as the Italian party with the largest number of votes and seats. In Merano it obtained nearly 12 per cent of the vote and became the second largest Italian party. And in the 1987 general elections the MSI emerged as the largest Italian party in the province with 10 per cent of the vote, tripling its 1979 performance. By contrast, the MSI vote elsewhere in Italy hardly reached four per cent.

The introduction of the 1969 package came about slowly; indeed, the last measures were adopted only in the summer of 1988. The South Tyrolese also complained, as in the days before the package, at the way in which the Italian government or the Constitutional Court rejected provincial laws, and this in turn gave extremists among them the opportunity to question the good faith of the government and to call again for self-determination. Many of those doing so were members of the SVP, and a number of them broke away from the SVP to form the (Tyrolese) *Heimat Bund*. The Italians were alarmed to note that the chairman of the party was Hans Stieler, convicted for terrorism in the 1950s; but the real party leader, and sole party representative in the provincial parliament, was Eva Klotz. She was the daughter of a prominent South Tyrolese terrorist, the late Georg Klotz, who used to be leader of the BAS and had been involved in escalating the violence after the death of Kerschbaumer.

The statutes and programme of the SVP approved by the 1973 party congress stated that, although the right of self-determination for the South Tyrolese people was inalienable, the party recognized the De Gasperi–Gruber Agreement as the basis for the national development of the Tyrolese minority within the Italian state. In the early 1970s, self-determination was interpreted to mean the right of a people or group to decide freely what legislative and administrative powers they should have to maintain their separate identity, and to demand these as a kind of 'inner self-determination'; separation, or 'external self-determination', would be sought only as a last resort if these demands were denied. This broadly remains the position of the SVP, but what the Heimat Bund argued for was that South Tyrol should either be given San Marino status or become a free state. In that way the South Tyrolese would be free of Italian control even if they were unable to return to Austria, and the members of the Heimat Bund were prepared to countenance violence to achieve this.

After a few incidents in 1986, 21 attacks were reported in 1987 and 13 more by August 1988. Although the aim of the bombing appeared to be to damage facilities, little attention was paid to the risk to human lives. Bombs were placed in cars and buses belonging to Italians and against the walls of houses inhabited by Italians, particularly politicians, as well as being aimed at traditional targets such as electric pylons and the Brenner railway line.

The last of those attacks, against a pipeline of an aqueduct, might have led to the bursting of a dam and the descent of more than one million cubic metres of water on nearby villages; and on one occasion machine-gun fire was opened on a *carabinieri* station in Merano.

One South Tyroler blew himself up when preparing a bomb. Two other South Tyrolese were arrested in 1987 and convicted for the bombing carried out in 1986, but since then the security forces have had no successes. Some of the bombs were accompanied by leaflets calling for one Tyrol, and after recent bombing, opposing leaflets have appeared signed by the MIA (*Movimento Italiano Adige*), threatening reprisals against the South Tyrolese community for its attempts to bomb the province out of Italy.

There is much speculation about the identity and motives of the terrorists. Most South Tyrolese condemn the attacks; many believe that the groups are linked to the MSI, and that the security services are to blame. On the other hand, there are still calls for self-determination for South Tyrol from the remnant of the BAS living in Austria and Germany. Apparently the 30 terrorists who are still active obtain funds with ease and still have sympathizers in South Tyrol.

ITALY SEEKS AUSTRIA'S APPROVAL

At the end of February 1988 the Italian government agreed with the SVP executive committee on measures that would implement the package in full. The Italian government therefore required Austria to make the declaration ending the matter, as provided for in the timetable. But Austrian policy takes its cue from the SVP, and within the SVP a strong movement led by Dr Alfons Benedikter was building up in opposition to such a declaration. There were three reasons for this:

i) There were 13 points outstanding which party hard-liners wished to see fulfilled before the package could be considered completed, some of them to do with language and court procedure.

ii) The Italians had not agreed that the package fulfilled the De Gasperi–Gruber Agreement, and so if Rome revoked any of the package measures Austria and the South Tyrolese would have no recourse except to ask the International Court to rule on that point; if the answer was negative, neither Austria nor the South Tyrolese would have any further recourse. And it was thought that, in view of the rise of the MSI, reflecting Italian concern about the future of the province, the Italian government might well resort to such action.

iii) In July 1988 the Italian government, on the basis of rulings of the Constitutional Court, decided to extend to the regions with special statute (and therefore Trento–South Tyrol and its provinces) the right to act with ordinary laws on grounds of 'national interest', to carry out national programmes either to annul or amend existing provincial laws or to intervene directly in spheres of activity in which the province had primary legislative competence. Even many Italian jurists consider these steps constitutionally questionable.

Dr Benedikter said that the Constitutional Court had approved a state law giving the government the right to give money to the city of Bolzano (with its 80 per cent Italian population) to build houses, even though housing fell into the primary legislative sphere of the province. He claimed that it was precisely such a step which had led to the crisis in 1957, the massive demonstration outside Bolzano and the downfall of the old moderate leadership. Between 1950 and 1960 the state had built 5500 dwellings, of which the South Tyrolese received only four per cent. Would more housing now be built in the name of 'national interests', in order to increase the declining Italian population of the province?

For the pan-Germans, neo-nazis and one-Tyrolers living in Germany and Austria, closure of the South Tyrol question would bring an end to their hopes. Their aim, therefore, is to put pressure on the SVP to advise the Austrian government not to make the declaration, or even to exacerbate the situation so as to cause the Italian government to over-react. Both German and Italian right-wing extremists would like to see this happen. The former hope for an outcome that would make the province ungovernable and perhaps force the Italian government to abandon the province; the latter hope for the ending of the package and a ruthless curtailment of provincial autonomy – indeed, its abolition – in defence of Italian national interests. The Benedikter group are therefore arguing that although the SVP executive committee may have decided to accept the latest Italian measures as fulfilling the package, it should be up to the party congress to ratify that decision and to advise the Austrian government on whether it should declare the matter closed.

In the meantime, as far as combating terrorism is concerned, Austro-Italian relations are good and Italy has no complaints. In November 1986 the two countries signed an agreement on the prevention of terrorism and the exchange of information. During a visit of the Italian

Minister of the Interior to Vienna in August 1988, the Austrians agreed
to help to discover the authors of the recent outrages and to help
Italy in the fight against 'terrorist groups opposed to the implementation of the package'.

Among measures envisaged is the strengthening of direct contacts
between the *questura* in Bolzano and the Innsbruck police. The Austrians said that at the request of the Italian authorities they had already
provided information on 40 terrorist incidents between 1984 and
August 1988.[11]

There seems to be no question, therefore, of Italy's vetoing, as in
1967, Austrian moves towards a closer relationship with, or even membership of, the European Community. But many South and North
Tyrolese feel that relations with the Community, requiring the removal
of Italy's objectives, are now a more important item on Austria's foreign
policy agenda than the South Tyrol question, and that this may modify
Austria's fervour in defence of its kin on the other side of the Brenner.

WHY IT ALL STARTED

The ability of the South Tyrolese to maintain their separate cultural
identity in their homeland depended not only on their being allowed
to go to German schools and use German when dealing with the public
authorities, but also on their finding jobs in the homeland, including
some relating to its economic development. Emigration in search of
jobs that could not be found in the homeland would weaken the group,
while the immigration of Italians to take jobs South Tyrolese could
not or would not fill could make the South Tyrolese a minority in
their homeland as well as in the nation, with little ability to control
their destiny.

Employment was therefore crucial; and it depended on circumstances
such as the decline of agriculture, the expansion of industry, the development of tourism, the size of the administration and the conditions
of access to it, the availability of housing, vocational training and
the availability of money. However, there is no evidence that attention
to these points would be at the expense of the Italian group in the
province and so affect the province's territorial destiny.

The second factor was the legacy of history. The injustice of the
decisions of 1919, the fascist measures of cultural genocide and the
fact that the South Tyrolese were forced to choose in 1939 between
abandoning their homeland or abandoning their cultural identity have

left a lasting bitterness and distrust of Italians.

The third factor was isolation. The Italians were seen as 'incomers'. Few, if any, Italians spoke German, and the South Tyrolese used Italian only in business relations with the administration. Social activities, such as cinemas and the theatre, were quite separate, if only because of the language. The Italians lived mostly in the big towns, while the South Tyrolese lived in – indeed owned – the countryside. The South Tyrolese considered mixed marriages to be ethnic treason. Schooling was separate, according to language. Moreover, Rome was a very long way away. Italian ministers rarely came to the province, and when they did it was the fears of South Tyrolese expansion that they understood, not the consequences of South Tyrolese decline.

The fourth factor was simply that the South Tyrolese had no means of making Italians hear, let alone act. They were a very small percentage of the national population, and therefore had no political power. And they could not reject Italian laws as Italy rejected provincial laws.

COULD IT HAVE BEEN PREVENTED?

With hindsight, could any early indications of trouble have been recognized? Certainly the 1954 SVP Memorandum was a warning – indeed, it said that there could be disturbances if the points in it were not met. An Italian official had written in the margin 'Then send for the police', which showed no understanding of economic or social malaise.

Could any steps have defused the situation if they had been taken earlier? The answer is that a more generous interpretation of autonomy, its swift fulfilment, and attention to the wishes of the very moderate SVP leadership were all needed, and their absence was the main reason for that leadership's fall and replacement by much more determined people.

For the sad truth was that the finest legal formulas that had stifled all chances of a dialogue between Rome and Bolzano were useless when it came to dealing with unofficial organizations and the violence that they brought with them. It was no credit to the way that Italy had handled the South Tyrol question that terrorists had seized the initiative which the Italian government had never agreed to undertake; nor that the terrorists were able to boast that it was their bombs that had provoked the setting up of the Commission of Nineteen.

Moreover, if the positive aspect of the Commission was that Rome had at last been pushed into establishing the contact with the South Tyrolese and beginning the dialogue that should have taken place 15 years previously, there was now a serious negative balance, namely the involvement of pan-Germanism and neo-nazism eager to profit from the conflict in order to prejudice the very dialogue that terrorism had brought about.

Under these unhappy conditions, and over the battlefields of past 'victories', fears and illusions, was conducted the retreat to reality. From being an entirely internal Italian affair, the question had been rendered international. From 'consultations', the parties had progressed to 'negotiations'. From a refusal to change the statute, change was at last accepted as necessary.

The overall element of uncertainty also played a part in the development of ethnic terrorism in South Tyrol. It had two aspects.

The first was uncertainty about the territorial destiny of the province. South Tyrolese were bitter at being denied self-determination in 1919 and 1945, but it is crucial to understand the Italian fears arising from their failure in 1946 to get Austria formally to renounce South Tyrol. That is why today Italians demand that Austria's forthcoming declaration is couched in terms that mean that the South Tyrol question is closed. Certainly the hostility to the Austrians and South Tyrolese at the time of the preparation of the 1948 autonomy statute was caused by the Austrian and the South Tyrolese insistence that the right of self-determination had not been abandoned. And even if a South Tyrolese return to Austria has been out of the question since the State Treaty of 1955, the present talk of 'San Marino Status' or '*Freistaat Südtirol*' (a free state) carries the same message: separation of South Tyrol from Italy. This has meant that although measures of the 1972 autonomy statute, fulfilling the package, are seen in terms of the protection and development of the South Tyrolese community within the Italian state, the Italians now see them in terms of the maintenance of the Italian presence in the province.

The second aspect of the uncertainty is the South Tyrolese lack of confidence that any laws passed by the provincial parliament can ever be guaranteed to be accepted by the Italian state. It has been pointed out that since 1974 the Constitutional Court has upheld the province in only 30 per cent of the cases submitted to it, and in 1987 alone, 44 per cent of the first-version provincial laws were rejected by Rome.[12] Now there is also the presumed forthcoming ability of the state to revoke or amend existing laws, to say nothing of the state's right to intervene, in the name of 'national interests', in the economic and social development of the province.

Thus, although the whole issue of minority protection hinges on cultural protection for the minority in return for the political security of the majority, the fact that neither was absolutely secured in South Tyrol gave terrorism its opening.

HOW TERRORISM WAS DEFEATED

Terrorism in South Tyrol was defeated, if not destroyed, by a combination of four factors:

i) The determined stand of the Italian government at home. It was made clear that Italy would not abandon South Tyrol, and this has enabled the government to enjoy absolute support in parliament and the country. South Tyrolese leaders know that they are not in a position to force Italians to grant 'external' self-determination, and the territorial destiny of South Tyrol is not really in doubt.

ii) The contents of the package amounted very largely to the 'inner' self-determination that the South Tyrolese had sought for so long. In the 1970s, with the acceptance of the package by Austria and the SVP, and as, albeit slowly, the measures of the package were being implemented, terrorism had the ground cut from under its feet. In principle, the package measures have made the South Tyrolese masters of their destiny. Terrorism's only real chances of revival would stem from an Italian reaction to the decline of the Italian community in the province, i.e. the revoking of measures in the package or the encouragement of Italian immigration with or without Italian-sponsored heavy industrial development.

iii) The determined stand of the Italian government abroad. The government did – eventually – take a hard line against the perceived benign attitude of the Austrians to the preparation of outrages and the existence of terrorists on Austrian soil, and as a result little was seen or heard of the terrorists for another 15 years. By vetoing talks with the European Community (EC), Italy gave the Austrians a sharp reminder of their European responsibilities.

iv) Simple good luck. On the one hand there was the Steiner incident, which in effect destroyed the indigenous South Tyrolese terrorism of the BAS. As a result, terrorists were forced over the border and the danger of a widespread, deep insertion of terrorism into the South Tyrolese community was checked. There was therefore no severe test of Italian statesmanship and of crisis management. On the other hand, there was the good fortune that the package was being implemented when there was an economic boom in the province. Even though this created problems elsewhere, the South Tyrolese community benefited enormously in that it was rural South Tyrol which gained from tourism, EC agricultural funds and Italian state infrastructural spending.

Significantly, the flight from the land was halted. The most recent figures show that there has been an increase in population in almost every rural commune since the 1971 census and, where there has been decline, that decline has been negligible.[13] By 1980 unemployment in the province was negligible, and although the provincial government introduced measures – at a time of stagflation and massive unemployment elsewhere in Europe – to damp down the economy and severely curtail construction work in the countryside, the most recent figures give the unemployment rate as 5.2 per cent, less than half the national average.[14] And as long as Germans continue to provide three-quarters of the tourists, there seems no reason why a satisfactory provincial economy cannot be sustained.

NOTES

1. A.E. Alcock, *The History of the South Tyrol Question* (London: Michael Joseph, 1970), p. 496. (Hereinafter *History*).
2. Ibid., p. 496.
3. Ibid., p. 496.
4. Ibid., p. 496 and p. 504.
5. The circumstances in which this letter came to be written, and the consequences, analysed in ibid., pp. 167–74, and pp. 280–2.
6. A. E. Alcock, *Geschichte der Südtirolfrage – Südtirol seit dem Paket 1970-1980* (Vienna: Braumüller, 1982), p. 174.
7. Autonome Provinz Bozen-Südtirol, *Südtirol-Handbuch* (Bolzano: Athesia, 1988), pp.51–63 (hereinafter *Südtirol-Handbuch*).
8. Alcock, *History*, p. 238.
9. Ibid., p. 426.
10. Alcock, *Geshchichte*, p. 97.
11. *Corriere della Sera* (Milan), 30 August 1988.

12. Dr. A. Benedikter 'Speciality Today' – 'Special Regions and Autonomous Provinces'. unpublished, but kindly made available privately, p. 19.
13. *Südtirol-Handbuch*, 1988, pp.182–4.
14. Ibid., p. 195.

2 Canada and the FLQ

BRITISH AND FRENCH CANADA

The relationship between Quebec and the rest of Canada, and between the French and British in the province, is complex, reaching back over two hundred years.

Large-scale British immigration and the creation of Canada in 1867 meant that French Canadians were a minority in a country where a British-dominated federal government held the broadest powers. Although confederation guaranteed certain language rights to the francophone minority at the federal level, recognized French civil law and gave French equal status with English in Parliament and in the courts, the threat of linguistic and cultural assimilation loomed large.

French Canadians were concentrated in the province of Quebec – the great majority in rural areas, with the British minority mostly in urban areas, especially Montreal. Industrialization and urbanization transformed the relationship between these two groups. Investment was concentrated in the hands of British companies, and capital from the United States directed itself towards the province's rich natural resources. Much of the labour for these industries was provided by French Canadians who had left the overcrowded rural areas.

Although they gained economically from industrial development and made up about 80 per cent of the province's population (30 per cent of the country's), French Canadians controlled less than 20 per cent of Quebec's economy. By 1961 the average income of francophones was 35 per cent lower than that of the English-speaking population. The combination of low wages and an essentially non-French management class contributed greatly to the radical nature of trade union activity in Quebec in the 1960s and the 1970s.

1960 AND THE QUIET REVOLUTION

The provincial election of 1960 marked an important change from the conservative approach of the *Union Nationale* administration to Liberal free enterprise, inviting foreign investment and control. In social areas like health, education and welfare the *Union Nationale* had deferred to the Catholic Church, with which it had close links.

Under the Liberal Lesage, the provincial government became involved in all aspects of the economy and pursued an active social programme.

The Lesage administration was determined to make French Canadians masters in their own home and created a number of state companies in vital industries, the most important of which was Hydro Quebec. The government also initiated programmes to help small and medium-sized French businesses. Quebec took exclusive responsibility for education, which was expanded and liberalized, as well as the welfare and health services. This attempt at a rapid state-led modernization became known as the 'Quiet Revolution'.

In parallel with this modernization many nationalist groups began to emerge, many favouring violence and some committed to the complete independence of Quebec. The groups advocating 'sovereignty' within the legal political system were drawn to the *Parti Québécois* (PQ, created in 1968) under the leadership of a former Liberal cabinet minister, René Lévesque, though some advocating radical change also joined the PQ.

However, some French Canadians believed there was an opportunity for greater change and benefits for Quebec at the level of federal government. Several prominent French Canadians, including Pierre Trudeau, joined the federal Liberal government, and quickly became the dominant political force in Ottawa. The most bitter fights involved those who had left for Ottawa and those who were seeking independence at the provincial level, and the election of Trudeau as federal Prime Minister in 1968 increased the tensions between French Canadian federalists and Quebec nationalists.

The growing Quebec middle class benefited from the 'Quiet Revolution', which brought them both control of a larger portion of the economy and employment in the rapidly growing public sector. By contrast, labour groups did not make any large material gains (though benefiting from improved labour legislation and unionization), and the more conservative rural areas were upset by the rapid pace of change and the extent of government intervention. These circumstances, combined with a 10 per cent swing to independence parties, contributed to the surprising electoral defeat of the Lesage administration in 1966.

GROWTH OF MILITANCY

The new *Union Nationale* government under Daniel Johnson faced an increasingly militant and violent union movement. This movement's fight was not only for conditions of employment; many radical union leaders had their own political agendas. Michael Chartrand, leader of the powerful *Central des Syndicats Nationaux (CSN)* in Montreal, wanted a revolution:

> We must destroy the capitalist system and reorganize the economy to meet the needs of the people. The CSN in Montreal will come to the assistance of all demonstrations, protesters and revolutionaries whose aims are the same as ours.[1]

Strikes were often accompanied by extensive vandalism and violence. Many companies or public sector organizations involved in labour disputes were the targets of bombings by the *Front de Libération du Québec* (FLQ).

Separatist sentiments were stirred in 1967 during the visit of French President Charles de Gaulle. He spoke to large crowds about 'the awakening of a people who want to be free to determine their own destiny in every respect' and at Montreal City Hall he uttered the now famous phrase *'Vive le Québec libre'*. His remarks helped to legitimize the separatist cause.

Demonstrations and protests over language accelerated. *Opération McGill Française* demanded the conversion of Montreal's largest English-speaking university into a French institution. For the 15,000 demonstrators who assembled in March 1969, McGill University was a symbol of English domination. There were also confrontations over the right of immigrant families to chose an English-language education for their children. In 1969 legislation assuring the right of choice inflamed Quebec nationalists who feared assimilation by the English-speaking minority.

Demonstrations turned increasingly violent. The St-Jean Baptiste parade on 24 June 1968, attended by Trudeau, deteriorated into a riot: 250 people were injured, and 292 arrested. The most serious incident came on 7 October 1969, when Montreal's 3,700 policemen and 2,400 firemen went on illegal strike. Unions and left-wing groups took the opportunity to attack the garages of the Murray Hill bus company, which was involved in a long-running dispute with the city's militant taxi-drivers. Several buses were set ablaze and the company's security guards fired on the mob, killing one person (an undercover provincial policeman) and wounding 30 others. Looting broke out, and the army was called in briefly to deter further incidents.

While the Quebec government attempted to chart its way through the hazards of language legislation and labour disputes, the federal government, with many of its key posts held by French Canadians, embarked on its own initiative. Ottawa had first examined the language question in 1963 after the initial stirrings of Quebec nationalism, with the Royal Commission on Bilingualism and Biculturalism, though the Commission's recommendations were not taken up. In 1969 the Trudeau government passed the Official Languages Act, which made the country officially bilingual. The Act also involved a controversial and costly programme to make the federal civil service bilingual, and to guarantee bilingual government services. Even at that early stage many English-speaking Canadians, especially those in the far west of Canada where there were few French-speakers, protested that Trudeau was showing undue favouritism to Quebec and inflicting bilingualism on what they saw as an English-speaking country.

THE FLQ APPEARS

The first attacks of the group which identified itself as the *Front de Libération du Québec* (FLQ) came on 7 March 1963, when the FLQ attacked three Canadian Army barracks in the Montreal area with Molotov cocktails. The FLQ described itself as 'a revolutionary movement made up of volunteers ready to die for the cause of political and economic independence for Quebec'. Its targets were 'all colonial symbols and institutions' including all vested interests of American colonialism, the natural ally of English Canadian colonialism. It called for 'independence or death'.[2] The FLQ emerged during the 'Quiet Revolution' when French-speaking Quebec was gaining a greater control of its destiny than at any time since the confederation but, although even the FLQ would have acknowledged that there had been some progress, change was not radical or fast enough.

Scattered bombings continued through April and May of 1963 targeted primarily at symbols of the federal government (post offices, mail-boxes and military establishments), and using dynamite stolen from subway construction sites. On 20 April a bomb attack on a Canadian Army recruiting centre killed a nightwatchman. A $60,000 reward offered by the Quebec government and the city of Montreal produced an informer who provided police with a list of about 30 FLQ members, though not all were involved in the bombings. A police swoop based on the informer's information led to the arrests of 23 people; all but two were held criminally responsible for the death of the nightwatchman, receiving sentences of up to 12 years' imprisonment.[3]

The arrests came at a critical point in the organization of the FLQ – a few days after its first serious attempt to organize itself. Eight FLQ members meeting on 1 June 1963 decided to reorganize the group into tightly-knit cells, with a 'central committee' in overall command. Changes were to include the division of the group into two distinct branches, a political branch (the FLQ) and a military branch (the *Armée de Libération du Québec* (ALQ)). Ironically, although the FLQ would exist in varying forms for another nine years, this was the closest it came to establishing a central leadership and structure.

When the FLQ began to reorganize in the summer of 1963, buoyed up by civil rights disturbances in the United States, the elements that made up the group had changed. Several members of the first network were still at large. Other cells, unconnected with the founding group, sprang up spontaneously and began to prepare for action. From then on, the FLQ was no longer a single organization but became a collection of loosely-connected though clearly distinct groups, a label to which all supporters of political violence laid claim. This situation continued through the decade. As Pierre Vallières wrote in the October 1965 edition of the FLQ publication *La Cognée* (The Hatchet):

> For all practical purposes, the FLQ is a vague collection of tiny, more or less active groups, whose members are all known to the police and each other. Only *La Cognée* carries on, although we cannot claim that it is really contributing at the moment to the theoretical or practical education of the revolutionary cadres. There is currently a lack, not only of grass-roots activists, but also of revolutionary thinkers.[4]

Even in 1970, during the shift to political kidnapping, the FLQ lacked central leadership or co-ordination. Given the spread of police informants and its own amateur nature, the FLQ could not have continued to exist in any other form. Bombings were indeed an 'infantile disorder'. They continued through the second half of 1963 and into 1964, aimed primarily at symbolic targets, such as the Queen Victoria monument and the Wolfe Memorial in Quebec city.

GOVERNMENT RESPONDS

In early 1964 the government responded by forming the Montreal-based Combined Anti-Terrorist Squad (CATS) which consisted of members from the City of Montreal Police, the *Québec Sûreté* (provincial police) and the Royal Canadian Mounted Police (RCMP), specifically the RCMP Security and Intelligence Service. Successful police operations in May 1964 led to the break-up of FLQ groups (acting under the banner of the ALQ); an FLQ 'fund-raising cell', which had carried out several bank robberies; and a group calling itself the *Armée Révolutionnaire du Québec*, which was involved in a robbery at International Firearms in Montreal that led to the deaths of two people in an exchange of gunfire with police.

In 1966 Pierre Vallières and Charles Gagnon were the first from within the FLQ to call for 'the construction of a specifically Québécois form of socialism'.[5] They took as their heroes Che Guevara and Mao but attempted to model themselves on the Algerian FLN. For them the fight had shifted from federalists versus separatists to the proletariat versus the bourgeoisie: 'The war for the national liberation of Quebec will be violent, organized, armed struggle'. After a short bombing campaign, targeted primarily at private sector companies involved in labour disputes, police arrested about 20 members of the Vallières-Gagnon network in September 1966, though the two principals left for the United States. Later that month they were arrested in front of the United Nations building in New York demanding 'political prisoner' status for those held in prison. Vallières and Gagnon were turned over to the Canadian authorities in January 1967, but did not come to trial for over a year. Their imprisonment became a *cause célèbre* in Quebec. In March 1968, with the publication of *Nègres Blancs d'Amérique*, Vallières became internationally known as the FLQ's chief ideologue.

FLQ activity accelerated during 1968–9 with a wave of bombings organized primarily by Pierre-Paul Geoffroy (a university student) and the *Front de Libération des Travailleurs du Québec*, though they later referred to themselves simply as the FLQ. Bombs were again directed at companies involved in labour disputes and also at the homes of city officials and federal offices in both Montreal and Ottawa. On 13 February 1969 a large bomb exploded at the Montreal Stock Exchange at the height of trading. This attack was designed to 'strike a blow at the heart of capitalism'.[6] Surprisingly no one was killed, though 20 people were injured, three of them seriously; in previous incidents separatist bombings had taken care to avoid casualties. Montreal police arrested Geoffroy shortly afterwards. In court he assumed full responsibility for the actions of the FLQ network and pleaded guilty to 129 counts related to 31 bombings, for which he received

124 life sentences. Although the imprisonment of Geoffroy removed the leader of that FLQ network, most of its members avoided capture. Within a few months the campaign resumed through 1969, but less effectively.

What is striking about the first five years of FLQ operations is how limited they were. The number of FLQ-related incidents decreased every year from 1963 to 1968, with the exception of 1965 when a revival of bombing attacks supported strike action. After 1966, symbolic attacks and bank robberies diminished, while the level of technical sophistication in bomb-making increased. Bombings made up 48 per cent of FLQ incidents, and 131 out of 174 acts of FLQ violence (75 per cent) were in Montreal.

FLQ members came from a variety of backgrounds, though most of them were students and young unskilled workers. In the early bombing campaigns the average age of those arrested was less than 19, while in the second half of the decade the average age of members rose towards the middle twenties. They were teachers and students, unemployed workers and workers in the public sector. A number of members were drawn from legal separatist and left-wing political groups, such as the *Rassemblement pour l'Indépendence Nationale* (RIN founded in 1960), and the *Front de Libération Populaire* (FLP), members of which constituted the café revolutionaries of their time. Recruitment was ill-organized, and relied substantially on friends and relations. As a rule there was not much continuity: those active in the early stages tended not to be active in the FLQ later in the decade, though there were a few notable exceptions.

ELECTIONS FAIL NATIONALIST ASPIRATIONS

The most important political event in Quebec in the first half of 1970 was the bitter campaign and controversial result of the April provincial election in which Robert Bourassa and the Liberal Party swept to power. With the newly formed *Parti Québécois* (PQ), the electorate for the first time had a real chance to vote for a party that favoured separatism. The Liberals captured 44 per cent of the vote and 72 seats in the 108-seat Assembly, while the PQ won only seven seats with about 24 per cent support. On the whole, PQ support was evenly spread throughout the province and only in the working-class east of Montreal was the concentration strong enough to yield seats. This was in stark contrast to the Social Credit Party, which benefited from rural discontent to win 12 seats on only 12 per cent of the provincial vote. Although the Liberal victory was expected, as well as the percentage vote distribution, the PQ felt the injustice of non-proportional representation. The upshot was that many in the separatist movement felt betrayed by the electoral process, and some resorted to terrorism in earnest.

MAY 7 COMMITTEE

The election result and a resumption of the FLQ bombing campaign generated activity at both federal and provincial government levels. In early May the federal cabinet Committee on Priorities and Planning, chaired by the Prime Minister, set up a special inter-ministerial committee chaired by the deputy Minister of Justice, Donald Maxwell, to work out an overall plan on law and order (it became known as the May 7 Committee). One of the Committee's tasks was to consider what steps should be taken if the War Measures Act was invoked in response to an insurrection, another was to examine means of strengthening the role of the armed forces and the RCMP in the maintenance of law and order.[7]

It was apparently on the initiative of the May 7 Committee that the Strategic Operations Centre (SOC) was established to bring together intelligence from various sources and to analyse it. The new unit assumed an important role in the managing of the coming 'October crisis'. Also during May, a deputy inspector of the RCMP Security and Intelligence Service in Montreal was transferred to Ottawa to set up 'G' Branch to deal with all 'separatist terrorist' activities, and to monitor the *Parti Québécois*; 'G' Branch was to work in liaison with the newly created SOC. Preparations for the activation of 'G' Branch continued through the summer of 1970, but were delayed by the events of early October.

With the renewal of bombing attacks following the 29 April provincial election, the Quebec government increased its anti-FLQ efforts. The Combined Anti-Terrorist Squad (CATS) was given a special adviser, Michel Côté, head of the legal department in the City of Montreal. By 28 May an FLQ 'fund-raising' network, believed to be responsible for about 30 armed robberies since 1969, was broken and five FLQ members were arrested. However, the police were unable to make significant progress against FLQ cells involved in the bombings. After a rash of dynamite thefts during the summer, the provincial government decided on a wide sweep to track down individuals believed to be involved in the thefts and bomb makings. According to the *Sûreté du Québec* there were 29 thefts of dynamite in 1970 involving 3,600 lb of TNT (4,600 sticks) and 5,708 detonators. The CATS was helped by information provided by an FLQ informer (recruited in March), and by a new explosives control law which gave it wide powers of search and arrest. It planned to start 'Operation Richelieu' on 5 October, the day on which the FLQ chose to act.

ROSE AND LANCTÔT

The central FLQ participants in the events of 1970 were groups clustered around two dominant but different personalities, Paul Rose, a special education teacher and member of both the FLQ and the RIN, and Jacques Lanctôt, a taxi-driver active in several radical-left protest groups including the RIN.[8] The two had met during the 1968 Jean Baptiste disturbances, though when they became involved in FLQ activities they at first operated independently.

Paul Rose, whose strength lay in organization, prepared for an extended struggle and a prolonged underground existence. The core of the group consisted of Rose (aged 27); his brother Jacques (22), a railway mechanic; François Simard (22), an apprentice electrician who had met Rose in the summer of 1969; Yves Langlois (22), a former court stenographer; and Claude Morency (21), a labourer. The Rose group concentrated first on fund-raising, primarily through the defrauding of American Express. This enabled Rose to rent safe houses in and around Montreal, buy vehicles and, most importantly, buy an isolated farm at Sainte Anne de la Rochelle, east of Montreal. The farm was to serve as a hide-out, training centre and possible 'people's prison' for hostages.

Unlike Rose, Lanctôt, (aged 24) was impatient and more of a man of action. Indeed, he had been active in 1963 when he was only 17. Other core members of the Lanctôt group included his brother François (21), André Roy (23), his friend and fellow taxi-driver; Marc Carbonneau ((37), a taxi-driver; Louise Lanctôt (23), Jacques' sister, an archivist; and her husband Jacques Cossette-Trudel (23), a teacher.[9] Frustrated by what he saw as 'endless' planning , Lanctôt decided on a political kidnapping – a departure for the FLQ but not surprising given Lanctôt's admiration for terrorist activities in Latin America.

The Lanctôt group drew up a list of foreign diplomats in Montreal and noted details of their travel and work habits. The first target,

Moshe Golan, the Israeli Consul, was perhaps chosen as a gesture of solidarity with the Palestinian movement, which many FLQ members admired, and the attempt to take him came during 'Quebec – Palestine Solidarity Week'. On 26 February 1970, Jacques Lanctôt and Pierre Marcil (25), an unemployed worker, were stopped by police because of a defective tail light on the rented van they were driving. Police found a sawn-off shotgun in the van. The two were charged with illegal possession of a firearm and released on bail. Lanctôt jumped bail and went underground. Following up their investigation, the police discovered a large wicker basket in the seized van and a note with media phone numbers and the word 'Golan' on it. The anti-terrorist squad subsequently issued warrants for the arrest of Lanctôt and Marcil for conspiracy to kidnap the Israeli consul. Marcil was arrested (he served four and a half years in prison) but Lanctôt, along with his wife and child, found refuge in the farm owned by Paul Rose who, though not involved, had known of the kidnap venture.

Other FLQ groups remained relatively quiet during the run-up to the 29 April 1970 provincial election, in which a third of French-speaking voters supported the PQ. After the election the FLQ groups resumed scattered bombing attacks, many in support of workers in labour disputes, and a robbery at the University of Montreal netted some $58,000. After several bombings in the English-speaking residential district of Westmount on 31 May, the Quebec Ministry of Justice offered a $50,000 reward for information. Bombing attacks aimed at a variety of targets in and around Montreal continued through May until mid-July. A departure from the normal pattern was the bomb set outside the Department of National Defence headquarters in Ottawa on St-Jean Baptiste Day (24 June), in which an operator at a communications centre was killed. On 16 July another bomb was defused near the Victoria Hotel in Quebec city, where newly-elected Premier Robert Bourassa was staying.

The second kidnapping target of the Lanctôt group was Harrison Burgess, the US consul. In early June the group rented a cottage near St Jérôme, north of Montreal, to serve as an operations base. Information from an informer responding to the reward offered during investigations into the robbery at the University of Montreal led to the surveillance of André Roy of the Lanctôt group, who was previously unknown to the police. Members of the Combined Anti-Terrorist Squad followed Roy to the cottage. On 21 June, 30 officers from CATS descended on the cottage and arrested Roy, his wife Nicole, François Lanctôt and Claude Morency; two others were arrested in Montreal.

At the cottage the police seized a variety of weapons and bomb-making materials, and $28,000 from the University of Montreal robbery. In a raid on an apartment rented by Lanctôt and Morency in Montreal, police found a copying machine, FLQ letterhead paper, a communiqué announcing the kidnapping of Burgess, a list of four demands and 250 copies of the FLQ manifesto. The break-up of the plot to kidnap Burgess became a double blow to the Lanctôt–Rose network when the police also discovered in the cottage the address of Rose's farm at Sainte Anne de la Rochelle.

Police raided the farm the next day but although all the key members of the Lanctôt–Rose group were there at the time, none was arrested. The police failed to find Paul Rose, Jacques Rose and Jacques Lanctôt, who hid in farm buildings. The other group members present answered police questions and gave false names (which the police failed to check). Although the group members avoided capture, the raid rendered the farm useless as an operations base. The 'headquarters' moved to a house rented by Rose at 5630 Armstrong Street in Saint-Hubert, a Montreal suburb on the South Shore. Lanctôt had failed to produce results and his action had led to the disruption of Paul Rose's careful planning, which had to begin again. Finances were a serious problem, and this was a key factor in a split between Rose and Lanctôt over the group's future.

Lanctôt himself was keen to free from jail his brother and his friend, and to restore the FLQ's image in the eyes of the Québécois. In early September, at the house on Armstrong Street, the group voted in favour of kidnapping an American diplomat to obtain the release of FLQ members held in prison. After losing the vote, Paul Rose, Jacques Rose and François Simard decided to re-establish a separate group and continue their long-term strategy. During that month two new members joined the Lanctôt group: Nigel Hamer (aged 23), an engineering graduate from McGill University (and the only English-speaking member of the group), who had been involved in the bombing campaign earlier in the year; and a young woman (aged 19) whose name has never been made public. The group now totalled seven. It was estimated that the total manpower available to provide support for the operation, in addition to the Lanctôt–Rose network, was about 25 people. When the Rose group heard of the planned kidnap the three decided to leave the country. On 24 September Paul and Jacques Rose and François Simard (along with Rose's mother and sister to act as 'cover') entered the United States by car.

THE KIDNAP OF JAMES CROSS

On 4 October the prospective kidnappers met at 10945 Des Recollets Street, where the hostage would be held, and made the decision to kidnap James Cross, the British Trade Commissioner. Until then the group had been undecided on the target. The list had been narrowed down to Cross and John Topping, the new US consul, who both lived on the same street in the Mount Royal section of Montreal. According to François Simard (of the Rose group), the original plan had never been to kidnap a British diplomat alone, for fear this would focus attention on the Anglo-French aspects of the conflict. The intention was to kidnap a British diplomat, as a protest against 'cultural colonialism', and an American diplomat, as an attack against 'economic imperialism'. Evidence also suggests that the kidnappers saw the abduction of Cross as a symbolic act and that a 'businessman' (probably American) was to be the next victim. Given their limited resources, the kidnappers opted for two consecutive kidnappings, rather than a double.

In the event, Cross was kidnapped at 8.15 am on 5 October by five members armed with two pistols and an M-1 rifle. He was bundled into a borrowed taxi and forced to lie on the back seat under a blanket. Five minutes after leaving his residence the party switched to another car and drove to the apartment at 10945 Des Recollets Street, where he was held for the next 59 days.

News of the kidnap had already become widespread when the kidnappers telephoned two radio stations shortly before noon to indicate where envelopes containing information could be found. The messages were picked up by the police, and contained a communiqué setting out FLQ demands and an eight-page manifesto. The demands, which were to be met within 48 hours, were:

  i) the cessation of all police activities designed to find the kidnappers of their hostage
 ii) the publication of the FLQ manifesto on the front pages of all major newspapers and its broadcast on Radio Canada during a special prime-time broadcast in which released FLQ prisoners would be permitted to read and comment on the text
iii) the release of 20 'political prisoners' in prison or in custody awaiting trial, as well as three others currently on bail, with permission to leave the country
 iv) the provision of an aircraft to fly them to Algeria or Cuba, accompanied by their lawyers and at least two reporters

   v) the rehiring of the 'Lapalme Boys', a group of dismissed postal truck drivers.[10]

  vi) a 'voluntary tax' of $500,000 in gold ingots to be placed on the aircraft with the political prisoners on their release

 vii) the publication of the name and photograph of the presumed informer who caused the break-up of the plot to kidnap Harrison Burgess in June.

REACTIONS AT NATIONAL AND FEDERAL LEVELS

At emergency meetings in both Ottawa and Quebec city the federal and provincial cabinets decided to act jointly, since they had overlapping responsibilities: the provincial government was responsible for criminal justice in Quebec (through the Ministry of Justice), and the federal government was responsible for the safety of foreign diplomats (through the Department of External Affairs), though it was clear from the start that the federal government was the dominant partner. After consultations with Quebec, the federal cabinet decided that they would not meet all the terrorists' demands and adopted a strategy designed to obtain the release of James Cross at the minimum cost in concessions. The strategy was threefold:

   i) to establish a dialogue with the FLQ and yield to the least excessive of its demands – the publication of the manifesto

  ii) to offer safe conduct and transport to a foreign country in return for Cross

 iii) to extend the negotiations as long as possible, to enable the police to locate Cross.

The Minister for External Affairs, Mitchell Sharp, initiated contact with the Cuban and Algerian embassies asking them to accept the kidnappers (but not any FLQ members held in jail), who might be given safe conduct in exchange for their hostage. Mitchell Sharp also moved to set up an External Affairs operations centre, under the direction of Claude Roquet, in the Parliament Buildings in Ottawa. It was manned 24 hours a day for the period of the crisis and was staffed primarily by External Affairs officers, though it also contained personnel from other interested government agencies, such as the Prime Minister's Office (PMO), the office of the Solicitor-General (responsible for the RCMP), the Department of Justice, the RCMP, the Department of National Defence (DND) and others. Its role was to collate, analyse and distribute information on the crisis to both federal and provincial government departments, but it represented only the particular interests of the Department of External Affairs, since the victim was a diplomat.

A completely separate and more central intelligence-collating group was the Strategic Operations Centre (SOC – see p. 41) initiated in May 1970. Also based in Ottawa, the members of the SOC included individuals with close links to the Prime Minister, including several members of the PMO. The core members of the SOC were: Jim Davey (PMO), the SOC director; Jean-Pierre Goyer (Trudeau's parliamentary secretary); Jean-Pierre Mongeau (PMO); sociologist Fernand Cadieux (PMO, and the Prime Minister's principal speech-writer during the crisis); Robin Bourne (PMO, and a retired colonel); and Arnold Masters (a Québécois of Irish descent and a deputy minister), in addition to representatives of the armed forces and the RCMP. Importantly, the SOC reported directly to Prime Minister Trudeau and his Principal Secretary, Marc Lalonde. Its function was to collate and analyse information on the situation in Quebec, to inform the Prime Minister, the cabinet and other government agencies accordingly, and to recommend action. Claude Roquet, director of the External Affairs operations centre, did not know of the existence of the SOC, nor did he have any contact with Jim Davey.

In Quebec city the central figures of the crisis headquarters staff surrounding Premier Robert Bourassa were Julien Chouinard, the premier's executive assistant (and former lieutenant-colonel in the Canadian Army), and his special adviser Paul Desrochers (former intelligence officer in the Canadian Army in the 1939–45 war). In Montreal the key figures in decision-making were the Mayor of Montreal, Jean Drapeau; the city's executive chairman, Lucien Saulnier; and legal adviser Michel Côté.

The police force initially responsible for finding Cross was the Combined Anti-Terrorist Squad (CATS), made up of officers of the City of Montreal Police, the *Québec Sûreté* and the RCMP. The group consisted of 20 city police detectives, about 30 provincial police detectives and an undisclosed number of RCMP officers; it was insufficiently prepared or staffed for the crisis, during which 300 bilingual RCMP officers were eventually involved in counter-terrorist activity in Montreal and approximately 300 more in other parts of the province. The city of Montreal police totalled about 3,700.

THE KIDNAP CRISIS

At noon the next day the kidnappers issued a second communiqué, along with a letter from Cross to his wife. The FLQ gave the authorities 24 hours to meet its demands, against the threat to 'execute' the hostage. A third communiqué was issued at about 6.00 p.m. containing another letter from Cross to his wife. The FLQ also requested the assistance of the media as the police, they claimed, were seizing documents before radio stations could pick them up.

Special cabinet meetings were held in both Quebec city and Ottawa. Mitchell Sharp publicly explained that the government regarded this particular set of demands as 'wholly unreasonable', so leaving the door open for negotiation. Both governments attempted to play down the hostage situation; the PMO announced that Trudeau still planned to go on his official visit to the Soviet Union, and Premier Bourassa indicated that he would go to New York on scheduled business later in the week. On the government side secondary actors took the lead positions – in Ottawa, Mitchell Sharp, and in Quebec city, Jérôme Choquette, the Minister of Justice.

The police began to piece together a suspect list and began arresting suspects; 27 were picked up in the early morning hours, but most were released after being put through an identification line-up. Jacques Lanctôt, given the attempted kidnapping of Golan and his brother's attempt to kidnap Burgess, was immediately a prime suspect and Mrs Cross identified a picture of him. The police also identified Marc Carbonneau's fingerprints on the first communiqué. In addition, an RCMP informer provided the names of most of the Lanctôt–Rose network, while a CATS source identified, among others, Lanctôt and Hamer. However, the police officers in charge of the investigation rejected the idea that Hamer was involved, and he was not put on the arrest list.

At 11.45 a.m., 15 minutes before the deadline, Justice Minister Jérôme Choquette (after consultations with Sharp) announced that the governments were prepared for discussions with the kidnappers and were waiting for a signal from them. At 1.30 p.m., a local radio station broadcast the fourth communiqué. This extended the deadline by 24 hours and demanded, as proof of good faith, that the manifesto should be broadcast and the police raids should stop; the first two original demands therefore became the minimum requirement for the government to show its good faith in the negotiations to come, though the second demand was reduced to a simple broadcast of the manifesto by Radio Canada during prime time. At 10.00 p.m., Sharp announced on national television that the government would arrange for the Canadian Broadcasting Corporation (CBC) to broadcast the manifesto. He also invited the FLQ to name a 'trustworthy person' to discuss the arrangements for the release of Cross.

The noon deadline passed without a communication. At 12.30 p.m. a local radio station broadcast the kidnappers' fifth communiqué, which repeated that the two demands of the previous day must be met and rejected the idea of a mediator. Police investigations and arrests continued throughout the day. There were reports that 250 soldiers of the Royal 22nd Regiment, a French Canadian regular army unit, had moved to Camp Bouchard, just north of Montreal.

That evening the French network of Radio Canada broadcast the FLQ manifesto. The document was a lengthy Marxist diatribe against both Canadian and Québécois institutions and government leaders, calling on the workers of Quebec to revolt. It was also, however, a populist document which identified specific groups with legitimate grievances which had been 'wronged' by the economic system and the government.

In their seventh communiqué (the sixth was lost in transit) the kidnappers announced that they were 'temporarily suspending' their threat to 'execute' Cross after the broadcast of the manifesto. The demands were reduced to the release of political prisoners and their safe transport to Cuba or Algeria, and a cessation of police activity. They promised that Cross would be released within 24 hours following the return of observers who were to accompany the prisoners. A warning was also made against any police attempts to rescue Cross; but this time the kidnappers did not mention their original demands, v, vi and vii (see p. 45).

Following his original schedule, Premier Bourassa travelled to New York to meet investment dealers and government officials.

At a press conference at 5.40 p.m. on 10 October, 20 minutes before the kidnappers' deadline, Justice Minister Choquette emphasized the dedication of the Quebec government to social reform and its desire to correct injustice. He called on the FLQ to understand the government's position and to contribute constructively to the solution of society's problems. Choquette said the government rejected the FLQ's demand for the release of prisoners, but added that normal parole procedures would be followed objectively and that, in cases of prisoners still before the courts, the cases would be considered with clemency. Choquette reiterated the willingness of the authorities to allow the kidnappers safe passage out of Canada on the safe release of Cross. One source later reported that, after watching Choquette deliver the government's final offer on television, Cross asked his captors what they were going to do. He was told that they would continue to hold him for a few more days, just to taunt the police, and then let him go.

THE CROSS NEGOTIATIONS

The authorities tried to block publication of FLQ communiqués, but the terrorists responded, and gained publicity, by sending duplicates to several media outlets. This phase lasted for two and a half days and was finally won by the FLQ. The second phase was the day and a half leading up to the broadcast of the FLQ manifesto, when the government tried to stall for time and draw the kidnappers away from communication through the media and towards direct and secret negotiations. At the same time it tried to delay as long as possible the publication or broadcast of the manifesto (even to the point of telephoning newspaper publishers directly). Once again, these efforts were undermined by the FLQ's provision of multiple copies to the media. Any good faith that had existed was destroyed when the terrorists' sixth communiqué, in which they responded to the manifesto broadcast in a conciliatory fashion, was never found because of the problems in delivery. The terrorists believed that the police had once again intercepted a communiqué, and in response issued a final ultimatum for the release of the prisoners. The government then drafted a final offer in such a way as to appease public sentiment, which sympathized with many aspects of the manifesto, while offering safe passage for the kidnappers.

The terrorists had undoubtedly gained widespread publicity and public sympathy for their cause, though they failed to win the release of the prisoners. They contented themselves with the propaganda victory. The authorities appeared to have bargained successfully for the release of Cross, but at the cost of widespread sympathy for the FLQ cause, opening the way to legitimizing it. Their miscalculation was to underestimate the strength of public support for FLQ aspirations.

THE TAKING OF LAPORTE

The Rose group had reached St Louis, Missouri, in the course of their 'fund-raising' tour in the United States, when they heard of the Cross kidnapping. They were surprised, not by the kidnapping, but that the target had been British and not American; they did not know of the terrorists' determination to proceed with consecutive kidnappings. They felt that Lanctôt had chosen the easier option, and that this undermined their chances of obtaining the prisoners' release. To help to strengthen the terrorists' bargaining position, they decided to return to Quebec and stage another kidnap.

By 8 October they had arrived in the Montreal area. Although they considered kidnapping James Lecoups, an American diplomat, this was considered too risky, as was their second choice. A third choice was Pierre Laporte, Minister of Labour and Immigration in the Quebec government, an influential political figure and a friend of Prime Minister Trudeau. Choosing Laporte had an added advantage in that he lived not far from where the Rose group intended to hold the hostage, the house at 5630 Armstrong Street. It was around that time that Bernard Lortie (aged 18), who had met Paul Rose in the Gaspé region in the previous summer, joined the group.

After watching Choquette on television rejecting the terrorists' final demands, the Rose group decided to go ahead and kidnap Laporte. On 10 October the Rose brothers, Jacques Simard and Bernard Lortie arrived by car at the Laporte residence in suburban Saint-Lambert, disguised and armed with two M-1 rifles and a sawn-off shotgun. Laporte, who was playing football with his nephew on the front lawn, was forced into the car and driven off. The nephew noted the license plate number and passed it on to the police.

After the abduction police activity accelerated significantly, and guards were assigned to all cabinet ministers and other public figures. Premier Bourassa (who had returned from New York that afternoon) moved into a heavily-guarded floor of the Queen Elizabeth Hotel in Montreal. The original kidnappers were completely taken by surprise, and there was no communication between the two groups of kidnappers for several days. However, the second FLQ kidnapping had a profound psychological effect on the provincial and federal governments and on the country as a whole.

The Rose group issued three communiqués during the following day. The first, received at 9.00 a.m., announced that the cell had kidnapped the minister and set 10.00 p.m. as the deadline for his 'execution' unless all seven of the original demands were fully met. The third communiqué (received at 5.00 p.m.), included a letter for Bourassa from Laporte, in which he told the Premier 'My life is in your hands' and urged him to make a deal over the prisoners.

Premier Bourassa met with his cabinet throughout the day in Montreal, and consulted with Ottawa and with Quebec opposition politicians. Five minutes before the Rose group deadline, Bourassa broadcast a statement asking the FLQ for a means by which to communicate. He was deliberately ambiguous about the possibility of negotiating an exchange, though he hinted at its likelihood.

The Rose group issued a communiqué which acknowledged the tacit acceptance of the FLQ's demands by the Quebec government and suspended the deadline for the 'execution' of Laporte but refused to negotiate the substance of the six remaining demands. The communiqué added that both Cross and Laporte would be 'executed' if the prisoners were not released. The disparity between the stated positions of the two groups delayed the appointment of the government's mediator Robert Demers, a lawyer with close connections to the Prime Minister. That evening Demers met with Robert Lemieux.

Meanwhile public pressure increased for Premier Bourassa to release the prisoners in exchange for the hostages. In a press statement, the PQ and its leader, René Lévesque, urged Bourassa to strike a deal quickly, 'since the government has implicitly accepted the principle of releasing the political prisoners'. Lévesque also suggested that the federal authorities should leave the negotiating to Quebec. Claude Ryan, editor of the large circulation French language daily *Le Devoir*, also supported negotiations as the most humane and realistic option.

EMERGENCY MEASURES

In Ottawa and Montreal, the federal and provincial cabinets discussed the possible introduction of the War Measures Act (WMA – which gives the police wide powers of arrest, detention and search) and the deployment of the army. The army would be used under the National Defence Act in aid of the civil power to take up the static guard duties, allowing the police to concentrate manpower on the search for Cross and Laporte. In Ottawa, army units took up positions to relieve the RCMP in the guarding of public officials, diplomats and government buildings, under a statute dealing with the provision of 'armed assistance' by one branch of the government to another. A team of army officers arrived at the headquarters of the *Québec Sûreté* to liaise between the provincial police and the military. (The *Sûreté* eventually became a joint operations centre.) Armed forces personnel at Mobile Command Headquarters, at Canadian Forces base Saint-Hubert, and units at Camp Bouchard were put on alert.

The two mediators met twice on 13 October, though no progress was made. Lemieux said that he needed further instructions from the two FLQ cells (with whom he was not in direct contact) before he could proceed. After meeting with his cabinet, Prime Minister Trudeau displayed a hard-line attitude in contrast to the perceived softening in Quebec city. He came out strongly against any negotiated release of prisoners and, in a now famous interview with a reporter outside the House of Commons, defended the use of the military:

> There are a lot of bleeding hearts around who can't stand the sight of people with helmets and guns. All I can say is: Go on and bleed. But it's more important to maintain law and order in society than to worry about weak-kneed people who don't like the looks of an army ... Society must use every means at its disposal to defend itself against the emergence of a parallel power which defies the elected power in this country, and I think that goes to any distance. So long as there is a power which is challenging the elected representatives of the people, then I think that power must be stopped and I think it's only, I repeat, weak-kneed bleeding hearts who are afraid to take these measures.

When the reporter asked how far he would go, the Prime Minister replied 'You just watch me'.

At RCMP headquarters in Montreal a list was drawn up of persons likely to be arrested if the WMA were invoked. The categories included:

i) individuals suspected of belonging to the FLQ
ii) individuals associating with the first group and in a position to help them
iii) individuals connected with the 'Vallières–Gagnon group' and with the *Mouvement de Libération du Taxi*[11]
iv) individuals in a position to advocate violence publicly and/or who had already taken part in violent demonstrations
v) individuals connected with various movements of the 'extreme left'.

The original RCMP list included 158 names. The Montreal Anti-Terrorist Section added a further 56, while the *Québec Sûreté* included the names of 140 individuals outside the Montreal area, chosen according to the RCMP criteria. In all, the draft arrest list contained a total of 354 names.

Paul Rose travelled to meet Jacques Cossette-Trudel, a member of the Lanctôt group (and for a time Rose was followed by police). It was the first communication between the two terrorist groups since the Laporte kidnapping, but they were unable to agree on a common approach on their demands. The Lanctôt group were conciliatory, refusing to kill Cross if the government refused to release the prisoners. The Rose group insisted on all the original demands, and refused to suspend the death threat against Laporte. They agreed that all communication with the authorities should be through the Lanctôt group, believing that this tactic would force the government to negotiate seriously. In a joint communiqué on 14 October, the terrorists suggested that both hostages would be released after the prisoners had been freed. The FLQ gave Robert Lemieux a free hand to negotiate on their behalf.

Troops continued to move into Camp Bouchard. The police arrest list was shown to Quebec Justice Minister Choquette (in consultation with the Premier) and two cabinet colleagues of the Prime Minister, Jean Marchand and Gérard Pelletier. All three removed a small number of names.

Bourassa's cabinet was divided on negotiating the release of the prisoners. That evening he announced that his government had not taken a final decision on the terms to be negotiated. At this point, fearing pressure from the federal government on the Quebec authorities, prominent PQ leaders such as Lévesque and newspaper editor Ryan called for the Quebec government to negotiate to save the lives of the hostages, and supported Bourassa in his earlier stand of favouring negotiations. Public concern mounted.

Students at the University of Quebec in Montreal boycotted classes after Robert Lemieux and Charles Gagnon had urged them to leave their classes and study the FLQ manifesto. Students at several other institutions went on strike in support of FLQ demands. A mass rally was scheduled for the Paul Sauvé Arena on the evening of 15 October, after which organizers planned to lead a march towards the City Hall.

The English language daily *The Gazette*, published excerpts from a 'secret report' of the RCMP, claiming that the FLQ had 122 active cells, 130 members and more than 2,000 sympathizers in its support network. A news agency in France published a communiqué from the 'délégation du FLQ en Europe', threatening attacks throughout Canada. In a television interview, FLQ mediator Robert Lemieux claimed (falsely) that the police had located the Rose group and were only waiting to find the Lanctôt group before attacking.

That evening, facing street demonstrations, numerous bomb threats and other demands on their manpower associated with the continuing search for Laporte and Cross, both the Montreal police and the *Québec Sûreté* requested assistance. This request was forwarded to the provincial government in Quebec city, who in turn asked the federal government for support. At 1.07 p.m., under the provisions of the National Defence Act, soldiers took up positions in the Montreal area 'in aid to the civil power'. They were deployed primarily in guarding public buildings and the homes of prominent persons. In Quebec city soldiers were deployed to guard the National Assembly building. The Quebec cabinet passed an order-in-council which placed all police and military forces under the command of the director of the *Québec Sûreté*. Thus, the chain of command was: the police director to the commander, Mobile Command (Saint-Hubert); to the Commander, 5th Combat Group; then down through the normal military command structure to the approximately 8,000 soldiers on the ground.[12]

That evening 1,500–3,000 people (estimates vary) took part in a highly charged rally at the Paul Sauvé Arena and were addressed by several speakers including Lemieux. After a reading of the FLQ manifesto, Pierre Vallières declared 'The FLQ is each one of you. It is every Québécois who stands up', as the crowd chanted 'FLQ, FLQ, FLQ'.

WAR MEASURES ACT

In Quebec city, after cabinet meetings and consultations with Ottawa, Premier Bourassa adopted a much tougher line in the negotiations. In his reply to the FLQ, he asked the International Red Cross or the Consulate of Cuba to act as intermediaries in the release of the two hostages. His government refused to release the 23 prisoners, but recommended the parole of five who had requested it; he promised safe passage for the kidnappers to the country of their choice, and rejected all other FLQ demands. Bourassa gave the FLQ six hours to respond.

After the announcement Bourassa signed a letter, drafted by himself and Trudeau's Principal Secretary, Marc Lalonde, asking Ottawa to invoke the War Measures Act:

> According to information in our possession and which is available to you, we are faced with a concerted effort to intimidate and overthrow the government and the democratic institutions of this province by the planned and systematic commission of illegal acts, including insurrection.[13]

A similar letter was sent to Ottawa by Jean Drapeau and Lucien Saulnier of the city of Montreal, which referred to an 'apprehended insurrection'. The letter was accompanied by a report by the Montreal police chief, Marcel Saint-Aubin, prepared with the assistance of Michel Côté.[14] It outlined the threat posed by the FLQ and, more importantly, the difficulties the police were having in tracking down the kidnappers:

> The extreme urgency in obtaining concrete results in uncovering all the ramifications of this organization and its seditious activities, and the volume and complexity of the evidence to be gathered and filed, finally the enormous task that we must carry out without resorting to unhealthy and undesirable repression, make it essential for higher levels of government to come to our assistance if we are to succeed. The slow pace of procedures and the restrictions resulting from the legal machinery and means at our disposal do not allow us to meet the situation.[14]

The letters from Quebec city and Montreal arrived in Ottawa at 3.00 a.m. on 16 October, the deadline set by Bourassa for a response by the FLQ. The federal cabinet was prepared to act, declaring that a state of apprehended insurrection existed in Quebec, and at 4.00 a.m. the War Measures Act was invoked. Using the powers granted by the WMA, the government declared the FLQ an illegal organization. At 5.00 a.m. a public announcement declared the Act invoked and the police, assisted by soldiers, started province-wide arrests (the WMA allowed for arrest without warrant and detention for up to 21 days), based on the lists drafted a few days previously. By 12.00 p.m. around 450 people had been arrested without warrant.

In the House of Commons, Prime Minister Trudeau defended the government's actions, though he sympathized with those who were concerned about civil liberties. Premier Bourassa took full responsibility for the decision to invoke the War Measures Act. He explained that the FLQ plan, which had begun with bombings and demonstrations, had progressed to kidnapping. The next stage, he believed, would include assassinations and the risk of anarchy; therefore, he concluded, the state had to act firmly. However, many opposition members in the House of Commons did not agree with the government's decision. New Democratic Party leader Tommy Douglas believed the government was dramatizing the situation to cover up its ineptitude. And according to the PQ leader René Lévesque, Quebec no longer had a government.

At the house on Armstrong Street, Pierre Laporte suffered serious cuts to his wrists and chest when he tried to escape through a window. François Simard, Jacques Rose and Bernard Lortie, who were with him in the house, bandaged his injuries but refused to take him to hospital. Laporte lost a considerable amount of blood. Meanwhile, Prime Minister Trudeau spoke on national television for the first time since the start of the crisis.

On 17 October the Lanctôt group issued its tenth communiqué which was intercepted by police and not broadcast. It claimed that the authorities had 'declared war' after first pretending to negotiate. It announced the suspension of the 'death sentence' on Cross, but added that he was a 'political prisoner' and would not be released until all FLQ activists had been set free. As for Laporte, the Rose group would announce a decision shortly. The Lancôt group had not been in communication with the Rose group, and Jacques Lanctôt later claimed that the communiqué had been intended to signal to the Rose group to keep Laporte alive. This was the last communiqué the authorities received directly from Lanctôt.

LAPORTE'S MURDER

At about 6.00 that evening, Pierre Laporte was strangled to death by François Simard and Jacques Rose. The four members of the Lanctôt group (though not all were present) accepted collective responsibility for his death. Laporte's body was put in the boot of the Chevrolet previously used to kidnap him. The car was left on the grounds of Won-Del Aviation in Saint-Hubert, near the Canadian Forces base.

At 7.00 p.m. an anonymous caller to a local radio station said that a package could be found in an abandoned car near the Saint-Hubert airport; this message was ignored as a hoax. An identical call was received at 8.30 p.m., and at 9.30 p.m. another call to the station gave the location of a communiqué which read:

> The arrogance of the federal government and its hireling Bourassa has forced the FLQ to act. Pierre Laporte, Minister of Unemployment and Assimilation (sic), was executed at 6.18 this evening by the Dieppe (Royal 22nd) cell.

After bomb disposal experts had checked the vehicle, Laporte's body was found at about 11.50 p.m.

At 3.00 a.m. on 18 October, Prime Minister Trudeau arrived at

the House of Commons, which was in session to debate the War Measures Act, and announced the death of Laporte. Some media sources
also erroneously reported the death of Cross. With the death of Laporte
there was an immediate swing of popular opinion behind the government. Claude Ryan gave his support, and René Lévesque wrote in
La Presse: 'This is not a time to split hairs. As of today the people
of Quebec must declare their support for the [provincial] government
in every way possible ...'.[16] Lévesque added, however: 'We believe
that the inflexible and uncompromising argument of reason of state
dictated by Ottawa bears a heavy share of the responsibility for the
tragedy we have witnessed'.[17] For his part, Premier Bourassa repeated
his offer of safe conduct to the Lanctôt group in exchange for the
safe release of Cross.

The police issued a warrant for the arrest of Paul Rose and Marc
Carbonneau. The publication of Rose's picture led to his identification
by a neighbour on Armstrong Street. Police investigating the house
discovered blood matching Laporte's, fingerprints of known FLQ
members and other evidence. In the house police also discovered the
address '3720 Queen Mary Road', where the Rose brothers and François Simard were hiding. (Police, however, did not follow up this information until 6 November.)

On 19 October the House of Commons approved the government's
action under the War Measures Act by 190 votes to 16, after it was
announced that the WMA would be replaced by new legislation within
a month (on 3 December Parliament passed the Public Order (Temporary Measures) Act, which provided for detention for up to seven days).
Both federal and provincial government officials attended the funeral
of Pierre Laporte, which took place under heavy security in Montreal
on 20 October.

A period of relative quiet followed Laporte's death, though police
investigations continued. On 25 October the Montreal municipal elections went ahead as scheduled with Mayor Drapeau's party capturing
93 per cent of the vote, defeating the *Front d'Action Politique*, a coalition
of leftist groups which at one point supported the goals of the FLQ,
though not their methods. The two FLQ cells were in a state of limbo.
The Rose group continued to hide out, but had no strategy apart
from avoiding capture. All eight members of the Lanctôt group and
James Cross were staying in the apartment at Des Recollets Street.
To ease the overcrowding, Nigel Hamer and one other left the
apartment on 21 October to liaise between the Lanctôt group and
the outside world. With the government refusing to negotiate, the Lanc-

tôt group were unsure of their prospects. At the beginning of November direct contact was re-established between the two groups for the first time since 13 October.

On 6 November, following up the address found on 18 October at the house where Laporte had been held hostage, Montreal police arrived at 3720 Queen Mary Road to carry out a 'routine search'. Three Rose group members (Paul Rose, Jacques Rose and François Simard) crawled into a specially built hiding-space behind a cupboard before the police were let into the apartment. Bernard Lortie and some other occupants were arrested. The three who were hidden remained motionless for about 20 hours until the police, who were carrying out a detailed search, left for a meal without posting a guard. The three then escaped.

On the same day, Nigel Hamer passed on a communiqué from the Lanctôt group to the authorities. Along with a message it contained a picture of Cross. Although the government banned publication of the communiqué, some media sources published the picture, in which Cross was apparently sitting on a case of dynamite.

CROSS RELEASED

Over 18 days, beginning on 7 November, two English-speaking RCMP officers eventually tracked down the Lanctôt group through standard police work. In an attempt to locate Lanctôt's wife, the officers, through the records of a moving company, traced the apartment which had served as a meeting-place for the two groups. From there they picked up the trail of Louise Lanctôt (Jacques Lanctôt's sister) and Jacques Cossette-Trudel, who were followed to 10945 Des Recollets on 25 November. That same day the RCMP picked up wire-tap information that led them to set up surveillance of a country house in the South Shore community of Saint-Luc, where (unknown to the RCMP at the time) Jacques Rose, Paul Rose and François Simard were hiding.

By 2 December the RCMP were convinced that Cross was being held at the apartment on Des Recollets. Louise Lanctôt and Jacques Cossette-Trudel were arrested shortly after leaving the apartment that afternoon. When they did not return at the appointed time the Lanctôt group realized that they had been discovered, and a series of negotiations began. The members of the group were given safe passage to Cuba in exchange for Cross. At 7.45 p.m. a Canadian Armed Forces aircraft left for Cuba with the kidnappers, along with some family members. At 2.00 a.m. on 4 December, after 59 days in captivity, James Cross was released.

On 22 December police began the search for the kidnappers. During the questioning of one of 11 suspects, police confirmed the location of the Rose brothers and Simard. The fugitives' hide-out in the cellar of the house in Saint-Luc was eventually found, and on 28 December the three surrendered to the police. On 18 November troops in Ottawa had returned to barracks; on 4 January 1971 the soldiers used in Quebec were withdrawn; and on 30 April 1971 the emergency officially came to a close.

THE AFTERMATH

Police action against the two groups of kidnappers dealt a crushing blow to the FLQ, while reaction to the murder of Pierre Laporte meant that a once sympathetic public virtually abandoned the Front. However, in its report of 1O December 1970 the federal government's analysis group, the Strategic Operations Centre, said:

> If anything, the FLQ are perhaps more dangerous now than they were prior to October. If the government has learned a lot about the FLQ, the FLQ has learned more about the government.[18]

The RCMP also produced a document based on the assumption of a continuing FLQ threat. *RCMP Strategy for Dealing with the FLQ and Similar Movements* advocated a policy of aggressive infiltration of FLQ cells and gave priority to the use of 'human intelligence' sources.[19]

Both these documents were approved at the 21 December meeting of the cabinet Committee on Security and Intelligence, chaired by the Prime Minister. In January 1971, the special RCMP Security Intelligence Service 'G' Branch, designed especially to deal with the 'separatist–terrorist' threat, was activated; its original deployment had been delayed by the October crisis. So the government began its active campaign against the remnants of the FLQ.

During 1971 and 1972 the RCMP Security and Intelligence Service heavily penetrated the remaining FLQ groups, to the extent that the RCMP set up fictitious FLQ cells which issued communiqués, stole dynamite and caused occasional explosions. In 1973 the RCMP broke into PQ headquarters and stole membership lists stored on computer tapes. Several acts committed by the Security and Intelligence Service during these operations were illegal. After a judicial investigation in 1981, 44 charges were laid against 17 active and former members of the RCMP. Charges included theft of dynamite, conspiracy, arson and theft.

The genuine FLQ cells mounted only sporadic bomb attacks and robberies, and were under constant police pressure. In December 1971 Pierre Vallières announced that he was leaving what was left of the FLQ to join the PQ in the fight for political sovereignty. The last active FLQ groups were broken by the end of 1972.

ASSESSMENT

Actions of the terrorists

By comparison with many other terrorist organizations, the FLQ must be rated as amateur. More importantly, as a group it did not constitute a serious threat to the stability of Canada. It lacked the organization or command structure to generate a co-ordinated assault on the government or to drive a wedge between the English and French communities, or between the 'proletariat' and the 'bourgeoisie'.

While claiming groups such as the Algerian FLN as its model, the FLQ showed an almost total lack of ruthlessness in its actions. During the group's entire active campaign (1963–72), not once did it deliberately plan to kill anyone. Those who died as a result of FLQ actions were killed accidentally as a result of bombings which had usually been planned to avoid injuring people or in shoot-outs during robberies that went wrong. The 'café revolutionaries' from which the FLQ drew membership and support were playing at revolution rather than pursuing it aggressively.

In Quebec there were no attacks on public establishments frequented by English patrons ('colonial' targets) or by the French Canadian elite ('revolutionary' targets). There was not a single bombing or shooting incident during the entire 'October crisis'. When one public official, Pierre Laporte, was killed, public sympathy for FLQ actions evaporated overnight.

Many of the operations mounted by the Rose–Lanctôt group in 1970 were marked by amateurism and impulsiveness. Only poor police work prevented the entire group from being arrested before the October kidnappings. The abduction of Pierre Laporte was a spontaneous action by the Rose group, who were ill-prepared to carry it out. They used a house which Rose had been living in for six months and which might have been known to the police, as well as a vehicle that was at Rose's farm during a police search in June. The group had so little money that at one point Laporte gave them $60 to buy food.

The FLQ nevertheless had some strengths. The bombing campaigns of the 1960s created fear and uncertainty among the population, but without a coherent strategy the FLQ failed to convert this effect into political leverage. However, by kidnapping a foreign diplomat in October 1970 the Lanctôt group forced the federal and provincial governments to take notice; they also achieved surprise. The hostage situation allowed them to play skilfully on the media by shunning direct talks with the government. The public nature of the negotiations added to the sense of involvement for those watching the drama, and also led to competition between media sources to be the recipients of FLQ communiqués. The extent and nature of the media coverage added to the tension and so helped the FLQ to create a climate of fear and crisis. The populist nature of the FLQ manifesto struck a sympathetic chord with the Quebec nationalist community, which in turn increased the pressure on the provincial government to negotiate the release of the hostages. These advantages sprang primarily from the efforts of the Jacques Lanctôt group. When the Paul Rose group burst on the scene, their priority was confrontation, not negotiation. Because of these conflicting strategies the propaganda and public sympathy gained by the Lanctôt group were eventually squandered.

The intelligence failure

The central problem in the response by the various levels of government to the FLQ was a failure in intelligence before, during and immediately after the October crisis. Not only did the intelligence services fail to forecast the FLQ's move to a different phase of operations (i.e. political kidnapping), but they also greatly over-estimated the strength of the FLQ.

There were several indicators of a change in FLQ tactics on kidnapping. By early 1970, a number of convicted FLQ members were being held in jail and at the same time terrorist organizations in several Latin American countries (with whom the FLQ was in sympathy) were kidnapping foreign diplomats to exchange for comrades in prison. In February 1970 the police accidentally uncovered the attempted kidnap of a diplomat, though they did not realize it until almost a month later. Then, in June, the Combined Anti-Terrorist Squad disrupted a second kidnapping plot aimed at a diplomat, and more FLQ members were arrested. Materials seized in the raids showed that the release of FLQ members in prison was one of the primary objectives. Still, the various intelligence groups (the RCMP Security and Intelligence Service, the intelligence unit of the *Québec Sûreté*, and the Montreal anti-terrorist unit) failed to give adequate warning to the appropriate government agencies or recommend significant preventive action. Instead, the primary focus was on the disruption of FLQ bombing groups, who had greater public visibility than potential kidnappers but were in fact more of a nuisance than a significant threat. So, on the day of the Cross kidnap, the police were geared for a sweep against bombing suspects.

In December 1970 the Strategic Operations Centre recorded the conclusion that the government should have been better prepared for the shift in FLQ tactics:

> In retrospect it is obvious that sufficient (although not complete) information was available to forewarn the government of the possibility/probability of an October crisis occurring, and to warrant some preventive or at least preparatory steps being taken prior to such a crisis breaking out.[20]

The fact that the federal government had recognized the intelligence shortfall in Quebec was demonstrated by the decision to create Branch 'Q' of the RCMP Security and Intelligence Service in May 1970, though the unit did not become operational until after the crisis.

The second intelligence shortcoming – the inability to provide an accurate estimate of FLQ strength – was demonstrated by the Justice Minister of Quebec, Rémi Paul, in October 1969 when he said there were about 3,000 terrorists in the province.[21] It is not clear where he obtained that figure, or how he defined 'terrorist'. At the height of the October crisis, a senior cabinet minister told the House of Commons that the government estimated that in the most pessimistic scenario there were about 3,000 terrorist members of the FLQ.[22] Again, the word 'terrorist' was not defined. Even the 'leaked' RCMP document (22 cells, 120 members and 2,000 active sympathizers) greatly exaggerated the size of the FLQ.

The level of accuracy was much the same when it came to the number of guns and rifles available. According to a senior federal cabinet minister, Jean Marchand:

We know that there is an organization that has thousands of rifles and machine-guns in their possession, and dynamite enough, about 2,000 lb, to blow up the heart of the city of Montreal.[23]

There had been a significant amount of dynamite stolen during the summer of 1970. As for weapons, however, after almost 5,000 police searches during the October crisis a total of 31 firearms were recovered. The Rose group were forced to buy one of the three weapons used in the Laporte kidnapping in a pawnshop after their return from the United States.

The FLQ contributed to the public perception that it was a large well-organized group. In an August 1970 interview, two alleged FLQ members in a terrorist training camp in Jordan announced their plan to return to Quebec and carry out 'selective assassinations' and wage urban guerrilla warfare.[24] The similarity between the attempt to kidnap Burgess and the successful operation against Cross gave the appearance of co-ordination between FLQ groups. Paul Rose, in issuing his group's first communiqué, referred to a decision to implement a non-existent 'Plan 3', giving the impression that there were a number of thought-out options available. The rapid kidnapping of Laporte after the government refused to give in to the Lanctôt group (18 minutes after the deadline) also contributed to FLQ mystique, underlined by the futile efforts of three police forces to find the kidnappers. In his letter to Premier Bourassa, Pierre Laporte wrote (or was told to write) 'We are in the presence of a well-organized escalation which will end only with the liberation of the political prisoners'.[25] And finally, at the time of Laporte's death, responsibility was claimed by an unknown 'Dieppe Royal 22nd' cell, invented by Paul Rose to suggest that several cells were acting as parts of a co-ordinated team.

When the police began to gather information after the Cross kidnap, informants provided the names of most of the people involved in both the Lanctôt and the Rose groups, even before Rose had kidnapped Laporte. The difficulty was that the police had no other information to go on, as the files on FLQ members were out of date.

Believing they were faced with a large, well-organized opponent, the police opted for the 'broad sweep' approach in sorting through intelligence information. This meant the systematic investigation of every piece of intelligence received – a task which quickly overwhelmed the small Montreal anti-terrorist unit (originally only 15 members) and required the services of more police personnel. During the crisis the police received an average of 12,000 pieces of information a day, each requiring verification; good information was lost in a flood of irrelevant data. The pressure on police manpower led to demands for army assistance with guard duty, and the slow progress in the investigations led to demands for the War Measures Act to be invoked. The amount of information received convinced police that the FLQ was large, and so the arrest operation, which eventually took in 497 people, was of corresponding size.

However, the arrest operation seemed to be aimed more at getting known sympathizers of the FLQ off the streets at a critical time in the crisis than at picking up those who were believed to have committed criminal acts. During the trials of those picked up by the police in October, no evidence that would support a criminal charge could be found in 435 of the 497 cases (87.5 per cent). Proceedings in 32 of the remaining 62 cases initiated under the Criminal Code or the War Measures Act were suspended in August 1971; only 30 people (6.5 per cent of those arrested) actually came to trial (with 16 people eventually sentenced).[26] If the five FLQ members in Cuba are included, the total number of those believed by the government to have been involved reaches 35. In Quebec the small and weakly organized FLQ met the WMA arrest operation with silence. It committed virtually no acts of violence in response, though there was always potential for a confrontation between FLQ supporters and the security forces.

The Macdonald Royal Commission on the RCMP Security Service in 1981 identified an additional problem: the lack of co-ordinated police intelligence resulting from jurisdictional disputes between the RCMP, the *Sûreté* and the Montreal police. Each force insisted on protecting its autonomy. The Combined Anti-Terrorist Squad, set up to co-ordinate police actions and exchange information, was relegated to a secondary role, and ceased to function after the kidnapping of Laporte. Another problem was RCMP distrust of the *Sûreté*. The RCMP had reason to believe that the FLQ or its sympathizers had penetrated the force. As a result, for example, the *Sûreté* was not given access to RCMP files. This hampered the exchange of information and complicated investigations.

When the October crisis was over, the Strategic Operations Centre greatly overestimated the potential threat the FLQ posed in 1971 and 1972. As a result, perhaps in an effort to make up for past failings, the RCMP mounted a series of 'disruptive' operations aimed at the FLQ and others, which were of dubious legality and had unfavourable consequences for civil liberties in the country. The RCMP's allegedly illegal activities in the 1970s touched off a political controversy that resulted in the removal of responsibility for intelligence from the RCMP.

Actions of the police and army

The police forces of Quebec and Montreal were reasonably successful in suppressing sporadic FLQ terrorism from 1963 to 1969, though they were unable to root out the highly decentralized and fairly spontaneous FLQ organization. However, the police were clearly unprepared for the October crisis; their actions disintegrated into 'improvisational disorder' and later 'chaos'.[27] Only the RCMP appeared capable of at least holding its own in the situation.

Obviously the central problems were to do with intelligence. However, in the realm of routine police work, both the Montreal police and the *Sûreté* missed several opportunities to close in on the terrorists. The *Sûreté*'s amateurism at times was 'almost unbelievable'. The following examples are illustrative and by no means exhaustive:

- The June 1970 *Sûreté* raid on the farm owned by Paul Rose: all the members of the Lanctôt–Rose group were present, but the police failed to find three FLQ members in a search and failed to verify the false names they were given by others.
- Although Paul Rose was a prime suspect in the kidnap of Pierre Laporte, his picture was not published until the day after Laporte's death. It was identified by a neighbour on Armstrong Street on the same day.
- An address found at the Armstrong Street house, which indicated where the remaining Rose group members were hiding, was not followed up for 18 days.
- *Sûreté* detectives identified Paul Rose at a subway station on 13 October but chose not to arrest him immediately. Rose lost the detectives twice while they attempted to follow him.

Although the army was given a 'high-visibility' role, its activities during the October crisis were generally low-profile. The army responded quickly and carried out its duties with great professionalism. The training required for Canada's overseas peace-keeping commitments was doubtless an invaluable preparation for support for the civil power. The army was not the target of any violent incidents, but the October crisis had stripped Canada bare of combat troops, and of the 1,200 soldiers deployed, 7,500 went to the Montreal area.

They would have been undermanned if they had faced an extended popular insurrection.

Actions of the politicians

In response to the Cross kidnapping, both governments played down the situation, and left the responsible ministers to manage the affair. The governments and the Lanctôt group appeared to be willing to accept a negotiated settlement short of their original objectives. The situation would have ended there if it had not been for the actions of the Rose group. It was during the Rose group's activities that the crisis became a political confrontation between the federal government and the FLQ at one stage, and between Prime Minister Trudeau and Quebec nationalists at a second. Seen simply as a response to FLQ terrorism, the governments' actions, though heavy-handed, overcame the threat.

Political structure

The result of the October crisis was the destruction of the FLQ and the clear drawing of political battle-lines for the next decade. For federalists, the defeat of the FLQ showed the need to fight Quebec separatism with a vigorous campaign from Ottawa, while for Quebec nationalists it confirmed that the only possible route to sovereignty or independence was through the legitimate political structure.

During the rest of the decade the federal government poured a significant amount of funding into Quebec to help economic growth, but also to raise the profile of the federal government. Programmes such as those of the Department of Regional Economic Expansion (DREE) directed a disproportionate amount of investment towards Quebec. For example, from January 1971 to March 1972 the province received 54.4 per cent of the money for new industries. Later in the decade this dropped to around 40 per cent, but was still proportionately higher than the amount received by any other province. During the 1970s the government also continued to pursue its policy of official bilingualism, and there was an accompanying rise in the number of French Canadians in the federal civil service. This perceived 'favouritism' toward Quebec did the Federal Liberal Party a considerable amount of political damage in western Canada, but the party's support in Quebec remained strong. In the 1972 federal election Prime Minister Trudeau won 56 out of 72 seats in Quebec, though popular support for the

Liberal Party dropped by 5 per cent in the province and the government suffered losses in other parts of the country.

After 1970 the Quebec government also launched a series of measures which touched on many of the issues which had come to the surface in the debate over Quebec nationalism, such as language, education and immigration. A sweeping language bill originally tabled in 1972 made French the official language of the province, limited access to English schools, required new immigrants to Quebec to learn French and made French the language of contracts in the province.

In 1976 René Lévesque was elected premier of Quebec, and the nationalist debate entered a new phase. In 1977 the PQ launched the 'Charter of the French Language' which legislated for the use of French in almost all government correspondence and communications and further restricted entry to English schools.

Most companies operating in Quebec were required to prove that French was the working language of their business, while the use of French was promoted in the areas of advertising, outdoor billboards etc.

One aspect of the legislation was the creation of a supervisory commission to oversee the implementation of the charter, labelled the 'language police' by the English minority. There was also an exodus of many English-speaking businesses from Quebec and several head offices were transferred from Montreal to Toronto. However, the PQ's 1976 electoral victory was not a mandate to pursue separatism. In the campaign Lévesque played down separatism (promising a referendum at a later date), and the victory was in part a result of the voters' dissatisfaction with the Liberals. In a 1980 referendum the PQ asked voters for permission to negotiate 'sovereignty association' with the rest of Canada as a first step towards separatism. The proposition was defeated by a 20 per cent margin, though the PQ was re-elected as the provincial government shortly afterwards.

Running parallel to the political situation in Quebec were the long-running constitutional negotiations initiated in 1968 to reassess the balance of power, and the relationship between the federal and provincial governments. Although the Canadian constitution and a Charter of Rights and Freedoms were 'patriated' from the United Kingdom in 1982, Quebec refused to ratify the agreement. The areas of dispute focused on the questions of minority language rights, the formula amending the constitution and a clause in the charter guaranteeing the free movement of Canadians within Canada (which had implications for access to education). It is illustrative of the political struggle between Quebec nationalists and Quebec federalists that all three of the people (including the Prime Minister) who signed the constitution on behalf of Canada were French Canadians, while the only province that failed to give approval to the constitution was Quebec. During the first term of office of conservative Prime Minister Brian Mulroney (also from Quebec), a package of constitutional amendments was agreed to by the ten provincial premiers and the federal government, the so-called Meech Lake Accord, as a compromise to bring Quebec into the 1982 constitution. The most controversial element of the Accord was the recognition of Quebec as a 'distinct society', allowing the provincial government to take such measures as were necessary to preserve Quebec cultural and linguistic identity. Although the Meech Lake agreement was approved by the Quebec National Assembly in June 1988, it was not ratified by all of the remaining nine provincial assemblies before the expiration of the two-year deadline in June 1990. The Liberal government in Newfoundland withheld ratification on the grounds that the Accord failed to offer sufficient protection for Quebec's English-speaking minority, while in Manitoba a native Indian member of the legislature used procedural rules to block last-minute approval, arguing that the amendments should also have recognized Canada's 350,000 aboriginal peoples as a 'distinct society'. The disagreement over the Accord was not a simple English-French split. At the forefront of the anti-Meech Lake campaign were former prime minister Elliot Trudeau and Jean Crétien, the newly-elected leader of the federal Liberal Party, who argued against any special status for Quebec and warned of the dangers to national unity of any further erosion of federal government powers. Still, the failure of the Meech Lake process was interpreted by many French Canadians as a rejection of Quebec and shortly afterward support for a nationalist option jumped sharply. Most importantly, Quebec premier Robert Bourassa, who had defended federalism in the past, appeared to have shifted to a more nationalist posture in the post-Meech Lake period. A provincial government committee was due to report in February 1991 to the premier on the constitutional and political options open to Quebec. It was widely believed that short of any constitutional *deus ex machina* retroactively to approve the Meech Lake Accord, Bourassa would call a referendum to pursue political sovereignty within Canada, similar to that proposed by the *Parti Québécois* in 1980.

Throughout the period of constitutional negotiations, politically-inspired violence in Quebec was limited to scattered vandalism against businesses with 'illegal' English signs, and one arson attack against an English rights association in Montreal. Should Quebec eventually choose to leave Canada, it will do so not as the FLQ had hoped with a bang, but with a whimper.

SUMMARY

The unpreparedness of the federal and Quebec governments to anticipate or react effectively to the relatively minor terrorist campaign mounted by the FLQ meant that the response in terms of politics and security was out of proportion to the threat.

Although this represented a victory for the FLQ, it also provided for the FLQ's destruction. The FLQ was a manifestation of the separatist movement, but it was the political element (the PQ) that was seen as the vanguard for change. No doubt many in the separatist political movement supported the FLQ in spirit, especially in the 1963–9 period of 'symbolic' terrorism which only rarely caused casualties; but the overwhelming majority of French Canadians did not support the actions of the Lanctôt group in murdering Laporte. The people of Quebec seemed to be willing to tolerate terrorism as long as no one was hurt.

This lack of support for violent terrorism can be linked to the fact that although there was dissatisfaction in French Canada over a number of socio-political issues, the option of pursuing change through the legitimate political spectrum was always available. There was not the isolation from the mechanics of change that often forces minority groups to resort to terrorism out of political frustration. No doubt the members of radical groups such as the FLQ did feel frustration, but the province as a whole looked to politicians, rather than terrorists, for change. Proof of this was the PQ, operating as a legal political party advocating separatism, which only eight years after its establishment formed the government of Quebec.

At the federal level also, French Canadians exercised considerable power. At the time of the October crisis the Prime Minister and several key members of the cabinet were French Canadians. In fact, since the 1930s a majority of Quebec-based seats in the Canadian House of Commons have been on the government side every year, except for short periods in 1957 and 1979. It took the Quiet Revolution to awaken Québécois to the need to assert control over their language, culture and economy. An overwhelming majority saw this as being possible through the existing political structure, with the important division running between those who believed it could best be done through a federal Canada and those who wished to achieve it in an independent Quebec state.

It is in this light that the political and economic programmes initiated by the federal and provincial governments during the late 1960s and the 1970s must be examined. The various economic programmes from which Quebec benefited, and the provincial language legislation (Bill 22 and Bill 101) were parts of the competition between the federalists and Quebec nationalists for the political hearts and minds of Québécois.

Although the October crisis added to the sense of urgency over these changes, the actions of the federal government (headed by Trudeau through virtually the entire decade) and the provincial government (until 1976) were aimed at keeping Quebec within confederation rather than being specifically directed at undermining separatist terrorism (which was not a significant force after 1970–1). In the final analysis, therefore, the strategy of the Canadian government against the FLQ terrorist threat was secondary to the much more serious political challenge to Canada posed by the separatist movement in Quebec.

NOTES

1. Louis Fournier, *FLQ The Anatomy of an Underground Movement* (Toronto: NC Press, 1984), p. 151.
2. Ibid., p. 13.
3. Ibid., pp. 36 – 41. By the end of 1967, all the participants in the first wave of FLQ activity were paroled. Georges Schoeters, a Belgian citizen, was deported after his release.
4. Ibid., p. 91.
5. Ibid., pp. 95 – 6.
6. Ibid., p. 150.
7. Government of Canada, *Commission of Inquiry Concerning Certain Activities of the Royal Canadian Mounted Police* (Macdonald Commission), vol. 3, August 1981, p. 269. The existence of this committee did not become public until a newspaper report of 23 December 1971.
8. Four other members of the Lanctôt family eventually joined the FLQ (out of ten children), and three members of the Rose family (out of five children).
9. The average age of those arrested for FLQ activity in 1963 was under 19 years. The average age of the known members of the Lanctôt–Rose network was around 24.
10. The 'Lapalme boys' were a unionized group of postal truck drivers who were replaced with another company by the Federal Minister of the Post Office in April 1970, triggering off a bitter and protracted labour dispute attracting the support and sympathy of many radical groups.

The FLQ carried out several bombing attacks on postal stations and offices in support of low-level attacks and sabotage on postal facilities conducted by Lapalme workers.

11. The *Mouvement de Libération du Taxi* was a militant group involved in the long dispute with Murray Hill and in other issues. Jacques Lanctôt, Marc Carbonneau and André Roy were members.

12. The status of the army was not altered by the declaration of the War Measures Act. At no time in the emergency was martial law declared or the civilian judicial structure in any way superseded.

13. Jean-François Duchaîne, *Rapport sur les Evénements d'Octobre 1970*, deuxième edition (Gouvernment du Québec, Ministère de la Justice, 1981) pp. 110–11.

14. As the War Measures Act was a federal statute, the letters from Montreal and Quebec city requesting that the Act should be enforced were not technically required, but they were thought to be politically expedient.

15. Duchaîne, pp. 113 – 15.

16. Peter Desbarats, *René: A Canadian in Search of a Country* (Toronto: McClelland and Stewart, 1976), p. 229.

17. Fournier, p. 257.

18. Duchaîne, Appendix, S.O.C. Document, p. 9.

19. Macdonald Report, vol. 3, p. 27.

20. Duchane, p. 24.

21. John Gellner, *Bayonets in the Streets: Urban Guerrilla at Home and Abroad* (Toronto: Collier-Macmillan, 1974), p.83.

22. Ibid., p. 8.

23. Lévesque, *Memoires*, p. 247.

24. Fournier, p. 207.

25. Gellner, p. 113.

26. Ibid., p. 93. Of those convicted – Paul Rose: two life terms for kidnapping and for the murder of Pierre Laporte; he was released on day parole in 1982. François Simard: life imprisonment for murder; he was released on parole in 1981. Bernard Lortie: 20 years for kidnapping; he was released conditionally in 1978. Jacques Rose: sentenced to eight years in his fourth trial in 1973 as an accomplice after the fact in the death of Pierre Laporte; he had previously been acquitted of murder, kidnapping and illegal confinement; he was released on parole in 1978. Michel Vier: eight years as an accomplice after the fact; he was released after serving four years. In addition, 13 other people served jail terms of not more than one year (Fournier, p. 271).

27. Duchaîne, pp. 253 – 6.

3 The South Moluccan Story[1]

THE THREAT

Roots of conflict

History

Until the 1939–45 war the Netherlands was a peaceful country with little serious crime. After the war the nation was reduced to serious poverty, and its energies were directed to rebuilding the country and to reabsorbing those returning from captivity. After ten years it became clear that the influence of the war went beyond rebuilding in a material sense: it had led to a more forceful, protagonist attitude in the population at large. Into the midst of this process the terrorist actions of the South Moluccans erupted as a total surprise.

The attitudes of the average Dutchman had for centuries been influenced by commerce with commercial centres around the world. However, the greatest wealth derived from the trade in spices with what is now Indonesia. In the 18th and 19th centuries, this vast area gradually became colonized, and emerged as Dutch East India. The instrument of the change was the VOC, the United East India Trade Company.

The Japanese captured and occupied Dutch East India from March 1942 until August 1945. Shortly before their surrender the Japanese had approved the setting up of an Indonesian independent state thus enabling Indonesian nationalist leaders to proclaim the establishment of the Republic of Indonesia on 17 August 1945, just prior to the landing of Allied liberation forces, the release of Dutch and other allied prisoners of war and civilian internees, and the re-establishment of Dutch rule. After a few years of military activity, interspersed with negotiations, the Dutch conceded sovereignty to the new state. Dutch is still widely understood there and in some areas it is still spoken. Many of the intelligentsia receive their education and training in the Netherlands. In particular, the relationship between the two countries, which was poor for a long time, has now improved, but it has taken a generation to heal the wounds of separation.

The Dutch saw their authority for the colonization of Dutch East

India in the church-supported concept of a 'historical role', which justified commercial objectives and military power. Since the area was 500
times the size of the Netherlands and half the world away, they delegated its management to a Governor-General. This government apparatus remained in force until 1948, though existing local customs and
forms of government ultimately responsible to a Dutch Resident were
maintained.

This immense territory was therefore effectively controlled by no
more than a handful of Dutchmen, even though the military were often
called on to maintain and, when necessary, restore order with severity.
The Royal Dutch Indian Army (KNIL) was formed of Dutch, or part-
Dutch, officers, though latterly members of the indigenous population
were admitted. The non-commissioned ranks and soldiers were entirely
recruited from the local population, predominantly from the group
of islands known as the Moluccas. The Moluccans were considered
particularly appropriate for military work in the tropics, and were
described by the Dutch as being 'loyal' and 'excellent soldiers'. This
Moluccan integration into the Dutch army aroused the hostility of
the other indigenous peoples towards the Moluccans.

Most of the Moluccans who entered the KNIL were from the South
Moluccan island of Ambon, and the Dutch colonial authority was
anxious to maintain the myth of the Christian, loyal Ambonese as
a professional soldier, even though revolts were frequent. The most
serious of these were in 1817, led by Pattimura, whose name is still
borne by an Indonesian regiment, and in 1858, 1860, 1864 and 1866.
In the knowledge that loyalty develops in parallel with a group's social
structure, the Dutch used this to set the different ethnic groups against
each other, and particularly the Ambonese against other population
groups to which they felt no loyalty. For example, it was common
practice for the VOC to send young indigenous men on punishment
expeditions or hunger-marches, with the objective of destroying the
social structure of the community.

Entering the service of the Dutch government was seen as going
into the service of the House of Orange or, it might be said, the Queen
herself. The loyalty that this implied was influenced by the Christian
religion, and was not found among the Islamic Ambonese. A young
man in a small village, accepted as a recruit for the KNIL, would
receive a so-called bounty, which he would usually hand over to his
parents. It was known by the Ambonese as 'head-money'.

Through colonial manipulation therefore, the Moluccans found
themselves between the Dutch and the the the rest of the indigenous popu-

lation. From time to time they strove to own the name and fame of Dutchmen; they came to meet the description given them by the Dutch; and gradually they became willing accomplices in the bloody colonial wars. As a result, in the colonial period the Moluccan people to a great extent lost their sense of history and identity.

In that colonial framework, the Moluccans' standards of law and order corresponded to those of the motherland, and many of those co-opted into the governing echelons studied at Dutch universities. They felt themselves to be the equals of, and to have equal rights with, the Dutch, and to be clearly superior to the rest of the population. When the Japanese occupation destroyed this colonial structure and imprisoned the local elite in particularly tough concentration camps, the seeds were sown for autonomy. After the war many of the Indonesian elite went to the Netherlands, where they easily found employment, particularly in government service, and were assimilated with few problems. Their presence was felt to be an enrichment of society and satisfied their prime wish to be Dutchmen.

Geography
Indonesia comprises more than 13,000 islands of which only about 3,000 are inhabited. The population is estimated at 175 million. The density varies widely, with about 65 per cent concentrated in Java and Madura. There are some 15 population groups in Indonesia, of which three are Javanese, and the largest numbers 15 million. About 90 per cent of the population are Muslim, but there are also 3.5 million Christians, 1 million Buddhists and as many Hindus. The official language is Bahasa Indonesia, but English and Dutch are also used, as well as the indigenous tongues of the different population groups.

The Moluccan islands have about 900,000 inhabitants living on hundreds of islands, of which the largest are Ceram, Halmahera, Buru and Ambon, where the capital which gives its name to the island is situated. Ambon has a population of about 700,000 and also has an important harbour from which primarily copper and spices are shipped. The designation South Moluccan is given particularly to the islands of Ambon, Haruku, Sapurua and Nussa Laut.

People
The Moluccans comprise many different races and socio-cultural unities, though there is a common thread in that the inhabitants have for centuries been primarily involved in fishing and agriculture and particularly the production of spices, including cloves. They have long

had a reputation as pirates, and their warlike character made them ideal for military recruitment.

Typically they are loyal to authority and were therefore devoted to the Queen of the Netherlands; indeed, with their soldierly instincts the army represented the only social group in which they could prove themselves. With the destruction of this identity they have little to fall back on, and tend towards aggression. There are few of the older Moluccans in the Netherlands who did not serve in the KNIL, and only a few who have enough education to articulate their interests and those of the South Moluccan groupings in general. It is they who almost automatically take the political reins in their minority group.

In negotiations with the Moluccans it is important to understand that there are three intense and independent communication structures which define their community: the breadth of family ties; the community of the village of origin; and the *pellas* – originally pirate co-operatives which acted and shared spoils in concert. The *pellas* have powerful threads and connections throughout the Moluccan community. Membership of a *pella* creates the obligation to give loyalty and preference to other members – particularly, nowadays, when choosing a marriage partner.

In personal relationships the most important factor is the *pangkat* ranking system, in which for example a European ranks 'higher' than a local, and a Christian 'higher' than a Muslim or a pagan. All the Christian Ambonese in the KNIL adhered to the Christian *pangkat*. Within these groups, military rank also affects decision-making. Today, nearly 40 years after the Moluccan's mass arrival in the Netherlands, the *pangkat* is still unassailable within group structures, particularly in the camps in which some of them still live.

Only a part of the population of Ambon, and an even smaller part of the Moluccas, has had this close identification with the Dutch. This is because Christian Moluccans were colonized in a different way from the rest of Dutch East India. From 1535 to 1605, before the Dutch set up their commercial centres, Ambon was occupied by the Portuguese, who imposed Roman Catholicism and various institutions on the Ambonese and in baptism gave them new names. When the area was surrendered to the Dutch in 1605, the Portuguese mission fathers left behind them 16,000 Moluccan Christians and the local chiefs insisted on continuing as they had been brought up.

The focus of attention on this group of Dutch Moluccans must not obscure the fact that there were two other larger and more important groups. First, there has always been a part of the population of the

South Moluccas which has been hostile to the Dutch. Mindful of exploitation and impoverishment under colonialism, these people embraced the proclamation of the Republic of Indonesia in 1945. To them, the KNIL were totally unacceptable freedom fighters, and they were strongly in favour of incorporation into Indonesia. Secondly, another group which did not identify with the Dutch comprised the many non-Christians, mainly Muslims, as well as a great part of the Christian population which did not live on either Ceram or Ambon. Such people did not fit in at all with the concept of the South Moluccans which had been disseminated successfully over the centuries by the Dutch and by the South Moluccans in Dutch service.

A third important group, neither predominantly Christian nor non-Christian, is formed by those South Moluccans educated and living in Indonesia. Although it is not the largest group, its members are intellectually and socially the most highly qualified. Most of them perform important functions in Indonesian society: they include the Governor of the South Moluccas, and many are doctors, priests, and engineers. A number of high-ranking officers in the Indonesian army are Moluccans. To these men, the Republic of Indonesia offered the possibility of rehabilitation and prosperity and some degree of autonomy for the South Moluccans. The political leaders of the Indonesian republic, mostly Javanese, knew well that it was incorrect to generalize about Moluccan support for the Netherlands. In general, feelings among the many Moluccan intellectuals outside Djakarta immediately after the war were entirely different from those of the Ambonese KNIL soldiers being released from Japanese captivity.

There was also for some considerable time an influential, republican, left-oriented movement under the leadership of the Moluccan Alexander Jacob Patty. His movement, *Sarekat*, gradually became more and more nationalistic (though the rulers of those days considered it 'communist'). He was finally arrested as a result of the influence of the village chiefs appointed by the Dutch, and was sent to Macassar. This caused great discord on Ambon. Patty later decided to merge his party with a larger group, the 'Radical Concentration', which had members in the *Volksraad*, the advisory council for the colonial government which had been set up in 1918. Today the portrait of Patty hangs in the building of the Ambonese synod – further evidence of how relations in the Moluccas change and how complex is the identity of this people.

Many Ambonese associations had been established at the beginning of the 20th century in what was then Dutch East India. Among these was the 'Ambonese Study Foundation', which was mainly funded by small contributions from the Ambonese KNIL soldiers. Among the recipients of grants from the Ambonese Study Foundation was J. Latuharharry, who studied in Leiden and in 1928 became the president of the *Sarekat Ambon*. His objective was to co-operate with the Indonesian nationalists. Since then, however, there have been many splinter groups formed as a result of disagreements on the level of co-operation to be given to Indonesia as it evolved.

As the main opponent of the left-wing *Sarekat Ambon*, there was on Ambon itself the *Sou Maluku*, which was founded in 1915 and was a federation of all kinds of intellectual groups as well as the Christian People's Union and the Ambonese Study Foundation. The *Sou Maluku* embraced the political rights of the Ambonese people, and in its fight for the autonomy of the Moluccas strongly opposed closer contacts with the Republic of Indonesia.

There was confusion in Indonesia after the surrender of Japan in 1945. British soldiers accepting the Japanese surrender on behalf of the Allied Powers found themselves fighting against Dutch KNIL soldiers, and Moluccans on both sides fought against each other, so that a system of signs and signals had to be worked out in an attempt to ensure that members of the same family, clan, tribe or *pella* did not kill each other. Within this confusion, the British and the Moluccan KNIL soldiers fought against a little army of KNIL deserters under the leadership of an ex-KNIL captain, Westerling. The API Ambon (Alliance of Ambonese Youth for the Republic of Indonesia) was continuously occupied in rescuing Moluccan families who risked their lives in the newly-formed Republic of Indonesia at the hands of Ambonese soldiers.

The 'Republic'

In Ambon itself, the new Republic of Indonesia appointed Dr Sumokil as General Attorney of East Indonesia. However, at a meeting on 23 April 1950, with just a few notables present – and under the threat of a hand-grenade held by a Corporal Tamaela of the KNIL, as well as the presence of red-bereted KNIL soldiers and ex-soldiers and men from the mercenary Westerling army – Dr Sumokil proclaimed the establishment of the RMS (*Republika Moluku Selatan* – the Independent Republic of South Molucca). The proclamation was made in the belief that the Netherlands, the United Nations and the United States would support it, but these assumptions proved wrong. Westerling commanded his mercenaries to keep out of the fight, and a pro-Indonesian Moluccan named Tahyatahia persuaded most of the Ambonese KNIL soldiers to remain neutral. The United Nations Commission for Indonesia (UNSEA) went by default as a result of delay. In the end the RMS stood alone in exile, and proved to be nothing more than a political fiction.

After heavy battles the country was again brought under the control of the central Indonesian government, but the guerrilla war in the bush interior of Ceram lasted for more than ten years. Dr Sumokil, the leader, was imprisoned and on 12 April 1966 was executed in Djakarta – an act which made a deep impression on the Moluccan community. What was seen as the uncaring reaction of the Dutch government, particularly of the Minister of Foreign Affairs, Dr Luns, caused further bad feeling. Militancy holds increasing attractions for South Moluccan youth and Dr Sumokil lives on as a hero to the Moluccan population, just as much as Pattimura. His widow, who has been living in retirement in the Netherlands since 1966, played a crucial role behind the scenes at the attacks on the train in De Punt and on the school in Bovensmilde in 1977.

No man's land

The situation in Indonesia became so complicated and hopeless that on the advice of their representatives living in the Netherlands, about 4,000 South Moluccan soldiers, and their families (about 15,000 people in all) emigrated to the Netherlands in 1951. The Dutch government was compelled to accept their arrival following a judicial decision that the soldiers should not be demobilized in a territory controlled by Indonesia, and the agreement of the Indonesian government that they should leave temporarily for the Netherlands.

The sudden and unexpected arrival of 15,000 South Moluccans in the Netherlands gave yet another dimension to the relationship that had lasted for four centuries between the Dutch and their former colonial subjects. Today in the relationship between Indonesia, the Netherlands and South Molucca, the emigrated Moluccans find themselves in a spiritual no man's land. Although most Moluccan families include a number of freedom fighters, they find themselves torn between all three elements. Many Christian Ambonese feel themselves to be 'black Dutchmen', just as their ancestors felt they were 'black Portuguese' in former times – a tendency which provokes in white Dutchmen feelings of both irritation and satisfaction.

Terrorism begins

Thus bungled decolonization brought some 4,000 homeless South
Moluccan soldiers and their families to the Netherlands. For years
this move was considered to be merely a temporary measure, and then
what had been feared happened: they became displaced persons. The
Moluccans claimed from the very first day that they had had a military
order to set sail, and that responsibility for what happened lay wholly
with the Dutch government. But the fact remained that their own objective, expressed before they left for the Netherlands, was to be demobilized while the Dutch still controlled New Guinea (which later became
the Indonesian territory of Irian), and to fight for the establishment
of an Independent Republic of South Molucca (RMS).

When they reached the Netherlands the soldiers and families were
warmly welcomed with a stream of letters from ordinary Dutch people
who thought that the newcomers' lives had been in danger and who
offered them generous accommodation. Swarms of reporters sought
statements from them and emphasized their loyalty to the Netherlands.
Large collections of money and clothes were raised. The lack of understanding of the true issues continued.

On the day they arrived the Dutch government dismissed these elite
soldiers from the Royal Dutch Army, and transported them to camps.
Deprived of military status, isolated in camps, forced into idleness,
saddled with a language problem and uncomfortable in a cold climate,
the Moluccans had nothing to sustain them but hopes, memories and
myths. The Dutch government had always been convinced that the
majority would return to the archipelago, and based its policies on
this conviction. In the first few years the state took care of everything,
even down to spending money; it was only in 1953 that the Moluccans
were given the opportunity, albeit within strict limitations, to find
employment.

The first attack
As repatriation became less and less likely and integration into Dutch
society largely failed, the RMS became the spiritual home of this displaced people, a straw at which to clutch in the hope of making sense
of their lives. The ambivalence of the Dutch government, the support
of right-wing movements, politicians and other influential people and
the need for a symbol all helped to promote the RMS as a dominant
political factor in the South Moluccan community. In particular,
Dutchmen who sympathized with the concept of an independent South

Moluccan state encouraged the community to see themselves in biblical terms as an exiled nation to be led back to the promised land by their leaders. Inspired by this growth of militancy, the RMS leaders, under the presidency of Manusama and the guidance of the Moluccan priest Metiary, founded the *Badan Persatuan* (Unity League of the People). This organization at first had about 80 per cent of the South Moluccan community behind it, but support crumbled as it found itself in competition with dozens of more active groups, a third of which eventually turned away from the ideals of the RMS. However, when Dr Sumokil's young widow arrived in the Netherlands in 1966, a group of young South Moluccans attacked the Indonesian Embassy in The Hague by night with Molotov cocktails. This attack marked the beginning of South Moluccan political violence in the Netherlands.

In the 15 years that had passed since their arrival, a second generation of South Moluccans had been growing up. These young people were less restrained by Christian ethics than their elders and were alive to the aspirations of the 1960s student movement, Che Guevara, the Black Panthers and the Palestinian cause. Increasingly resentful of their ageing leaders who had sought redress for their grievances by democratic means, the younger generation turned to more violent means. Mock military manoeuvres, organized at this time with the connivance of the Dutch government, lent credibility to the concept of preparation for armed action. Within the paramilitary sections of the South Moluccan community such as the KPK (Corps for the Maintenance of Order), this concept was particularly developed. In 1970 it culminated in the occupation of the Indonesian Embassy in Wassenaar, a suburb of The Hague, on 31 August, just before the visit of the Indonesian President Suharto.

As the colonial past receded, Dutch feelings about the RMS changed, and when an anti-communist administration came to power in Djakarta, understanding of the RMS ideal diminished still further. Doubts were raised as to how far the feelings of the South Moluccan islanders could legitimately be interpreted by Moluccans who lived in the Netherlands and sympathized with the RMS. Nevertheless, the RMS in the Netherlands is still the only organization with a true Moluccan identity, though many young Moluccans in the Netherlands resent its polarization into left and right wings. The terrorist actions of RMS members become more understandable when seen against this background.

Campaign of violence

In the 1970s the Netherlands saw a number of terrorist actions by various groups, of which only a small number were by South Moluccans: over the decade 112 actions started on Dutch territory, and 36 ended there. In the course of these there were 49 deaths, among them those of six terrorists, and in total more than 40 terrorists and more than 500 victims were involved. In the same period, the Dutch government was subjected to demands backed by terrorist action elsewhere in the world; in one case it refused to give asylum to terrorists, and in two cases it gave help or offered mediation.

Major incidents

31 August 1970, Wassenaar (near The Hague).   A group of 33 heavily-armed South Moluccan terrorists occupied the residence of the Indonesian Ambassador and took 30 hostages. A policeman was killed.
DURATION: 12 hours. DEATHS: 1. OUTCOME: Surrender and, after trial, light sentences.

1970–75.   In October 1970 the Dutch Prime Minister and the Foreign Minister made clear to the President of the RMS that the Dutch government wanted nothing to do with a political solution to the South Moluccan problem. Although the government later modified this hard-line policy, its attitude hardened towards South Moluccan political activity, as well as towards the community's paramilitary organizations. Discord in the community expressed itself in arson attacks, riots at trials of South Moluccans and a number of confrontations with the police in The Hague. In December 1974 South Moluccan youths assaulted the Peace Palace in The Hague, involving the police in serious fighting. In April 1975, a conspiracy to kidnap the Queen of the Netherlands was only just thwarted.

2 December 1975, Wijster (in the north of the Netherlands).   Five South Moluccan terrorists hijacked inter-city train no. 734, from Beilen to Hoogeveen; 79 passengers and railway personnel were taken hostage, of whom 24 escaped out of the last set of coaches during the first two days. During the first three days, the terrorists murdered in cold blood three hostages in the first set of coaches. Two hostages from these coaches succeeded in escaping, and five hostages were released.
DURATION: 12 days. DEATHS: 3 hostages. OUTCOME: surrender.

4 December 1975, Amsterdam. South Moluccan terrorists took 36 hostages in the Indonesian Consulate, among them 14 children, members of the consulate and of a travel agency established in it, and some visitors and pupils from an Indonesian school. At the outset of the action four people jumped out of a window; one of them died from his injuries.
DURATION: 16 days. DEATHS: 1 hostage. OUTCOME: surrender.

23 May 1977, De Punt (in the north of the Netherlands). Nine South Moluccans hijacked inter-city train no.747 from Assen to Groningen: 96 hostages were taken, of whom 42 were released in the first hour. After intensive negotiations two pregnant women and one sick man were released. During the storming of the train six terrorists and two hostages were killed, and of the 49 rescued passengers six were wounded.
DURATION: 19 days. DEATHS: 8. OUTCOME: forceful intervention by marines.

23 May 1977, Bovensmilde (in the north of the Netherlands). Four South Moluccan terrorists took five teachers and 125 schoolchildren hostage in a public elementary school; 20 Moluccan children were immediately released. During very complicated negotiations one teacher and all the other schoolchildren were released.
DURATION: 19 days. OUTCOME: intervention by marines.

13 March 1978, Assen (in the north of the Netherlands). Three South Moluccan terrorists, calling themselves suicide commandos, occupied the provincial government centre (Provinciehuis) and took an unknown number (at least 50) of hostages. One hostage was murdered immediately and another died from bullet wounds inflicted by a South Moluccan during the storming.
DURATION: 28 hours. DEATHS: 2 hostages. OUTCOME: intervention by marines.

Analysis

Pressure and demands
The conspirators at first intended the occupation of the Indonesian Ambassador's residence in Wassenaar in August 1970 to take place simultaneously with the occupation of the Indonesian Embassy in The Hague and the Indonesian Consulate General in Amsterdam but the

leaders of the KPK persuaded them to concentrate on the single target. The date was changed from 17 August, Indonesian Independence Day, to the date of the visit of President Suharto, who was held responsible for the death of Dr Sumokil. Some of the 33 South Moluccan terrorists involved did not even know each other, because they were drawn from different wings of the RMS. Their errors included unintentionally killing the Dutch policeman on guard; leaving behind in a car the pamphlets containing their demands; allowing the ambassador to escape; and failing to realize that the head of the Indonesian secret service was among the hostages.

Their main demand was that President Suharto should hold official talks with Manusama, the President of the RMS, within 48 hours in the presence of a mediator appointed by the United Nations. President Suharto had rejected an earlier request for such talks and as he had not arrived in the country by the time of the attack he had merely to delay his visit. In the end the terrorists gratefully accepted the mediation of Manusama and Metiary and were satisfied with the Dutch government's promise that the Prime Minister would open talks with Manusama, the content of which would be passed on to the Indonesian government. When the South Moluccan leaders confirmed that they agreed with this proposal, loss of face was avoided and the occupiers surrendered.

Following the events in Wassenaar, the Dutch government reviewed its social policy towards the South Moluccan community and arranged for the Ministry of Culture, Recreation and Social Work to co-ordinate all the various government or private activities on behalf of the South Moluccans. This found no favour with the South Moluccans, many of whom deemed it insulting that their case should be handled as a social rather than a political problem. The talks with Manusama led to nothing, and as a result there were hunger-strikes and symbolic protests. The government's response to these was to make clear that its policy was that the majority of South Moluccans would stay in the Netherlands, and that discussions about political aspirations were closed. Internal divisions among the South Moluccans meant that money provided by the government for social and cultural activities was not productively used, and this, together with the government's continuing and increasing antagonism to the political plans of the South Moluccans, undoubtedly provoked the next spate of terrorist actions in 1975. Social and employment difficulties were also contributory factors.

An important factor in the deterioration of relations was the granting of independence to Surinam on 15 November 1975, and the Queen's accompanying declaration that every nation had a right to independence. A week or two later the train hijack and the occupation of the Indonesian Consulate in Amsterdam started – in some ways not an unsuccessful operation, by comparison with earlier actions. The train hijack showed the dangerous immaturity and cruelty of the young Moluccans, all of whom came from the community at Smilde. (Train hijacking was not a new idea. In September 1975 four members of a Palestinian–Syrian group had been arrested in Amsterdam as they planned to hijack the Warsaw Express.) The Moluccans stopped the train by pulling the emergency brake, wounded the driver, and 20 minutes later shot him to death. To bring pressure on the government they shortly afterwards murdered two more people. One of the terrorists and one of the hostages were wounded when a terrorist accidentally fired his Sten gun, and both people were taken to hospital. After the killing of the third hostage, for which the terrorists had first asked God to forgive them, one terrorist started to weep and two others threatened to hang themselves, at which point the hostages consoled and mentally supported their captors.

The occupation of the Indonesian Consulate two days later restored Moluccan morale. The action came as a total surprise to the Dutch population, to the South Moluccans in general and even to the terrorists on the hijacked train, and seems to have been entirely spontaneous. The attackers did not know the way to the Consulate and arrived there by tram, each carrying his own weapons. Their demands were much the same as those of the terrorists of the Wassenaar group in 1970: the raising of the South Moluccan question at the United Nations and the opening of talks between the RMS's *Badan Persatuan* and the Indonesian government, with the United Nations and the Dutch government as participants. They also demanded that the government should admit on television that it had committed a great injustice to the South Moluccan people, and that the usual bus should be provided to take them to be flown to an unspecified destination: by this they probably meant East Timor, where they could expect to obtain help from the *Fretilin* liberation movement. The co-operation of *Fretilin* had probably been secured by a Dutch businessman, H.J. Owel, who had also helped to finance the 1970 action in Wassenaar. As usual the terrorists demanded the release of all South Moluccans in captivity, whether for criminal or political offences. The exchange of captives was to take place at the airport.

All the demands were variations on the standard theme heard in other kidnapping cases, but with the additional demand for direct contacts between the Moluccan leaders and either the Dutch or the Indonesian government. The terrorists excused their behaviour by reference to the thousands of Moluccans who had died for the interests of the Netherlands.

Moluccan reactions

At the start of the Wassenaar occupation a *Badan Persatuan* representative clearly distanced himself from the affair and even condemned it, but one day later the official leader, the priest Metiary, supported the action in the name of the *Badan Persatuan* and even praised the participants. The same happened over this first dual action. To begin with, Manusama, the President of the RMS, officially condemned the action, calling the soldiers 'terrorists' and even offered to use his KPK militia to storm the train. At a later stage, he reversed his position and offered to replace the hostages in the train with prominent South Moluccans.

Manusama's whole-hearted support of the actions was prompted only by the fact that the international press had seized on the stories; he then increased his political involvement by sending telegrams to authorities all over the world and a request to Portugal (which had protested at the United Nations against the Indonesian attack on Timor) to support the South Moluccan case in the United Nations. He was, therefore, both preaching and promoting the Moluccan question and at the same time offering his services as a mediator in the train hijacking.

The success of every agreement with the authorities was overstated, and inevitably disappointment and renewed action followed. Many defeats were necessary before it became clear that the political solution of the Ambonese question was no longer in Dutch hands. The outcome of both the 1975 actions was surrender without any concessions other than government agreement to talk with the South Moluccan leaders. The conclusion of these two actions was the last time that the traditional South Moluccan leaders restored their authority; future actions were directed against not only the Dutch government but also the South Moluccan leaders themselves.

The actions that followed in May 1977 at De Punt and Bovensmilde were again double actions, and both involved trains. They lasted longer than the 1975 actions and ended with force: the 1975 murders had put the Dutch government in a position from which it could not withdraw without serious loss of face. However, the fact that the authorities

had shown particular concern when children were involved demonstrated the value of children as bargaining counters, and pointed the
way for the future.

Once again, the events of May 1977 came as a total surprise. In
January 1976 the Dutch government had opened talks with the RMS
leaders and these had led to the setting up of the 'Köbben–Mantouw
Commission' – named after its two presidents, one Dutch, and the
other South Moluccan. This commission was charged with seeking
solutions to the conflict that had arisen because expectations and political ideals had been fostered among the South Moluccans which the
Dutch government could not share, though it acknowledged their existence and seriousness. The work of the commission revealed that the
gap between the radical young and their leaders was unbridgeable.
The young felt betrayed, and determined on new action – this time
against the Dutch government and the South Moluccan government
in exile. At the beginning of 1977 'messages' – genuine or not – from
political prisoners on Ambon and requests for help from a liberation
movement on Ceram contributed to the decision to act. In addition
a number of South Moluccans had been imprisoned in the belief that
more actions were planned, and their comrades felt that something
must be done to liberate them.

The demands made on the morning of 23 May 1977 contained no
new elements: release of the imprisoned South Moluccans and the cessation of Dutch political and material support for the 'fascist dictator-
ship' in Indonesia. The two actions might have ended peacefully if
it had not been for Dr Sumokil's widow, who handed a note to the
terrorists indicating that they would be able to land the aircraft they
had demanded in the African state of Benin. Careful official enquiries
had made it clear that this was not the case. However, the note encouraged the terrorists to break off negotiations, and at this point it was
feared that a ritual slaughter could follow; the authorities therefore
stormed the train and school.

Action in 1978 followed the publication in January of that year
of the government paper entitled *The Problem of the South Moluccan
Minority in the Netherlands*, in which, among other things, the government denied the legality of the proclamation of the RMS in 1950 as
'a motive for the actions which followed'. A further spur to action
was the fury felt by some militant young South Moluccans at the so-
called orientation journeys of South Moluccan leaders to Ambon,
designed to confront South Moluccans in the Netherlands with the
changed realities in their homeland. Two promoters of these orientation

journeys were personally threatened and one was even the victim of an unsuccessful murder attack. In addition, the author of the South Moluccan 'national anthem', Docianus Sahalissy, considered by some young South Moluccans to be a sort of Che Guevara of the RMS, had some months previously arrived in the Netherlands and had spread alarming stories about the way in which the Indonesian authorities were 'destroying' South Moluccan culture.

The attack on the centre of the provincial government of Drente, the Provinciehuis at Assen, was preceded by a rigorous arms search among the South Moluccans, which was greatly resented. The 'South Moluccan Suicide Commando' consisted of what were generally described as 'quiet, unspectacular boys', of whom two had recently lost their mothers and one had close contacts with the brother of one of the dead train hijackers. It was in the Provinciehuis that Max Papilaya, the real leader of the 1977 action at De Punt, had worked as a registration clerk, and 500 metres away from it he and the other 'martyrs' were buried. So, for the first time, a Dutch government building, in which hundreds of employees worked, was the target.

The three terrorists began by taking hostage the driver of the taxi in which they had gone to the Provinciehuis, hoping that this would help them to keep secret the fact that they were such a small group. For the same reason, they kept appearing at the windows during the occupation wearing different sweaters. As soon as they had forcibly entered the building they started firing wildly around with the intention of killing many people – though in fact none died. A short time previously a Palestinian suicide mission in Israel had cost the lives of more than 30 people, and the Dutch authorities bore this in mind when planning their strategy.

The demands were mailed to the government. Once again, they included the release of the South Moluccans in prison, a bus to the airport, a getaway plane – and $30 million. The package did not contain any political demands because the terrorists took it for granted that these would be well enough known. They later declared in court that they had murdered one victim in front of the other hostages to prove their seriousness of purpose. They also shot and wounded several people outside the building, including a press photographer.

As their deadline approached the terrorists left the negotiating to the hostages themselves who, with guns at their heads and knowing how to make sure that their appeals would reach the Prime Minister, could apply pressure most effectively. Just as the terrorists were preparing for their first double execution, marines stormed the building and released all the hostages. One victim, who had been first on the execution list, was hit by a terrorist bullet and died a month later from his wounds.

This time there was no question of any solidarity with the terrorists in the South Moluccan community. These terrorists were isolated not only in the general way in which South Moluccans felt isolated, but also because their own community rejected their identification with 'heroes' from earlier actions. They were condemned to 15 years' imprisonment.

The targets
The first action was directed against Indonesia and the next two were against Indonesia and the Netherlands, while the actions in 1977 were directed against the Netherlands and the traditional RMS leaders. Just before the last action of March 1978, against the Dutch government, the terrorists tried, but failed, to murder the much-respected South Moluccan leader Kuhuwal. So the target moved from the prime enemy to a less important enemy, and finally to the terrorists 'own group'.

The move was also from right to left and included a growing willingness to use violence, even against children. Tactics changed: they became more refined, and so made a non-violent solution to the conflict more difficult. Objectives also changed – from rescuing the homeland to extracting friends from prison, and releasing the terrorists' own inner turmoil. Condemned terrorists wrote to the South Moluccan community that in every liberation fight concessions had to be made and victims had to die so that one could free oneself from apathy and lack of courage. In their own words: 'The political dimension has become the expression of a psychological dimension'.

The results
The most striking feature of these terrorist actions is the total lack of political success. A South Moluccan Republic did not take effective shape and never will. Although the world now knows about the Moluccan case, this has led to nothing but a few conferences and meetings with politicians on the periphery of the United Nations. No country has recognized the republic and it has gained no support.

Perhaps the most important result has been a widening gap between the South Moluccans and the rest of the Dutch population. The terrorists established a reputation as a cruel, stubborn people, living in self-chosen isolation as a foreign nucleus in Dutch society and regularly causing problems. That most of them did not want to accept Dutch nationality on the terms offered, but on the other hand were willing to profit from the social security and goodwill of Dutch society, has created a bad opinion of them. Their claim, after 45 years, still to be treated as soldiers provokes intense irritation. At the same time, the South Moluccans' own unity has not been strengthened, nor have these terrorist actions given them a new identity. They are split into a large number of small groups, all with differing political and social opinions. None of the convicted South Moluccan terrorists has been released from Dutch prisons or from any form of captivity in Indonesia, but the next terrorist action is likely to show the same spontaneity and lack of preparation as those in the past, as well as even greater cruelty and violence.

The traditionally authoritarian and barely democratic relationship between the South Moluccan leaders and their peoples has been damaged, though some concessions have been made to the younger generation. The RMS means different things to different generations: for the elder generation it serves to maintain an identity; for the younger generation it is the only tie that holds them together and which might come to represent them in the outside world.

As for the Dutch, those who were wounded and the relatives of those who were killed have suffered grievous hurt which may last all their lives. Many victims, mutilated psychologically as well as physically, have transferred their hurt into a hatred of the Dutch government and into support for the South Moluccans. A few act as unwelcome mediators and irritating critics, and nearly all have translated their deep lack of security and safety into demands for financial or other support from the government.

Intense criticism from the victims' relatives often followed the terrorist actions. It is understandable that the parents of children held hostage were repeatedly on the point of taking matters into their own hands and rushing the school. It was not easy for negotiators to pursue a long-term strategy in the face of such emotion; it is a factor that has to be taken into account when deciding whether to terminate an incident peacefully or by force. Still more difficult were the relationships between the relatives at home and those who were rescued, whose often positive attitudes towards the terrorists appeared incomprehensible.

All in all, weighing the numbers killed and wounded on both sides against any benefit gained, it is clear that from the South Moluccan standpoint the whole sequence was highly counter-productive.

The media

The South Moluccan terrorists were never well organized; their intellectual leadership was weak and the use of the media was neither well-planned nor in the least subtle.

The public's right to know conflicts with the hostage's right to survive and the terrorist's desire to succeed. Since governments prefer in general to release as little information as possible, and the media want as much information as possible, conflict between government and the media is inevitable. During the occupation of the Indonesian Consulate, the terrorists claimed that the fight of the RMS had achieved world publicity. They also claimed to have broken a conspiracy of silence between the Netherlands and Indonesia on the RMS and claimed that publicity had been behind the postponement of the state visit of President Suharto – a decision which they said paid homage to Dr Sumokil, the 'freedom fighter'. That the Dutch government recognised Manusama as a mediator and that new inspiration for the struggle was given to South Moluccans around the world, were also seen as evidence of success.

During the occupation of the Indonesian Ambassador's residence the press did not reveal that among the hostages was Abdullah Hassan, who was not only the head of the Indonesian secret service, but also a brother-in-law of President Suharto. If this had been reported, the terrorists would have had a powerful lever with which to force Suharto to the negotiating table. Nor did the press report that the editor-in-chief of a Dutch newspaper was on the train in the 1975 hijacking. On the other hand, during the last of these terrorist actions, the occupation of the Provinciehuis at Assen in March 1978, the media reported in full the names of all the hostages and the tragic consequences of the action.

Profile of a terrorist

Max Papilaya was the leader of the train hijacking at De Punt in 1977. Of all those who had tried to build or repair good relationships with the Dutch, Papilaya had tried hardest. He was continually trying to arrange meetings between the two groups, and warmly supported any proposal for community activity. His clarion call was 'One must adapt', and at school he had done well and been totally accepted. But again and again all these efforts led to nothing: there was no response from the Dutch.

That Papilaya's benevolence turned to such hatred can be explained only by the most powerful feelings of inadequacy and suppressed aggression, at the base of which lies the ambivalence that has always characterized the relationship between the South Moluccans and the Dutch. It was apparently Papilaya's failure to compensate or to subli-mate this drive that tipped the scales. He is no exception: seemingly well-integrated Indonesian Dutchmen often display strong symptoms of hatred under the uninhibiting influence of, for example, anaesthetics. The fact that even the most irresponsible terrorists were often described by their victims as 'such nice boys and girls' is also related to this phenomenon.

For Papilaya and many other South Moluccans there were no obvious reasons for their feelings of discrimination. Their housing was quite adequate by Dutch standards, and not a few had cars; they were appreciated at work and at home. What had happened illustrates the strength of inborn, as opposed to adopted, social and cultural values. The continued frustration of Papilaya in his drive for self-confidence and recognition provoked a stronger drive for aggression, which des-troyed his chances of adapting.

Impact on society

The impact of the terrorist actions on society was rapid and deep. Holidaymakers abroad identified with the victims and listened to the radio all day while the actions provoked negative feelings towards anyone who was not white: a number of such people were assaulted by revengeful Dutchmen who made no distinctions of race or origin.

Hindsight shows that certain behavioural elements were constant in South Moluccan actions. For example, religion and the Bible are inseparably associated with all South Moluccan revolts as well as figur-ing in the actions reviewed here, though to Western eyes the form they take may appear so rigid and primitive as to be virtually unrecog-nizable. There appears to be a double identification – not only with the religion of the ruler and therefore with authority as personified by its officials, but also with God – which is very ambiguous in char-acter. Being primitive and formal, it fits into the Moluccans' traditional and educational framework, and through identification it justifies behaviour which is in conflict with the inner values of that same religion. It is precisely this element which has for centuries bewildered Wes-terners.

The beginning of the terrorist actions was at a prayer meeting, and the frequent and visible use of the Bible while at the same time hostages were being murdered in cold blood was incomprehensible to the Dutch. Such behaviour may appear strange, but the South Moluccan concept of religion is so unusual that genuine co-operation and the sharing of common experience with other minorities in the Netherlands or with the Dutch people themselves is blocked.

Another point, less specific but recognizable in the Christian Moluccan group, was the personification of their feelings, both positively and negatively. Hence their intense drive for equality with and likeness to the Dutch was personified in the Queen, as once it was in the Resident or the army officer. In the same way, the denial by the Dutch of any such equality has led to personally directed hatred. The sensitivity and vulnerability of the South Moluccans can therefore be transformed into a literally mortal hatred, in which the victim plays a symbolic role. Historically, there is a logical line linking Resident Van de Berg, who was murdered in cold blood with his wife and children during the Pattimura revolt in 1817, just a day after his arrival; the policeman on guard in front of the Indonesian Ambassador's Residence when it was stormed in 1970; the train driver in April 1975; the young uniformed conscript soldier and a randomly selected older person on that train; and the two murders at the Provinciehuis at Assen in 1978, of a man wearing spectacles and a red shirt and a high provincial public servant, both unknown to the terrorists. All these victims had one thing in common: an attribute identified to a bewildered questioner in 1818 by a Moluccan who was equally puzzled to be asked the question 'Why all this?' and responded 'They are Dutch, aren't they?'.

Other examples of this personified hatred were the 'balcony scene' and its variations. The 'balcony scene' occurred during the occupation of the Indonesian Consulate when victims were subjected to public display, bound and blindfolded and threatened with guns. This was a humiliating display of power which was seen by millions on television and in press photographs. Other incidents included the refusal to allow seriously wounded victims to be carried away and the abandoning of dead bodies to lie outside a train for days, without being identified. One must question whether it was not in fact political exploitation and subjugation that made the South Moluccans the most-feared KNIL soldiers in the past. In such collective psychological qualities there may be a passive self-selection stronger than the Dutch administration's own selection. This possibly contributed to the separation between those who stayed behind and those who continued to try to prove themselves soldiers. It is curious that revenge was never undertaken against the authorities responsible for deaths caused in retributive actions against the Moluccans. It was only random victims who experienced Moluccan aggression.

Further insights into the South Moluccan culture sometimes came during the negotiating process, for example, the significance of the *pella*. It was noticed during one of the actions that a Moluccan intermediary, a generally respected physician who knew almost all the hijackers personally, was getting a hostile reaction in his attempts to communicate with one of them. At a certain point, the tone of the conversation changed completely and became a cordial exchange, in which the classical South Moluccan hierarchy re-established itself. It transpired that both he and his contact, unknown to each other, were members of the same *pella*. This relationship was shown to be crucial to the selection of any intermediary or contact.

THE RESPONSE

A system emerges

The starting point
The murder of the Israeli participants in the Munich Olympic Games in 1972 prompted the Dutch government to draw up a scenario to anticipate similar actions in the Netherlands. However, when the hostage-taking started in Deil in 1975 this scenario appeared to have been forgotten, and the clumsiness of the political administration provoked extended discussions and action in The Hague. It had become quite clear that more skill was needed in preparing for and dealing with events of this kind, and in particular that the involvement of the lower echelons of the administration was essential.

This led to a better statement of the guidelines, but even so the handling of a hostage-taking at the French Embassy in September 1974 was feeble and largely contravened the guidelines. It is true that a complicating factor on this occasion was the continual French pressure to capitulate to demands. Furthermore, the Prime Minister, who assumed responsibility for the negotiations, ignored the carefully thought-out distinctions between matters which should be handled at local level and vital points which needed approval from the centre. The result was that the Dutch saw television pictures of the triumphal exodus of terrorists, accompanied by US$3 million, on a free flight to Libya.

After this, and following intensive study, matters were better handled – as for example at Scheveningen prison, where the administration performed well and policy was satisfactorily put into practice. The terrorists were arrested, and there were no political concessions or hostage deaths. This was probably the first time that the hard line had resolved a hostage-taking without death or injury. Continual refinement of procedures finally led to the smooth co-ordination of government actions, as well as a clearly-maintained policy line.

The command chain

From the outset every terrorist action was taken to be an infringement of the law, and responsibility therefore rested with the Minister of Justice. The Crisis Centre (see **Organization and Operation** below) was set up under his jurisdiction, but with the participation of other ministers. The Minister of the Interior was involved, since the mayors and, through them, the Municipal Police report to him; the Department of Internal Security (BVD) is also responsible to him. The Minister of Justice is head of the public prosecution service and therefore the ultimate head of the government police, the Rijkspolitie. What this means is that the maintenance of the law is the responsibility of the Minister of Justice, and the maintenance of public order is the responsibility of the Minister of the Interior.

The Prime Minister was usually among the other ministers on the crisis team. If trains or aircraft were involved, the team might include the Minister of Traffic and Public Works; if schools were involved, the Minister of Education might be included. If other countries were drawn into the affair, the Minister of Foreign Affairs might be seconded. Professional co-ordination rested with the Secretary-General of the Ministry of Justice.

Where hostage-taking had a political dimension, the legal line prevailed, and procedures followed consultation with the Minister of Justice; supervision was provided by the Attorney-General; and the conduct of the police was in the hands of the General Prosecutor. All this was laid down in a 'hostage-taking circular'. Police gave priority to the rescue of hostages before the capture and prosecution of the terrorists, and this guideline gave judicial authorities the opportunity to arrange decision-making. In practice the role of the Prosecutor was nil, since he was over-ruled by the Attorney-General, whose own freedom to make policy was in turn subject to the Minister of Justice.

Since it is the law that is concerned with committed or continuing offences, the rule of law was paramount, and harmony between the judicial and the public order spheres was essential.

Legal issues

Between October 1974 and December 1975 the questions of competence and responsibility in a terrorist incident came up for discussion on a number of occasions. Although the supremacy of the judiciary was established, these questions were repeatedly the subject of debate, on the grounds that problems could arise from the relationship of the different governmental levels, from the freedom of action of the mayors (who have the prime responsibility for maintaining public order) and from the fact that decisions made by the crisis centre might not accord with the law.

Proclamation of martial law, or even a state of war, during a terrorist incident was repeatedly rejected, as indeed was any change in legislation, on the grounds that the penal code already contains articles relating to murder, the unlawful deprivation of liberty, the illegal possession of arms and the causing of grievous bodily harm, and is therefore adequate to deal with terrorism. Recently a special committee recommended to the Minister of Justice that the planning of serious crimes such as murder and kidnapping should be made a criminal offence.

The declaration of a State of Emergency was considered but rejected at the time of the double terrorist attacks and the frequently suggested enforcement of the Law of Exceptional Competence for Civil Authorities (*Wet Buitengewone Bevoegdheden Burgerlijk Gezag*) was found to be equally unacceptable. In short, the extra latitude that could have been created by the adoption of special powers was never considered advisable.

On at least one occasion, however, the government did act outside the law. Between 1971 and 1975 government policy against terrorism was largely reactive. When President Suharto's visit was postponed, the police were instructed to ban any South Moluccan groupings or associations from The Hague, but the Minister of the Interior later admitted in the Second Chamber that the government knew that there was no legal basis for these orders. In December 1975 the Justice and Interior Ministers, the Attorney-General and the Queen's Commissioners decided – just in time – that problems of this kind would have to be addressed pragmatically.

Police and military

Apart from the municipal police (*Gemeentepolitie*), under the jurisdiction of the mayors, the Netherlands also has the government police force (*Rijkspolitie*) under the Minister of Justice, which in general covers the smaller municipalities and is organized by districts. The military police force (*Koninklijke Maréchaussée*) is a separate body with only limited policing competence towards civilians. Its ultimate chief is the Minister of Defence; in civil matters it can take action only within the framework of a special law and is always subordinate to the regular police, but to meet the occasional needs of the legally appropriate authority, or to dispose of extra manpower on a temporary basis, detachments can be made available with the consent of a Queen's Commissioner (a co-ordinating governor of one of the 12 provinces of the Netherlands).

Under the pressure of the terrorist actions from 1970 to 1975, provisions were made to draw on police and military resources as necessary. To provide an armed intervention capability, 'Special Assistance Units' (*Bijzondere Bijstands Eenheden*, BBEs) were formed from a company of conscripted marines, consisting of three platoons. Of these, two are always kept in a state of readiness and the third is a training platoon which will take the place of one of the other platoons when it is demobilized. These marines are rigorously chosen young men who have specifically requested the posting as part of their military service, under professional officers. As with other non-political units, these platoons operate only under the command of the regular police authorities, and their secondment and deployment are subject to a well-balanced governmental, judicial and organizational system.

This applies also to assistance given by other soldiers – normally no more than guard and cordon duties. For this purpose, a battalion from the armed forces is chosen each month to keep itself in readiness for action, and no other group may be used in this way. These soldiers have on occasion been used for other tasks, for example the construction of a barbed-wire barrier around the school during the 1977 attack, but such work requires the personal permission of the Minister of Defence. Both the police and the military police have light armed vehicles at their disposal.

In addition the authorities can call on two units of marksmen, one police and one military, whose disposition is subject to strict rules. These marksmen are on permanent training, though the police unit is also used for normal police services and can be called on directly by means of a special procedure. The request for support of whatever kind must pass from mayor to Queen's Commissioner and then (if it is beyond the latter's authority) to the Minister of the Interior and other appropriate ministerial colleagues. In this way, fundamental decisions about the secondment and use of these resources is reserved to the competent authorities, who therefore must be represented at every level of decision.

Investigation procedures are of course reserved to the police, as is the practical execution of designated police work, but in the early 1970s steps were taken to co-ordinate the investigation of terrorist crimes. The Central Investigation Information Service (CRI) dates from February 1972, and in September 1973 a new department was created to apply itself to the collection of information about this type of crime – the Information Centre for Special Affairs (ICBZ). In 1974–75, initiatives were taken to set up a national support group to combat terrorism, the LBT (*Landelijk Bijstandsteam Terreurbestrijding*), which became effective in 1975 and consists of delegates from the government and municipal police forces. The LBT has two tasks: to collect information about terrorist crimes and to support local police in the fight against such crimes. A district attorney was appointed general leader. It was in 1973 that at local level the police in the larger cities started to form units of marksmen.

At the end of nearly all the terrorist actions there was much criticism of the Dutch intelligence services, both the CRI (see above) and the interior service, the BVD. These criticisms do not seem to have been justified. The Moluccans formed a tightly closed group, mistrustful even of each other. The only substantial information that emerged came from normal police sources and welfare workers able to get access to them. The terrorist actions were unrehearsed and unexpected, even to the South Moluccan community, and appeared to be spontaneous. The only preparation was a prayer meeting on the eve of an action, and the terrorists had to find their own arms. In such circumstances little can be expected of an intelligence service.

However, with the measures which have been described and the acceptance of the law as the weapon with which to fight terrorism, the early inefficiencies gradually gave way to a well-oiled and functional response system.

Organization and operation

Command Post

The Command Post (CP) was established as close as possible to the place of the terrorist action. It was in fact an advance police post with a multiplicity of tasks, predominantly of a technical police nature, which included erecting the necessary barriers, taking care (eventually) of supplies of food to the hostages, organizing observation posts (visual, infra-red, heat sensoring), installing and manning telephone taps, making initial contact with the terrorists, providing covering fire for escaping hostages, keeping unauthorized personnel away from the site, setting up (or removing) telephone lines and escorting ambulances, technicians and intermediaries.

Policy Centre
The members of the Policy Centre (PC), under the presidency of the Attorney-General, consisted of the mayor(s) involved, the local district attorney, the Queen's Commissioner and the chief of the municipal and/or government police. Apart from these, there were permanent places in the PC for two advisers, one the behavioural expert and the other the press and PR adviser (see below). Separate accommodation was required for the administrative, technical and secretarial staff, and for the information and message centre which dealt with the collection of all possible information from outside, including radio and television broadcasts from home and abroad. The PC also required a room from which a number of policemen could serve as links between the PC and the CP, and between the police chief and his staff and other contacts (this section could also be used to edit the enormous stream of mostly irrelevant information coming from outside, before passing selected items to the PC).

The technical requirements of a PC have been found to be:

- Close proximity to the site of the action and the CP.
- Meeting areas for members of the PC, including secretarial, police, administrative and technical support staff, as well as one or two locations where telephone contact can be maintained with the terrorists. All these areas should be interconnecting. A separate room should be reserved for the reception of visitors, and provision must be made for a canteen and for a recreational area, with a television set for both recreation and information.
- Isolation from other buildings and the capability of protection against possible attack (this is the responsibility of the police chief and district-attorney).
- Sleeping accommodation and facilities for those who have to remain on duty for extended periods.
- Reports rapidly and properly prepared.
- A private telephone line, or at the very least a direct line to the Ministry of Justice, adjacent to the room used by the permanent staff of the PC.

● As well as police staff, there must be people who will tape all discussions with the terrorists, and if possible all other discussions. And although discussions with the terrorists are conducted from a separate room, they should be relayed through speakers to other areas so that they can be followed by everyone present in the PC.

Crisis Centre
The Dutch experience suggests that rooms should be set aside in the Justice Department or some other suitable location directly connected to the minister's office, to provide a meeting-room and secretary's office. The secretary-general (permanent under-secretary) from whom the line of command runs should be located near by, with his staff. The minister himself should be connected through his secretary with other departments. The direct telephone line between the PC and the Crisis Centre should be in the office of the secretary-general. There should also be a press adviser in the Crisis Centre (see below) acting as spokesman for the Ministry of Justice. All heads of service departments should be immediately available, together with transport facilities such as cars and helicopters and their guards.

Press centre and press adviser
In the Netherlands the role of the official spokesman for the authorities, in this case the Ministry of Justice, is unique. He is no extension of the press, in that the obtaining and transmission of information are entirely the responsibility of the media and since he has no political responsibility for that information, he need not be concerned for his position. He therefore provides a screen for the authorities, and during the major terrorist actions he was the prime contact point for the media.
    Basic principles governing the giving of information to the media were, and still are:

● In principle, the government tells the truth.
● It may be necessary in special cases (temporarily) to withhold part of the information.
● There are two points on which in no circumstances is information given: plans for later offensive action and surveillance (bugging).
● Press conferences are held every two hours, at times announced at the beginning. The background objectives of these are to prevent false rumours; to trace, if possible, what the press knows from its own sources; and to contradict or deny incorrect press reports.

It should be remembered that the Dutch people and their government were devastated by the overwhelming impact of the vision of a train brought to a standstill in the midst of Dutch countryside by a group of terrorists, with unsuspecting passengers under threat of death. It was easy to identify with the victims. The terrorists had expected that most of the publicity would be given to their planned escape by air to a foreign destination, and initially they had no idea of the tremendous sensation they caused. In the United States, the news item was regularly featured on coast-to-coast television. The press of 12 nations had about 1,000 journalists covering the story.

So that the spokesman could give a responsible report of the current situation which had the approval of the authorities, it was found necessary for him to be present at meetings of the PC, and to be fully briefed about the negotiations; he was unlikely, therefore, to be taken by surprise. The spokesman also advised on the impact which the giving of certain information to the media might have on the outside world, and on the feelings, ideas and expectations of media representatives. In the Crisis Centre he maintained contact with the chief editors of the press, radio and television, developing a confidential and professional relationship with them.

To keep the numbers of media representatives manageable during the train hijack, 150 press cards were issued daily. This procedure has been used only rarely to deny admission to unreliable or unwelcome 'reporters'.

The behavioural expert

The behavioural expert was added to the PC team at an early stage, on the grounds that a view on the psychological structure and group relationships of both the terrorists and the victims could be of value. This was indeed the case, but the behavioural expert was of use in other ways too. He contributed to the evaluation of the complicated interreactions between police, media, public opinion, politics, terrorists and victims, all of which influence each other, and he could assess the resistance to stress of all those involved, not least the members of the PC, the CP, the police and the soldiers. Other, unforeseen circumstances further justified the presence of this adviser, for example the 'balcony scenes' during the occupation of the Indonesian Consulate. He advised on the problems caused by the flood of suggestions, not only from the outside world but even from members of the PC, such as that gases should be employed or tranquillisers put in food. And he gave advice on handling parents intent on rescuing their captive children, as well as detecting and advising on frictions developing in the Centre itself.

The lessons

The first phase

Certain lessons can be drawn from the Dutch experience of South Moluccan terrorism. Although each terrorist action is different, there are common factors. The first phase of an action is usually marked by great uncertainty and chaos, and however adequate the authorities' preparations and guidelines, it cannot be expected that all the people involved and the resources required will be available. In addition, the information about what has happened will be muddled – sometimes non-existent, sometimes obtainable only in confused form from released hostages or press reports.

Because it is normal for some time to elapse before precise information can be obtained about what has happened and about the number and identity of terrorists and victims and the demands being made, counter-measures must be prepared with great care. This is the phase with greatest risks for the victims, partly because of the great stress and tension under which the terrorists are operating, and partly because of the risk of incorrect measures being taken by the authorities and individuals.

There is a major difference between actions which take place in a small town or in the country and those that occur in a large city. In a city, there is greater availability of resources and personnel. In the South Moluccan example, government attention was so concentrated on the main argument and handling of the incidents that normal government activity was disrupted. One of the most significant lessons learnt was that terrorist incidents should not be permitted to distract the government unnecessarily.

The following points will need to be covered in instructions on dealing with serious terrorist actions. Because it is the local authority police who receive first news of the action, it is assumed that these instructions will be directed to them:

- There must be a proper procedure for informing the authorities.
- Most importantly, and with all possible speed, a large-scale barrier must be erected at the scene of the crime.

    This is best arranged in two circles, an outer one passable only by residents and an inner one which is not accessible to anyone without the permission of the legal authorities; in particular, the media must be refused access. The erection of these barriers is more difficult, but at the same time even more urgent and necessary, in a densely populated area. Experience has shown that media representatives do not hesitate to use devious means and to spend large amounts of money to get close to the scene. During the attack on the Indonesian Consulate there were instances of reporters hanging by their legs out of windows, microphone in hand, trying to make contact with either the attackers or the victims. There is also the possibility of the news media interrupting negotiations, or passing undesirable information to the terrorists.

- The setting-up and locations of the Policy and Press Centres, and the time and place of the first meeting, must be declared in accordance with the written and spoken instructions of the authorities. These procedures should be in writing and, most importantly, be regularly practised.

- Manning levels in the police must be brought up to strength, and special support units mustered.

- From a technical point of view, for subsequent study and reports to Parliament, it is advisable to maintain a written diary of events, as well as tape-recordings. Practice, however, reveals inherent dangers in this. The stress of the situation, with terrorist threats and hostages' lives at stake, may produce records which lawyers can use against the authorities or state. In the Netherlands, judges have a tendency to demand more information than is strictly required for a prosecution, and this can have deleterious side-effects, such as the compulsory disclosure of the tactics of the negotiators.

- Instructions must clearly state the limits of the responsibilities of all personnel involved, particularly those who may make first contact with the terrorists. Any such people who do not have full authority to negotiate must make this absolutely clear to the terrorists, but at the same time they should indicate that everything possible will be done to get in touch with the appropriate authorities as soon as possible. This early contact provides a good opportunity to offer to organize field dressings, medicines, ambulances and medical support in case of need; an appeasing attitude can take some of the tension out of this critical phase. No discussions should be started at this stage, particularly of a moral or reproachful nature. In brief, the role of the person who makes first contact is to avoid imposing any further strain on the terrorists, while at the same time making clear that he has no mandate for action.

- Instructions must be clear on the question of giving information to the media. The chaotic nature of the first phase can give rise to ill-informed media criticism. In the Netherlands, however, as preparations improved and there was greater experience of this type of crime, both the speed and the quality of the government response greatly improved.

Use of force in Moluccan hostage cases

The greatest risk to hostages was at the time of forceful intervention, by government forces, and it was therefore essential that clear policy lines were laid down at the highest level to establish the maximum provocation and violence that victims should have to endure before this step was taken. In this connection, the 'balcony scenes' mentioned earlier are of great significance. The objective of this gruesome and humiliating display of power involving bound and blindfolded victims at the Indonesian Consulate was to intimidate the administration through the negotiator, and to force concessions.

A situation of this kind may last for some hours, during which one victim may be replaced by another, who may even have volunteered for the ordeal as part of the co-operation between attackers and victims or perhaps for tactical reasons. Sometimes the exhibited victim is under obvious threat from a concealed or partially concealed armed terrorist. Such victims have been told that their ordeal would be 'only for show', but there is no certainty of that and this behaviour could be termed physical and psychological torture. It is certainly sadistic, and failure to take it seriously may have disastrous results.

It was the role of the behavioural expert to advise on the seriousness of the South Moluccan terrorists' intentions, and the degree of distress being experienced by the victims. During the first train hijacking, the train driver, a soldier and a randomly chosen civilian were tied up and shot, and their bodies were thrown overboard; this was followed by a refusal to allow the dead and wounded to be carried away. Society's reaction to this scene, featured frequently on television, had a major impact on the decision of whether or not to storm the train.

At one time various criteria were suggested – they now seem both cynical and amateurish – whereby a maximum of one, two or three hostage deaths would be the signal for intervention. The problem that arose was that the terrorists tried on two occasions to give the impression that they had killed hostages, by firing off bullets, and it was impossible to verify this. In the absence of precise information, different evaluations were sometimes proposed, and personal experience naturally played an important part in reaching correct conclusions. As the surveillance apparatus became more sophisticated, evaluations became more accurate and therefore of more value in the negotiations. Nevertheless, there was always the risk that such provocative actions by the terrorists would lead to premature or ill-prepared counter-measures, and it cannot be too strongly stressed that such matters should be carefully considered and incorporated in the guidelines for Policy Centres, or their equivalents, to avoid a clash of views and opinions.

Given the diversity of the places in which actions may arise (in the Netherlands these included the train stranded on a bend in the track in the middle of remote marshland, the Indonesian Consulate in a residential area in Amsterdam and the isolated and largely glass-walled school in Bovensmilde), it is practically impossible to have a ready-made model governing forced intervention. An emergency plan, formulated at the start of the incident, is, however, essential.

Such plans give moral support to the authorities against capitulation to the terrorists which both simulation and actual practice have proved is otherwise likely. In the first 24–48 hours of an action, characterized by chaos and acute danger, the existence of the plan will remove the likelihood of precipitate action and will help bring a degree of stability. In the next phase a fragile equilibrium emerges, particularly between the hostages and their captors, and negotiations can begin. The supply of food and clothing, and everything else that contributes to the normalization of the situation, must continue, without concessions to the terrorists. The guidance of the behavioural expert is essential at this stage.

At the same time, in case there is to be police/military action, information is needed as quickly as possible about the construction materials and internal lay-out of the buildings under attack, and this may involve obtaining drawings and plans from the local authority. Equally, the location of both hostages and attackers must be identified, and contingency plans must be prepared to make necessary resources available.

The time it takes to amass these resources is often longer than might be expected. Four or five days must be allowed, and continual monitoring is necessary to take account of changing circumstances. Secrecy is important at all times. The arrest of the terrorists must be organized in advance, to prevent criticism of it in court by defence lawyers, and such plans will require the approval of the Crisis Centre.

The negotiator
As the negotiations progress it is extremely important to obtain the release of at least some of the hostages. To avoid a public outcry, the Crisis Centre may well give priority to the release of any children involved, even though it is unlikely that the terrorists would harm

them. From a technical point of view, however, it is more important to make contact with hostages who can give information about the situation at the centre of the action. It is most valuable if those released can give the numbers of hostages and terrorists, the terrorists' armaments, ages, attitudes, cohesion, technical knowledge, guard rotas and everyday routine, and the disposition of different groups, as well as some idea of the probable stress resistance of both hostages and terrorists.

The same information is always sought from intermediaries or, as they were often called by the Dutch government, 'contact persons'. Some use was made of those South Moluccan leaders who were considered by the Dutch authorities to be reliable and who were accepted by the terrorists. Non-Moluccans who were friends of the terrorists or close associates were also used – in one instance a Chinese doctor. The situation sometimes became complicated, in that each intermediary had his own aims and objectives and played his own game, so that negotiations were sometimes misused in the pursuit of private rivalries or interests. Constant evaluation is therefore essential.

In discussions both before and after their contact with the terrorists, the authorities tried to indoctrinate these intermediaries with the official viewpoint and extract from them all possible information. The evaluation and weighing of such information and claimed achievements often involved putting the intermediaries under great pressure to make it possible to understand fully what had happened and so to formulate correct policies.

From the above, it can be seen that an ideal intermediary is someone with an open view of the position of the terrorists, who never loses sight of the objectives, who attempts to create a positive relationship with the terrorists, battles to save the lives of the hostages and is indefatigable. Experience shows that such a negotiator should preferably not be recruited from the ranks of priests or lawyers, and certainly not from relatives, who are likely to meet with the most violent threats from the terrorists. If it proves necessary to use diplomats, careful control will be necessary, since they will, naturally, seek to benefit their own country, and perhaps to derive some later advantage from the situation. The negotiator must have endless patience; never lose face; always know how to strike the right note in discussions without ever slipping into humility; in no way ever convey the impression that he is himself competent to institute actions (this eliminates the majority of police officials); be able to adapt rapidly to changing situations, states of mind and attitude; never display nervousness; be able to display decisiveness when necessary; and always be available. His voice should be soothing, and he should never try to convince or to dominate – which is usually counter-productive. Depending on the circumstances, but preferably early on, it is desirable for the negotiations to progress from the 'I – you' to the 'we' mode. Continuously, however, he must remain alert to the reactions he is receiving and be able to assess how far these are changing, perhaps as the result of changes in the stress resistance of the terrorist(s) or as an indication of a change in the group's cohesion. This is, of course, a counsel of perfection, but an acceptable model might be that of an elder brother who is independent of both sides but is making an all-out effort to assist in bringing matters to the best possible conclusion.

Although the vital teamwork between the civil administration, the Ministry of Justice and the police improved during the course of the South Moluccan terrorist incidents, some problems persisted. Some officials in the Policy and Crisis Centres were also involved in the day-to-day management of municipal or provincial matters. This meant that they could not be present all the time, and even their substitutes alternated. As a result co-operation was harder to maintain. Consistency of reaction is vital, and these changes were detrimental to that. The substitutes were gradually withdrawn from the framing of policy, but this diminished motivation and the value of their views, itself giving rise to friction. Tactics were devised to ensure that the most important decisions were delayed until the appointed officials were available, and this in turn placed an additional responsibility on the negotiator. Substitution caused no problems for the police, since they are accustomed to crises of this kind.

None of those in authority had previously been subjected to such stress, which meant that the strongest personalities had to be chosen; however, all those involved greatly appreciated being part of a closely-knit group.

The media
From the standpoint of crisis management, the media have a negative influence. Even the 'quality' press will sometimes behave irresponsibly, as for example when, on the eve of the forceful recapture of the Indonesian Consulate in Amsterdam, an article was published which purported to describe exactly how the building would be stormed, including a photograph of the vehicle to be used – a lorry-mounted crane with a high-level working platform. Additionally, an ambulance train which was kept ready for emergencies during one of the train

hijackings was frequently identified as an armed train from which the counter-attack would be mounted. These 'news' items obviously influenced the negotiations and often, quite unjustly, led the terrorists to believe that the authorities could not be trusted. During the train hijack and the attack on the Indonesian Consulate in Amsterdam the terrorists were greatly encouraged to hear that the right-wing Christian group of the Evangelical Broadcasting Company (EO) was 'full of understanding', and the news that the RMS community backed them also boosted terrorist morale.

On several occasions the lives of hostages or kidnap victims have been endangered by publication of their names, social position and background. As one hostage in the Provinciehuis at Assen said: 'I heard my death sentence on the radio'.

On the other hand, Dutch experience shows that the media can be manipulated. It was enough to describe information as 'confidential' to ensure its dissemination. The government used the media repeatedly to publish statements from the Prime Minister and the Minister of Justice against allowing hijackers to leave the country, reiterating that those who were responsible for killing or wounding hostages would be subject to the rigour of the law.

At first, negotiating tactics left an open connection between the terrorists and the media, to allow the former to let off steam and to express their demands: the population were surprised to hear terrorists broadcasting their demands live over one of the public channels. There was a technical advantage in this, in that it pre-empted the usual condition made by terrorists that their demands should be published. After this point such contacts with the terrorists were reserved exclusively to the Policy Centre.

Mistakes

It is important to make advance plans for the reception and care of released hostages. On one occasion the failure to do this had distressing consequences: a conflict in perceived responsibilities between the regional health authorities, the Dutch Red Cross and the military health service resulted in the delayed and inaccurate identification of dead and wounded victims, so that it was some hours before even the Policy Centre had a list. Relatives were understandably upset, and there was criticism of those responsible.

At the first train hijack in Wijster the actions of a sergeant of the *Rijkspolitie* caused great frustration and annoyance to the terrorists (and severe repercussions for the hostages). It was he who had first contact with the terrorists, using a loud-hailer. This method of communication instantly causes aggression and the sergeant's error was compounded by his blunt and repetitive reaction to the terrorists' demands. It was a long time before empathy could be restored – by telephone. Similar experiences underline the need to exercise care in deciding who is to make first contact.

When the contact is with foreign terrorists or those with an inadequate command of the language, they should not be confronted with a negotiator who is completely fluent in their language. In preference to language professors, young people who do not display superiority in their use of the language, and who will follow instructions from the Policy Centre, should be chosen.

Interpreters were needed to listen in to tapped conversations. Indonesians with experience in the Moluccas used for this purpose slowly translated the bulk of the material, and they did so under fear of reprisals. Their translations often conveyed an inexact picture of the terrorists' state of mind and emotions, if only because all offensive expressions were bowdlerised or omitted. The express order to translate literally later produced material of some value. On the eve of surrender in the Indonesian Consulate, imperfect translations indicated that the hostages' lives were in danger, and for some hours armed intervention was seriously considered. This did not, however, take place.

THE FUTURE

South Moluccan nationalism in the Netherlands is a product of Dutch colonialism, poor decolonization and a failure by the immigrants to integrate into the post-colonial motherland. As it became clear that the South Moluccans were going to stay, on the recommendation of a committee they were moved from the barracks in which they had originally been accommodated to new buildings. Recently, however, the Dutch administration lost a case against the South Moluccans, when it was refused permission to rehouse the last groups in well-furnished, newly built houses, on the grounds that they did not wish to move: in fact, they did not wish to shed their soldier culture. So for the time being, the barracks situation will continue, probably until the death of the last South Moluccan in the 60 families still remaining there.

Those who, mostly half-heartedly, agreed to be moved to group accommodation in newly-built blocks continue to function as a closed community; in spite of easy naturalization procedures, over 60 per cent voluntarily remained without nationality or the right to vote, and their social integration was seriously hampered by the language barrier, lower educational standards and a different life-style.

From the outset, the Dutch authorities put no obstacles in the way of South Moluccan progress towards social and cultural independence. The heart of the problem was that the Moluccans perceived their struggle as a political fight for independence. The prospects of success on these terms were nil.

The basic concept of government welfare was that it should provide the seed-bed in which individual and collective self-awareness could begin to flourish. In the 1960s the prevailing climate had been favourable towards such social issues and was strongly orientated towards the Third World.

However, when it appeared that the South Moluccan revolutionary spirit had been broken, political attention immediately lessened, and this had repercussions on government policy. While it is true that there have been very few political confrontations since then, it is equally true that 60–70 per cent of South Moluccans under the age of 30 are unemployed, as compared with 40–50 per cent for other minority groups and 14 per cent for the nation as a whole.

South Moluccans are known as rough customers: for example, they are hardly welcomed as opponents in sport. They are themselves living under strong internal social pressures, in that an austere educational system at home, and the behaviour it induces, contrasts strongly with the freedom that exists in Dutch society at large. Their command of the Dutch language is sadly lacking. While Moluccans have always recognized the importance of education, not least as a means of achieving the longed-for equality and acceptance, life is not easy for them in Dutch schools, since their whole language culture has been virtually static for centuries.

As a result of the terrorist actions the South Moluccans' non-integration with Dutch society is now partly at the wish of the Dutch themselves, whether explicitly expressed or not. This factor, high levels of drug addiction, long-term unemployment and the inability to rediscover a political identity are the fundamental reasons why South Moluccan youth in the Netherlands is disoriented and increasingly severs ties with the older generation.

Insight into the problems of minorities, combined with a positive attitude to them, does not necessarily ensure the ability to communicate. One of the main lessons to be learnt from the South Moluccan tragedy is that this ability is not easy to acquire.

At first, government departments had no concept of the problems faced by immigrants, or indeed of those faced by their own employees working in this field, and as far as they could they ignored them. When the immigrant population was still relatively small, few came to the attention of the authorities, though when they did language and communication problems immediately ensured that there was little response to questions asked. The vicious circle of small demand and poor response maintained this isolation.

But the numbers of immigrants increased, government departments opened their doors, and the problems of giving service, help and information became well recognized. By contrast with the excellent arrangements made by central government, local authorities were at first unable to cope. Gradually they attempted to set up a means of dealing with these problems within existing departments and working methods. They often recruited new employees who were themselves of immigrant origin, but this gave rise to two new problems: first, the immigrant employee became overworked, since all complaints, questions, demands and communication problems were loaded on to him; and secondly, some institutions insisted that new employees should be re-educated to deal with their colleagues in the Dutch manner. Help given to immigrants diminished. The employment of immigrants is thus not in itself sufficient to provide professional help for minority groups, and government departments came to realize that, to provide adequate service for their new clients, they had to enhance the expertise of their Dutch employees.

Dutch policy

The administration has declared that its policy is to ensure a fair distribution of welfare and the elimination of social disadvantage, and that therefore the professions generally must be made more available to all, including immigrants. This in turn requires that in every department as many members of staff as possible must be able to relate to immigrants, and to the Netherlands as a multicultural society. Although in the Dutch context the term 'minority' refers simply to numbers, in general it will have to be used to describe the relative power of the group in question. The official definition of 'minority' by the United Nations takes this into account: 'A minority is a non-ruling group in population which has ethnic, religious or linguistic traditions or other important marks which distinguish it from the rest of the population, and which it wishes to maintain'.

The only hope

The tragic irony is that while the Netherlands grants immense help to a minority group, that group largely rejects Dutch nationality and refuses to make proper use of what is so generously offered. The only hope may be for gradual assimilation through mixed marriages. It is rare for a Dutch girl to marry a Moluccan boy but the converse is not uncommon, and this prompts the belief that the approach to minority problems should be widened by not thinking so much of integration and the promotion of the minority culture, but instead moving in thought and actions towards women's emancipation. In nearly all minority population groups, women have an inferior status to that of men.

Emancipation of Moluccan women in the Netherlands is well advanced. There have been some serious incidents involving ill-treatment and even manslaughter, coupled with mental and psychological identity problems, associated with the move towards female emancipation, but such set-backs cannot stem the tide. The loosening of the traditional and authoritarian bonds which have fettered and inhibited the women has resulted in, and has been promoted by, intermingling with people from other groups, in this case perhaps particularly the Dutch. It is to be hoped that this erodes the phenomenon of the minority group. In the Dutch context, it is even possible that these emancipated women may be able to generate an impulse towards re-emigration by the South Moluccans, more probably and perhaps more desirably to other parts of Indonesia or other parts of the world where they might feel more at home than in the Netherlands, and be able to make a fresh start.

A return of the Moluccans to Indonesia is certainly possible but would naturally be on the terms of the government there. This would not, however, coincide with the present wishes of the Moluccans in the Netherlands.

Politically, the position is clear and incontrovertible. The Dutch government cannot go back on the Paper of 1978 in which it stated (and it has subsequently repeated) that 'there are no legal, historical or factual reasons of either international or national character which would support a case for the establishment of an independent or autonomous Republic of South Molucca'. Relations between the Netherlands and Indonesia are improving daily, and individual Moluccans may derive advantage from this, but the seriously disturbed relations between the indigenous Dutch and the immigrant South Moluccans will take generations to restore.

NOTE

1.   This chapter is based on a number of lectures, in particular that delivered to the 25th General Press Institute Assembly of the International Press Institute in May 1976 in Philadelphia and the May Eden Lecture in 1978 at the University of Aberdeen.

4 The Neutralization of the Red Army Faction

INTRODUCTION

In the 20 years preceding its unification with the German Democratic Republic (GDR), the Federal Republic of Germany (FRG) had lived with terrorist attacks. This chapter concentrates on the *Rote Armee Fraktion* (Red Army Faction or RAF) which has perpetrated most of these attacks and was the longest-lasting and most virulent extremist group in the Republic. It is impossible to tell when this particular kind of criminality will come to an end, though within the band of opinion still broadly known as the 'New Left' the RAF is now largely isolated and what once appeared to present a serious challenge to the state has been reduced to an isolated group of disgruntled individuals. The RAF is no longer able to disseminate its policy or justify its operations to anyone outside its own reduced circle, but the murder of the Deutsche Bank chief, Alfred Herrhausen, on 30 November 1989, and the attempt on the life of Hans Neusel in July 1990 showed that it is nevertheless capable of further attacks. It still has a small hard-core membership and it seems able to recruit new members; what is more, now that it is thrown back upon itself its attacks will probably be more precipitate, more difficult to predict and more brutal than they were in the past.

The individuals who were later to form the RAF first came together in 1968, when they committed an arson attack on a store in Frankfurt. Other attacks followed against US military facilities and symbols of the West German state. The group operated in West Berlin as well as in larger cities and urban areas throughout the country. In the later phases, from the mid-1980s onwards, the RAF extended its target range to include the 'military industrial complex', concentrating on NATO facilities and the arms industry.

When the RAF began its terrorist activities, the government had the task not only of finding and arresting the terrorists but also of draining the field of sympathizers. From the beginning the RAF accompanied its criminal acts with propaganda aimed at discrediting democracy and winning 'comrades in arms'. The government learned to respond to this campaign by enforcing the law and winning public support. In the end the government succeeded in winning away sympathizers by public relations and its 'no negotiations' attitude, though the RAF contributed to its own reduced appeal by committing strategic and tactical mistakes. The RAF's inability to win public sympathy through violence and killings bolstered government efforts, and even prominent members of the New Left who had at first shared its theoretical objectives dissociated themselves from the violent methods it adopted.

Over the years, those who sympathize with the terrorists' aims have changed and so has the way in which they provide support. At first the RAF's concept of 'armed struggle' attracted the attention and later the sympathy of a body of intellectuals. In the main this lasted until the RAF moved on from committing crimes to obtain money, vehicles, weapons and personal documentation, to perpetrating attacks in which people died or were wounded.

During this second phase the terrorists continued to enjoy some public understanding of their objectives but not of their violence. Sympathizers who until then had defended the RAF's aims now concentrated on criticizing the security authorities as a way of condoning RAF violence. As they saw it, the RAF was using 'counter-violence' against unjustified state violence. After 1977 this argument was harder to justify because of the murders of the Federal Attorney-General Siegfried Buback, the banker Jürgen Ponto, and West German Industries Federation President Hanns Martin Schleyer.

Even the RAF's most fervent sympathizers on the far left dwindled after it shot and killed a US soldier on 7 August 1985 to obtain his identity card. The murder led to severe criticism by the New Left, which continues to this day but which reached a peak in the course of heated discussions at the 'Frankfurt Congress' over the first two days of February 1986. About a thousand people attended this leftist gathering with the original purpose of showing support for the RAF. However, an overwhelming majority condemned the brutality of the group's attacks and since then support for the RAF has been confined to individuals who belong to the non-clandestine members or the 'legal arm' of the organization.

At no time has the RAF depended on financial support from outside the Federal Republic, nor has it obtained its weaponry from other than internal sources. In the early days there was some initial contact with Palestinian groups, particularly the Popular Front for the Liberation of Palestine (PFLP), though this never developed into training

or logistic co-operation. In June 1970 core members of the group travelled via Damascus to Jordan to undergo military training in a Fatah
camp, but before this could take place Jordanian troops had driven
the Palestinian fighters out of the country. In particular, Horst Mahler,
the lawyer who was later to defend RAF founder-member Andreas
Baader in court, spoke out against Middle East training; and in general
the RAF, unlike the other groups, Revolutionary Cells and 2 June
Movement, was far too independent and arrogant to seek help and
advice.

In effect co-operation with other terrorist groups has been minimal.
Attempts to set up a united guerrilla front in the 1980s failed when
the RAF's would-be partners in France (the leaders of the international
section of the French group *Action Directe*) were arrested. Contacts
with the Italian Red Brigades never appreciably influenced the RAF's
capability to mount actions, nor did expressions of solidarity with
the Spanish First of October Anti-Fascist Resistance Group (GRAPO)
in 1990 signify tactical co-operation.

THE THREAT

Beginnings

From the mid-1960s the liberal intelligentsia accepted the protest movement in the Federal Republic, aware that the pressure for reform on
many issues, such as education, had been initiated by extra-parliamentary movements and not by the established parties. The model for
West-German student protest was the protest movement in the United
States, which concentrated on opposition to US military involvement
in Vietnam. Close academic contacts existed between West German
universities, particularly Berlin, and universities in California and on
the east coast of the United States. When televised mass student demonstrations reached their peak on the campus at Berkeley, California
in 1964, they provided the impetus for student movements in France,
Italy and West Germany.

The West German New Left movement gradually emerged over the
next two years, convinced that neither Moscow-line communism nor
West German social democracy as artificially established by the allies
after the 1939–45 war provided a proper model for the state. Core
groups formulated the protest, which a broader student band practised
and developed. Politics, sociology and psychology faculties provided

recruits for the demonstrations. The theories of Herbert Marcuse, and especially his rejection of the basis of contemporary Western society, influenced many students. Hundreds of young people attended lectures in Frankfurt by Professors Adorno and Horckheimer who taught sociology and philosophy and argued that the violence of the state stimulated the terrorist phenomenon.

The appearance in 1966 of the 'Grand Coalition' between the conservative Christian Democratic Union (CDU) and the German Socialist Party (SPD) under Chancellor Kiesinger also stimulated protest. The protesters saw this alliance as a betrayal of democracy, effectively removing political opposition, and therefore the prospects for reform and change, and confirmed their suspicion that the new West German state was basically rotten with 'rulers' trying to maintain power by unacceptable alliances.

The student movement, with the support of a vociferous segment of liberal and left-wing professors, joined the campaign against new legislation of emergency laws which were to apply in times of war or social upheaval. In this phase, 15 attacks over Easter 1968 were directed at US and West German state targets, as well as at the conservative Springer publishing house, where 38 people were injured. At the same time a debate on violence developed within the movement, differentiating violence against property from that against people. The former was seen to be justified in the struggle against what the movement characterized as repression, and particularly against state institutions considered to exercise that repression.

In August 1968 the Warsaw Pact troops invaded Czechoslovakia and one result of this was that in the autumn of that year the campaign against the emergency laws collapsed. The student protest movement split into those who concentrated on making a theoretical Marxist analysis of the Federal Republic, and the activists intent on building a revolutionary organization. In February 1971 the RAF emerged from this transitional phase committed to the concept of the 'armed struggle'. Up to this point the name Red Army had only been used by the Japanese group which had hijacked a plane to North Korea in 1970. In a letter to the North Korean Workers' Party (17 November 1971), the Germans explained that the term *Fraktion* meant not a splinter group from a formerly undivided movement, but a group forced to work unlawfully because of the prevailing repression; it was not in itself a party, though indeed in organization, practice and concept it was a necessary component of a communist party deserving of the name. Among the leftist intelligentsia a current of thought justified this armed struggle in the

wake of the failure of the protest movement, which they argued had
been forcibly suppressed by the 'establishment'.

The first RAF operations aimed at creating a logistic basis for future
operations. Funds were largely obtained by armed bank robbery and
during the build-up there were three bank raids in Berlin on 29 September 1970 from which the group netted DM220,000. Further raids
followed, accumulating to some DM1.7 million by 1974.

Sympathizers welcomed these attacks, and even some who were not
politically committed hesitated to condemn them. The meticulous preparation and the precision and daring exhibited in the raids attracted
admiration. Some saw the terrorists as latter-day Robin Hoods with
the police playing the role of the corrupt Sheriff of Nottingham's men.
Sympathizers with no RAF connections lent support though today
most of them find it hard to justify their involvement.

In November 1970 a professor in Hanover put a flat at the disposal
of Ulrike Meinhof and two other RAF members. From 24 December
1970 until 8 January 1971 a Stuttgart secondary-school teacher let
other members use his flat. In January 1971 another teacher in Stuttgart
accepted packages from RAF members and later delivered them to
other colleagues. A month later a Heidelberg doctor rented a safe
flat in Hamburg for the group. In mid-March 1971 another teacher
from Stuttgart put his car at its disposal. At the end of the month
a doctor in Hamburg rented a flat for Gudrun Ensslin. In September
1971 an actor from the Stuttgart State Theatre hired a car for the
group. The following January an Esslingen psychologist rented a safe
flat in Frankfurt which was used by the RAF until June 1972.

These supportive acts by people alienated by the political system
are among the many examples of otherwise law-abiding and democratic
citizens helping the terrorists during the early phase of their operations.
RAF activists exploited this sympathy without scruple, often conceal-
ing their own identity and their true intentions. In many cases the
sympathizers were politically naive and displayed an inadequate grasp
of reality as they unhesitatingly supported perpetrators of serious
crimes.

The West-German Nobel Prizewinner Heinrich Böll suggested in
Der Spiegel on 10 January 1972 that 60 million people (the population
of the Federal Republic) were hunting a mere handful of young people
– though the RAF rejected his opinions and those of other sympathizers
as coming from mere liberals. Many newspaper articles favourably
compared the behaviour of the sympathizers with that of citizens who
had given refuge to resistance fighters fleeing from the Gestapo. This

type of sympathy made it more difficult for the police to elicit co-operation from the public, and so hampered criminal investigations.

The first murders

In 1972 the RAF moved to a more violent phase directed against people (see chronological appendix for detailed list), though many of its members had already been arrested for less serious crimes.

A series of bomb attacks – 15 explosive devices in six locations – began on 11 May 1972 with an attack on the headquarters of the 5th US Corps in Frankfurt in which one US officer was killed. On 12 May attacks followed on the State Criminal Office in Munich and on the police headquarters in Augsburg. On 19 May two bombs detonated in the Springer publishing house in Hamburg injured 38 people, some of them seriously. Five days later there was a heavy attack on the headquarters of the US Army in Europe in Heidelberg: three soldiers died.

These attacks were intended to encourage other organizations and groups of the New Left to align themselves with the RAF. To this day there are still those on the revolutionary left who argue that violence wins support, in spite of all evidence to the contrary. Indeed the RAF's failure to attract support led some members to argue for and to practise greater brutality.

THE ROUTINE OF VIOLENCE AND PROTEST

In 1977 the RAF kidnapped Hanns Martin Schleyer in an attempt to secure the release from prison of founder-members Ensslin and Baader. In a parallel action, a Palestinian commando hijacked a Lufthansa aircraft that landed in Mogadishu (Somalia), where a special unit of the Federal Border Guards, GSG9, stormed it on 18 October. In the early hours of the same day, Ensslin, Baader and Jan Carl Raspe took their own lives in the Stuttgart–Stammheim prison. The next day the kidnappers murdered Schleyer. These events were seen as a defeat for the RAF, which took 18 months to prepare new actions.

Again they met with failure. On 25 June 1979 the RAF attempted to blow up the then Supreme Commander of NATO in Europe, Alexander Haig, on his way to NATO Headquarters near Brussels. On 31 August 1981 members carried out a bomb attack on the NATO Air Force Headquarters in Ramstein (Pfalz) in which 18 US soldiers and two German civilians were injured. On 15 September 1981 General Frederick H. Kroesen, C-in-C of the US Army in Europe was lucky to escape death from two RPG-7 rockets fired at his car. Thereafter the RAF tried to develop a new strategy of an 'anti-imperialist front in Western Europe', an idea developed in a 'discussion and planning paper', copies of which were found in safe flats in Frankfurt and Karlsruhe in July 1984, when police arrested six members.

In December 1984 the RAF launched its '84–85 Offensive'. In the first days of December those in prison went on hunger-strike, demanding prisoner of war status. On 18 December an RAF commando attempted a bomb-attack against the NATO school in Oberammergau, though the bomb was defused in time, and the lives of some 30 people were saved. Three days earlier the French terrorist group *Action Directe* (AD) and the RAF had published a paper entitled *For the Unity of Revolutionaries in Western Europe* in which they announced the formation of a 'united front for the struggle against NATO imperialism'. Accordingly, on 25 January 1985 in Paris, AD terrorists murdered the French General René Audran in front of his flat, and a week later two RAF terrorists shot the German armaments manager Dr Ernst Zimmermann in his house near Munich.

The hunger-strike and the so-called commando operations were accompanied by attacks and attempted attacks by the 'legal periphery' of the RAF. During the hunger-strike there were 15 explosive attacks and 25 cases of arson, half of which were directed against military targets. After Dr Zimmermann's murder the prisoners came off their hunger-strike, justifying this by saying that the anti-imperialist front had not yet attained the political, practical and organizational level needed to limit 'the state's open aim of annihilation'. The RAF nevertheless maintained that rapid progress towards the unification of West European guerrillas and improved terrorist performance were possible.

As if to demonstrate this, on 8 August 1985 the RAF carried out a heavy attack on the US Rhein Main Air Force base near Frankfurt, where they exploded a car-bomb which killed two Americans and injured 11 passers-by. On the previous day two RAF terrorists had shot dead the US soldier Pimental in order to steal his identification card to enter the base.

Pimental's murder was widely criticized by the 'legal periphery', so much so that the RAF felt compelled to excuse its action in a paper entitled *To Those Who Fight on Our Side*. In spite of this evidence of the difficulties it was experiencing in justifying its terrorist actions to its sympathizers, the RAF carried out further murders. On 9 July 1986 it assassinated Professor Dr Karlheinz Beckurts, board member of Siemens AG, and on 10 October it killed the Foreign Office Ministerial Director Gerold von Braunmühl. Two years later, on 20 September 1988 it attempted to kill Secretary of State Hans Tietmeyer, who was responsible for International Monetary Fund decisions in the Ministry of Finance. And on 30 November 1989 it murdered the Deutsche Bank chairman in Frankfurt.

IDEOLOGY

From the start the RAF faced the dilemma that, although it wanted to struggle for the proletariat, hardly any of its members came from that class. Andreas Baader (1943–77) was the son of a historian; Gudrun Ensslin (1940–77), a clergyman's daughter, graduated in philosophy and languages; and Ulrike Meinhof (1934–76) was an art historian's daughter who had studied philosophy and sociology. Jan-Carl Raspe (1944–77) was a sociologist and the son of a chemical factory director. Most of the 17 members of the 1970 nucleus were students; of the females one was a junior barrister, another was a medical assistant and two were journalists. The larger circle of activists who joined in 1971–2 came from much the same background. In the main, even their supporters and sympathizers were not only drawn from the middle classes but in many cases held the sort of jobs that are typically preferred by intellectuals. In particular, the group's composition reflected the explosive emancipation of women at that time. Meinhof, Ensslin and a score of others are examples of a phenomenon which distinguished the membership of ultra-left groups in West Germany from extreme right-wing groups.

The members of the RAF believed with Lenin that the leadership of a revolution belonged to the enlightened element of the working class, but they have never openly discussed this thesis. Only Horst Mahler argued early on that the proletariat in capitalist countries had evolved into a 'workers' aristocracy' and that Lenin's interpretation of the proletariat was not therefore a fit 'revolutionary subject' for the RAF. Mahler spoke to intellectuals whose origins were not working-class, and argued that they should be considered an advance guard. He maintained that it was not industrial labour but the revolutionary elements in the student body who were the present-day custodians of revolutionary conscience.

In the eyes of many intellectuals, the task of the 'student elite' – to work for the interests of labour – had been betrayed by the 1968 attack on the Springer publishing house. While Springer itself was accepted as a target for attack, the workers in the building were not. As fewer people accepted the RAF's methods, so the group lost support, though as noted above some sympathizers turned to criticizing the criminal investigation methods, the way in which prosecutions were carried out and the sentences imposed.

Three pamphlets that Horst Mahler and Ulrike Meinhof published between April 1971 and November 1972, which accompanied and justified the first RAF violence, are still the definitive framework of the RAF's strategic concept. Because they are couched in language which to a very large extent can be understood only by intellectuals and which does not therefore motivate the working class, they have served as ideological justification to only a very narrow readership. After Baader, Ensslin and Jan-Carl Raspe had committed suicide in prison in 1977, the RAF theoretical basis grew still narrower, and attempts to embark on new theoretical discussions foundered: they followed acts of violence and were no more than efforts to justify the attacks ('the primacy of practice'). Forward-looking ideas were not forthcoming. Many former supporters were now voting Green, and those who did not wish formally to dissociate themselves, at least distanced themselves from murder, calling it counter-revolutionary. Admittedly, 'a liquidation [murder] could be an expression of revolutionary struggle; if however it becomes policy in itself, it deteriorates into left-wing self-justice', according to a 1987 discussion paper by an 'autonomous group' of the alternative left from Frankfurt–Main.

AN EYE TO PUBLICITY

In spite of the mistakes it has made in other respects, the RAF has from the beginning shown skill in publicity. Although the public soon forgot the names of policemen shot by the RAF, the terrorists killed remained in the public memory because later atrocities were carried out in their names. Much capital was made also from the force-feeding of prisoners during their hunger-strikes. State institutions generally were depicted as disregarding human rights, and the RAF prisoners as undergoing treatment that could be likened to torture. Solitary confinement, for example, became known as 'isolation torture'. From 1972 onwards the principal code words of this campaign were 'sensory deprivation', 'extermination imprisonment' and 'planned murder'.

The campaign was initiated by RAF members in prison and organized by their defenders outside. The prisoners were elevated to the status of martyrs, and the constitutional actions of the state were branded as a 'strategy of annihilation'. The campaigners argued that conservative forces were using the fight against terrorism to set up a 'police and surveillance state'. RAF suicides in jail were 'massacres' – an accusation that led to the establishment of an independent committee which confirmed that Baader, Ensslin and Raspe had indeed taken their own lives.

In frequent speeches to New Left groups and at universities, defence lawyers attacked the way in which sentences were imposed on terrorists. The lawyer Klaus Croissant, who was arrested on 23 June 1975 and later given a conditional discharge, moved to France on 11 July 1977 and made accusations of this kind in interviews to French newspapers and on French television. He was arrested in Paris on 30 September 1977 and extradited in November to the Federal Republic, where it emerged at his trial that he and other lawyers had facilitated communications between leading RAF members in jail. Ten defence lawyers had not only acted as messengers, but had also smuggled into the prisons weapons for a planned break-out and had themselves organized and participated in terrorist acts.

This knowledge reduced the readiness of opinion-formers to stand up for the terrorists' rights. After Schleyer's kidnap, in the course of which the driver and three policemen were killed, those who until then had spoken up for the terrorists and had appealed for understanding for their motives were silent.

REACTIONS

The intellectuals

Mindful of pre-war German fascism, many intellectuals genuinely feared that the state might over-react to terrorism. At the beginning of 1976 Heinrich Böll published *The Lost Honour of Katharina Blum*, a novel telling the story of a woman who embarks on a love affair with a man without knowing that he is a terrorist. The heartless probing of a newspaper correspondent into her private life and foolish questioning by police officers finally leads Katharina Blum to shoot the reporter. In the preface Böll writes: 'The characters and the treatment of this story are imaginary. If in this account similarities emerge between certain journalistic practices and those of the *Bild-Zeitung* [published by Springer], such similarities are neither intended nor unintentional, but unavoidable'. The book was filmed and subsequently shown a number of times on West German television, most recently in 1986.

In May 1977 Heinrich Böll and the writer Günter Wallraff published *Reports on the State of Mind*. Böll's contribution satirized the security authorities' investigations into terrorism. Wallraff contributed a summary of investigations which he said he had been subjected to on suspicions of his belonging to a terrorist organization. Both contributions attempted to prove that the security forces had themselves created the grounds for suspicion that they were then investigating.

Immediately after the murder of Siegfried Buback, Attorney-General of the Federal Supreme Court, in Karlsruhe on 7 April 1977, the writer and poet Erich Fried wrote:

> This piece of flesh
> thought it was doing justice,
> but did injustice.

In Fried's eyes Buback was only a 'part of the injustice'. Overall the poem did not focus on the murdered man but branded as injustice the prosecution of murderers and enemies of the West German constitution. The student newspaper *Göttinger Nachrichten* expressed itself still more clearly. Two weeks after the murder an anonymous 'obituary' signed 'Mescalero' read:

> My immediate reaction, my consternation, after the shooting of Buback can be quickly portrayed: I could not, did not want to (and still do not want to) conceal my furtive delight.

In June that year 44 professors and four lawyers republished the Mescalero obituary, claiming that the gesture defended free expression and that they hoped to stimulate 'a rethinking of the conditions of violence in our society'. Together with the obituary and other material was a 1905 article by Rosa Luxemburg on the assassination of the Tsarist Governor-General. By associating this assassination with Siegfried Buback's murder, the sponsors identified the Federal Republic with Tsarist Russia.

Government and the churches

The government and the Socialist Party, as well as the Catholic Church, questioned the responsibility of such attitudes and considered their effect on the terrorists and the climate of opinion surrounding their acts to be highly dangerous. Former Chancellor and SPD leader Willy Brandt reacted to Schleyer's kidnapping by publishing an appeal on 8 September 1977. He maintained that the sympathizers were 'responsible for the terrible deeds to an incomparably higher degree than those fanatics who pull the trigger of the machine-pistol'. Without them the assassins would be helpless. They formed the 'background encouragement in front of which the murderers can act as heroes ...'. Without such psychological support, clandestine life-styles and murder could not be sustained. It provided 'the nourishment, equipment, and sanctuary without which the terrorists could not cling to their absurd and bloody dreams of the People's War'.

On 21 September 1977 the German Conference of (Catholic) Bishops published a statement which said, among other things:

> Numerous faculties in our high schools and universities have for years taught and recommended non-acceptance of, and violence against, developed industrial societies. Can one avoid the thought that the terrorists obtained their ideological armoury here and desired to translate their false and Utopian theories into fact? We must ask ourselves whether perhaps certain conflict theories in the field of education have led to a spiritual misdirection among young people.

> In the mass media, and even in the classroom, there were, and are still, attempts to degrade and ridicule our state, its constitution, its laws and its representatives ... Frequently the concept of justice, order and institutions has been characterized as the embodiment of the reactionary and the outdated.

The Protestant church was more reserved in its condemnation. Indeed, during the 1970s there was a strong body of Protestant opinion that felt that the West German democratic system was unjust in certain respects, and in the early years a number of clergymen had provided RAF members with cars, flats and passports.

Labour and the Communist Party

Neither the unions nor the orthodox West German Communist Party (DKP) condemned the terrorism. The unions took the view that terrorism did not affect labour relations and that it fell to the government to respond to the threat. The DKP studiously avoided commenting because the RAF quoted Lenin in particular in support of its actions.

COUNTERMEASURES

The search for RAF members was difficult, and it still is. They are intelligent, work clandestinely, enjoy the support of a circle of sympathizers (now reduced, but still there), operate in an open society and are determined to resist arrest with lethal weapons. Success for the security authorities depended to a great extent on support and information from the man in the street, and such information was lacking during the early phases of operations between 1970 and 1972. When the state showed itself determined to counteract terrorism through large-scale searches the public at first became more willing to provide information, but then their willingness to help the security authorities decreased. Essentially this was a reaction to the widespread presence of the police, for example causing traffic jams at road blocks. Between 1975 and 1977 the number of wanted lists on display in the Federal Republic diminished considerably: the police were able to display only a quarter of the number of posters they had previously put up in small shops. The authorities were losing the confidence of the public, who began to believe that it was more dangerous to support the state than to support those who fought it.

The case of Dr Traube published in *Der Spiegel* in February 1977 is an example of how public concern was brought to bear. Dr Traube was the manager of a nuclear plant and had met some members of a terrorist organization in his holiday home near Bonn. The security services, with the authorization of the Ministry of the Interior, had bugged the residence from 2 January until 29 February 1976. As a result of the disclosure of the bugging, however, a parliamentary committee investigated the facts and the Interior Minister Werner Maihofer was forced to resign in June 1978.

Nevertheless more than 100 West German terrorists were arrested. The Ministry of the Interior was responsible for this effort, even though law enforcement in the Federal Republic is a provincial responsibility in the hands of every state (*Land*) government. The Federal Criminal Agency (BKA) and the Federal Office for the Protection of the Constitution (BfV) set about co-ordinating operations that crossed *Land* boundaries, and in order to cope with terrorism country-wide the government set up a number of working committees on which each *Land* was represented. The *Länder* are naturally jealous of their independence and although in practice co-operation on federal criminal matters is reasonably effective, in spite of the small print laid down in formal agreements neither the BKA nor the BfV can compel the

Land authorities to act against their will. It is certainly true that sometimes better co-operation would have led to more effective policing.

The general search measures available to the police were not, as a rule, sufficient to achieve success: the police found they lacked the sources of intelligence necessary if their searches were to be efficiently targeted.

Terrorist activity caused the security authorities to increase recruitment and to invest in computerized methods. The number of jobs in the Federal Criminal Agency increased from 933 in 1969 to 2,500 in 1977. This office has been expanded to serve as the central information and communications office for countering terrorism. The collection and processing of intelligence are undertaken with the most modern electronic equipment by the Federal Office for the Protection of the Constitution (Intelligence Service), which studies all aspects of terrorist activity.

The increase in personnel and technical aids obliges the security authorities to use their resources with care, since when they seek to uncover terrorist organizations and arrest violent criminals they must resist the temptation to cover the Federal Republic with a search-net reminiscent of George Orwell's 1984. Over-reaction plays straight into the hands of the terrorists, as loss of public support in the mid-1970s showed.

Academic research

Perhaps the most imaginative of the government's measures was the decision by Interior Minister Gerhart Rudolf Baum to research the phenomenon of German terrorism. Between 1979 and 1984 a group of well-known sociologists, psychologists, historians, lawyers and philosophers researched and compiled four volumes entitled *Analyses of Terrorism* for the FRG Ministry of the Interior.[1] Those involved came from the widest spectrum of political opinion. The first volume deals with 'Ideologies and Strategies' and analyses the arguments with which terrorist organizations explain and justify their activities. The second evaluates the biographical facts of those who turned to political violence. The third analyses the organization, structure and hierarchy of terrorist groups, methods of recruitment and the alienation of members of the groups from society when they are under pressure from the terrorist organizations. The last volume, which was published in two parts, deals with sociological processes and reactions. The first of these parts explores problems of legitimacy and questions of social and political integration, and is partly based on the results of a poll on the relationship of the young to the state and the democratic system. The second part analyses the interaction between terrorism, government response and socio-cultural reaction. The effect of this research was to prove to the intellectual establishment that the government was open to ideas, and to win that establishment's approval of subsequent government policy.

Other related research compared terrorism in West Germany, France, Italy and the Netherlands, and looked into such questions as whether the development of terrorism was in any way dependent on certain structures of society, economic conditions or government policy. The research provided arguments for discussion not only within universities but also in the media, and convinced many that terrorism was not the right way to change society.

New laws

New laws also helped to combat terrorism, though generalized responses were viewed sceptically: they easily become prey to routine, and terrorists have proved ingenious enough to adapt to them easily.

Since the passage of a law in 1971, hijacks and attacks on aircraft have carried a penalty of at least five years' imprisonment, and manslaughter in this context carries a prison term of at least ten years. In that same year the law was extended to include kidnapping, and a law against taking hostages was introduced. In addition, in 1976 a law was passed against those supporting and encouraging serious violent crimes.

The rights of the defence have been partly changed. It is now possible to exclude a defence attorney from a trial if he is suspected of being involved in the crime of which the defendant is accused, and it is no longer permissible for one lawyer to defend several persons on trial for the same crime. The possibility of carrying on the trial in the absence of the accused (for example during a hunger-strike) was extended in 1974.

In 1976 a law was passed increasing the penalties for membership of a terrorist organization. The law on the arrest of terrorists was strengthened, and control of written communication between the defence attorney and his client was instituted. In 1977 a further law was passed preventing contact between terrorist suspects and their defending lawyers if these contacts increased the chances of escape.

A law passed in 1978 aimed at improving the methods of detection following the attacks on Federal Attorney-General Buback, on Ponto (chief executive of the Dresden Bank) and Schleyer. The Schleyer case was something of a watershed in the development of police methods: it drew attention to legal inadequacies and indicated which powers were of particular importance to the police. An emergency provision allowed searches to be conducted in all apartments in an apartment block. During a large-scale police search, control points were allowed on roads to establish the identity of everyone on the road. Refusal to co-operate is punishable, but once an individual has been ruled out as a suspect, the information must be destroyed. The principle of this police trawl was enshrined in law in 1986. The police are now able to gather information on everyone's movements so as to create a net in which the potential terrorists can be trawled. The law stretches to the automatic reading of passports and identity cards: the transfer of such data is permitted only on special powers granted by a judge or by the prosecutor's office in writing, and remains effective for only three months. Moreover, a defence attorney can be removed if there are indications that he is planning a crime together with his client. The use of dividing panels has been authorized during discussions between the accused and his lawyer, so that nothing can be handed over.

Response during terrorist assaults

Even if they have been brought to the highest possible level of efficiency, improved personnel and technical resources will not on their own prevent terrorists from committing crimes. Apart from the search apparatus, three important factors have proved relevant to combating terrorist crimes successfully:

   i) security for vulnerable persons and institutions
  ii) constant attention to terrorist organizations and their activities by means of intelligence, and
 iii) a decisive government approach to the terrorists, especially during and after an attack.

During the 1970s, computer-assisted detection methods improved dramatically. Much public discussion and explanation were needed to allay public anxiety over the new technology and to counter criticism that the measures would turn the Federal Republic into a state which invaded the citizen's rights of privacy. In the event a computerized information system linked the intelligence gathered by the various intelligence-gathering agencies – namely the Federal Office for the Protection of the Constitution, the *Länder* equivalents, the BKA's Department for the Protection of the State, the Federal Intelligence Service and the Military Intelligence Service. There is also an information index classified according to persons, institutions and movable and immobile objects or facilities. Lastly, a computerized card-index of clues has been set up, so that links between the clues can be swiftly identified.

In addition, the use of information compiled and processed by non-police authorities, such as electricity and gas board customer details, has proved helpful in solving terrorist crimes. The information has been used both to identify a terrorist where his characteristics are known, and to reduce the number of potential suspects by making comparisons with police data. For example, RAF members thought to be living under false names in Frankfurt were assumed to pay their electricity bills in cash. Those who paid in cash and were living under false names could be identified by excluding others such as car-owners, pensioners and insurance policy holders whose names appeared on other registers. To counter the misuse of such data a Data Protection Act was passed in 1977, following the Swedish Data Act of 1973. Other countries followed – Austria (1978), Denmark (1978), France (1978), Norway (1978), Luxembourg (1978), and the United Kingdom (1984).

Even with these methods the police have been unable to solve many terrorist crimes. Infiltration and the use of informers have been tried, but on occasions have brought disrepute since some infiltrator agents have broken the law.

The issue of a court's reducing a sentence in return for information leading to the capture of other terrorists was hotly debated in the mid-1980s. A law passed in December 1986 allowed limited pardons but excluded those who had committed murder. At the same time, the sentences for founding a terrorist organization were doubled and it was made an offence to distribute publications that instructed people in the use of violence. It was also considered wise to provide the Federal Prosecutor's office with powers to prosecute foreign terrorists active in the Federal Republic, rather than leave it in the hands of the *Länder*.

A successful terrorist action is usually followed by further violent crimes, for nothing succeeds like success. The April 1975 occupation of the West German Embassy in Stockholm and the murder of two West German diplomats, aimed at securing the release of terrorists from FRG prisons, resulted from, among other factors, the government's yielding to terrorist demands during the kidnapping of CDU leader Peter Lorenz in February. By contrast, the government's resolute behaviour during the attack on the Stockholm Embassy was followed by a lull in serious attacks over the next year and a half.

The media

Every terrorist attack is unique and requires a response determined partly by the situation. Experience suggests that during an attack, the authorities should never react in the way in which the terrorists expect them to: such a reaction breeds repeated attacks. The state must always demonstrate that it will not give in to blackmail and that it will not tolerate violence. The publicity given to terrorist actions, which to some extent is part of the actions themselves, makes it even more difficult for the government to maintain a firm attitude. During the Stockholm siege, Swedish Television had a camera focused on the embassy for several hours. After the 1977 kidnap of Schleyer, the terrorists' first ultimatum demanded that one of the prisoners whose release was demanded should inform the commando unit, via public television, once they had been set free. In their third message the kidnappers demanded that a video tape of Schleyer reading a letter should be broadcast. Video tapes and polaroid photographs with ultimatums and announcements were constantly sent to the domestic and foreign press. During the Schleyer case the German press, at the government's request, refrained from publishing this material and so the terrorists lost the publicity they had expected.

LESSONS FOR THE FUTURE

After 1992, with the removal of border checks at internal EC frontiers, some of the security measures applied in West Germany in the 1970s and 1980s may need to be adopted by other EC countries. It is worthy of note that, before the unification of Germany in 1990, approximately 100,000 people were detained in border checks at Germany's frontiers every year, of whom about 50,000 were recognized from wanted lists and the other 50,000 detained as a result of 'hunches' by West-German police, border guards or customs officials. After 1992, border checks will need to be replaced by spot checks and, since anyone entering, say, Greece or Italy will be able to move freely to Germany, France or the United Kingdom, greater international exchange of information and access to data may be needed. In particular, improvement of some of the national police computers may be required (Belgium so far has not got one) and more frequent use of electronic linkage between them may be justified, to check whether there is any need to detain or investigate criminal or terrorist suspects picked up at spot checks, and on whom there may be data held on other national computers. There may also be a case for the introduction of ID cards in countries which do not have them (notably the United Kingdom and the Netherlands), and possibly for both ID cards and passports, and perhaps also visas issued by EC consulates in certain countries such as Syria or Libya, to include machine-readable data, including biometric data (e.g. records of finger print, retina, vein pattern or DNA data in digital form). Harmonization of data protection legislation to prevent or detect abuse of such data or of powers to use them may also be necessary.

NOTE

1. *Analysen zum Terrorismus* (Opladen: Westdeutschen Verlag GmbH, 1981 – 84)

APPENDIX: ATTACKS BY THE RED ARMY FACTION

11 May 1972	Bomb attack on the headquarters of the 5th Army Corps of the US armed forces in the FRG in Frankfurt by the 'Commando Petra Schelm'.
12 May 1972	Bomb attack on the police headquarters in Augsburg and the State Criminal Office in Munich by the 'Commando Thomas Weissbecker'.
16 May 1972	Bomb attack against judge Buddenberg at the Federal Court in Karlsruhe by the 'Commando Manfred Grashof'.
19 May 1972	Bomb attack on the Springer tower block in Hamburg by the 'Commando 2 June'.

24 May 1972	Bomb attack on the Headquarters of the US Armed Forces in Europe in Heidelberg by the 'Commando 15 July Red Army Faction'.
24 April 1975	Occupation of the German Embassy in Stockholm by the 'Commando Holger Meins'.
7 April 1977	Murder of the Attorney-General of the Federal Supreme Court, Siegfried Buback, in Karlsruhe by the 'Commando Ulrike Meinhof'.
30 July 1977	Murder of the Chief Executive of the Dresdner Bank in Oberursel, Jürgen Ponto. Responsibility claimed by 'Susanne Albrecht from a Commando of the RAF'.
25 Aug. 1977	Bombing of the office of the Attorney of the Federal Supreme Court in Karlsruhe.
5 Sept. 1977	Abduction of the President of the Employers' Association, Hanns Martin Schleyer, in Cologne by the 'Commando Siegfried Hausner'. Schleyer was murdered on 19 October 1977.
25 June 1979	Bomb attack on the Supreme Commander of NATO, General Alexander Haig, in Mons, Belgium by the 'Commando Andreas Baader'.
31 Aug. 1981	Bomb attack on the Headquarters of the US Airforce in Europe in Ramstein by the 'Commando Sigurd Debus'.
15 Sept. 1981	Attack on the Commander-in-Chief of the US Armed Forces in Europe, General Kroesen, in Heidelberg by the 'Commando Gudrun Ensslin'.
18 Dec. 1984	Attempted bombing of the NATO training school in Oberammergau by the 'Commando Jan Raspe'.
1 Feb. 1985	Murder of the Chairman of the Board of Directors of the MTU (Motor and Turbine Union) and President of the BDLI (Federal Organization of the German Aviation Industry), Dr Ernst Zimmermann, in Gauting, Munich by the 'Commando Patsy O'Hara'.
8 April 1985	Bomb attack on the Marine Technology Planning Society of International Ship Studies (ISS) and attempted bomb attack on the firm Project Management Office (PMO) in Hamburg by 'Illegal Militant, Fighting Unit Jonas Timme' (sic) (Johannes Thimme).
9 May 1985	Bomb attack on the pump station of the NATO Pipeline at Gromlich Badbergen (NI) by the 'Fighting Unit Johannes Thimme'.
7 Aug. 1985	Murder of US soldier, Edward Pimental, in Wiesbaden.
8 Aug. 1985	Car bomb attack on the car park of the Rhein Main Airbase in Frankfurt by the 'Commando George Jackson' of the RAF and *Action Directe*.
15 Aug. 1985	Attacks on the area of the military depot (Pomcus Depot) of the US Army in Munchen Gladbach by the 'Fighting Unit "For the Building of the Anti-Imperialist Front in Western Europe"'.
13 Oct. 1985	Bomb attack on the area of the establishment of Daimler

	Benz in Swabian Gmund (BW) by the 'Revolutionary Cell, Fighting Unit Ulrike Meinhof, Fighting Unit Gudrun Ensslin'.
9 July 1986	Murder of the Chairman of Research and Technology for Siemens, Karlheinz Beckurts, and his driver in Strasslach (Munich) by the 'Commando Mara Cagol' in a car-bomb attack.
24 July 1986	Bomb attack on the Fraunhofer Institute for Laser Technology in Aachen by the 'Fighting Unit Sheban Atlouf'.
25 July 1986	Car bomb attack on the firm of Dornier in Immenstaad (BW) by the 'Fighting Unit named after a female companion who was killed by a guerrilla rocket attack at a meeting of International Socialists in Lima'.
11 Aug. 1986	Bomb attacks on the land of the Federal Border Police in Swisstal Heimerzheim (NW) by the 'Fighting Unit Crespo Cepa Gallende'.
13 Aug. 1986	Bomb attack on the Administration buildings of the US firm Westinghouse Signal Tools in Wuppertal by the 'Fighting Unit' (no specific name).
8 Sept. 1986	Car bomb attack on the Federal Office for the Protection of the Constitution (BfV) in Cologne by the 'Fighting Unit Christos Tsoutsouvis'.
15 Sept. 1986	Bomb attack against the Panavia Aircraft and the NATO MRCA Management Agency (NAMMA) in Munich by the 'Fighting Unit Anna Maria Ludmann'.
10 Oct. 1986	Murder of the Foreign Affairs Ministry head of the political division of Foreign Affairs, Gerold von Braunmühl, in Bonn by the 'Commando Ingrid Schubert'.
16 Nov. 1986	Bomb attack on the computing centre of the Science Centre of the US firm IBM in Heidelberg (BW) by the 'Fighting Unit Hind Alameh'.
19 Dec. 1986	Bomb attack on the German Society for Good Management Co-operation (DEG) in Cologne by the 'Fighting Unit Rolando Olalia'.
21 Dec. 1986	Bomb attack on the Kurt Schumacher Picture Centre of the Friedrich Ebert Foundation in Bad Munstereifel (NW) by the 'Fighting Unit Mustafa Aktas'.
20 Sept. 1988	Attempted murder of the Secretary of State in the Finance Ministry, Hans Tietmeyer, in Bonn by the 'Commando Khaled Aker Red Army Faction'.
30 Nov. 1989	Murder of Deutsche Bank chief, Alfred Herrhausen, by the 'Commando Wolfgang Beer'.
27 June 1990	Attempted murder of Hans Neusel, State Secretary at the German Interior Ministry.

5 Italy: The Problem of Ultra-Leftist Violence

THE TERRORISTS: FACTS, FIGURES AND CAUSES

Although 487 named left-wing terrorist groups have appeared in Italy since 1969, only three have made any long-term impact: the *Brigate Rosse* (BR) or Red Brigades; the *Nuclei Armati Proletari* (NAP) or Armed Proletarian Nuclei; and *Prima Linea* (PL) or Front Line. All three of these groups believed in the violent overthrow of the state and in an ill-defined 'socialist' society based on Marxist-Leninist and Maoist principles, but their structures, tactics and strategies varied considerably.

The Red Brigades was formed in Milan in 1970 by the fusion of a group of young ex-Communist party members in Reggio Emilia (they had been expelled for their extremist views), and a Milan group whose members were largely factory workers. BR organization has evolved in accordance with the ideas of succeeding generations of leaders, but the group owes its continuity to its being both tightly compartmentalized and clandestine.[1] Almost from the start it set out to form an armed, clandestine vanguard to educate and lead the proletariat towards revolution. It rejected the spontaneous violence advocated by others on the extra-parliamentary left.

The *Nuclei Armati Proletari* first emerged in 1972 and was strongest in Naples, though it had important bases in Rome and Florence. It began as a movement in the prisons, designed to politicize criminals into believing that injustices should be combated with violence against the state. Its members were less ideologically inclined than those of BR and their organization was less tightly controlled. Over four years NAP committed four murders, six woundings, three kidnaps and innumerable bank robberies. By 1976 most of its members had been caught, sentenced and imprisoned, or killed in gun-battles with police. Those who remained merged with BR.

Prima Linea was formed in about 1976 in Turin from the most extreme elements of the extra-parliamentary left. Unlike BR, PL saw itself not as an elitist armed vanguard, but as 'a service structure for the proletariat'. Its members kept closer to the factory floor than those

135

of BR. Nevertheless, by the late 1970s violence had become so competitive that there was little to choose between the two groups in terms of ability and readiness to shoot and kill. Between 1976 and 1980 PL carried out 16 murders and 23 woundings. No one has reliably estimated PL membership, since there were many part-timers, but there may have been as many as three thousand in the PL 'orbit'. The organization operated throughout northern Italy.

During the late 1970s, when it was at its strongest, BR had about 500 members, of whom about 50 were full-time and lived clandestinely. The others held down normal jobs, kept their own names and enjoyed the conventional ties of family and friends. Columns were established in Milan, Rome, Turin, Genoa, Naples, the Veneto region and (briefly, with little success) in Sardinia. This chapter concerns itself primarily with the state's reaction to this organization.

The victims

Between 1970 and 1980, BR committed 55 murders (the first in 1974), 68 woundings and was responsible for 11 kidnappings.[2] Its most intense activity came in 1978, when it carried out 106 attacks. The 55 murder victims in this decade comprised 31 security force members, six judges, five company executives, three prison officers, three prisoners, one politician, one factory worker, one journalist, one lawyer, one prison health inspector, one company employee and one commercial representative.

The following table includes later statistics and records all forms of terrorism in Italy, not only that of the far left.

To these figures must now be added the victims of the two terrorist attacks of 1988 – the car bomb, claimed by Islamic Jihad, that exploded outside a US services club in Naples on 14 April and killed five people, and the BR murder of Christian Democrat Senator Roberto Ruffilli two days later in Forli, near Bologna.

Far-left groups were responsible for 74.5 per cent of the attacks and for 150 of the deaths (including that of Ruffilli). In geographical terms, 87.2 per cent of all terrorist attacks were carried out in 16 of Italy's 95 provinces. The worst hit was Rome, followed by Milan, Turin, Naples, Bologna, Reggio Calabria, Padua, Bari, Florence, Genoa, Brescia, Palermo, Venice, Bergamo, Trieste and Catania.

Table 5.1   Analysis of terrorist attacks 1969–87

Year	Total incidents	Attacks involving injuries	Injuries	Deaths
1969	398	3	19 (17)	88
1970	376	2	7	50
1971	539	2	2	—
1972	595	3	5	2
1973	426	5	40	61
1974	573	7	26 (20)	199
1975	702	14	10	7
1976	1 353	13	10	6
1977	1 926	45	13	34
1978	2 379	67	35	54
1979	2 513	66	24	101
1980	1 502	48	125 (85)	236
1981	634	34	25	16
1982	347	17	23	42
1983	156	11	10	3
1984	85	6	20 (15)	134
1985	63	11	20	146
1986	24	3	2	2
1987	8	2	3	1
Total	14 599	359	419	1 182

Note: Numbers in brackets indicate injuries sustained in right-wing terrorist attacks.

Finance and motivation

As for financing, Italian left-wing terrorists were basically self-sufficient. At first, BR and the other groups were funded by wealthy left-wing Milanese intellectuals, including millionaire publisher Giangiacomo Feltrinelli, but after disagreements over strategy in 1971–2 BR began, with great success, to rob banks. Other raids were made on post offices and jewellers' shops. Kidnapping also provided funds. BR bought weapons regularly on the black market (at first often in Switzerland, later in the Middle East) and stole from armouries or from armed security guards, or simply used forged licences, a practice which was relatively simple until 1978. Between 1975 and 1979, 13,297 long-arms and 15,652 short-arms were stolen.

Between 1981 and 1983 the terrorist left amassed the equivalent of about £3.8 million from only 12 robberies. These groups never depended on foreign or outside sources for funding.

Those attracted to political violence came from a broad spectrum of society: many worked in the large factories of Turin and Milan, but a large minority were university-educated and a few had been university teachers. There were two 'generations', born respectively in the first and second halves of the 1950s; there were more females participating in the second generation, and they tended to have high educational qualifications.

It is impossible to point to any single cause of left-wing violence. Italy's emergence from a fascist, peasant society into a modern industrial democracy brought about deep political, industrial and social changes which created opportunities for such violence to grow. At least a part of the original inspiration for BR came from the previous generation of partisans (mostly communist) who had helped to liberate Italy in 1945, and who looked on in dismay as post-war Italy clung to the remnants of its fascist past and at the same time came increasingly under the dominance of Western capitalism. Their sons were attracted to BR when they saw that the amnesty of 1946 had opened prison doors for some 40,000 former fascists who in many cases returned to their former positions in the armed forces, police and public administration. Partisan fighting manuals went the rounds of the far left as the new generation inherited not only the spirit of heroic resistance against an unjust system, but also the material legacy of weapons, technical experience and instruction.

Another factor was the student 'revolution' of 1968, when young people gained their first experiences of confronting authority and of acting independently as the New Left. The student revolution spilt over into the workers' struggles of 1969–70. The violence was relatively low, but workers' struggles provided the emerging extra-parliamentary groups with a cause.

A further important precipitating factor was neo-fascist thuggery and in particular the terrorist attack of 12 December 1969, when a bomb exploded in a central Milan bank, killing 17 people and injuring 80. Even the President of the Republic tried to blame the far left and numerous leftists were arrested. For the far left, the reaction showed the lengths to which the state would go to obscure, disregard or disbelieve the challenge from the right (20 years and seven trials later there is still no final judicial verdict on who planted that bomb, even though no one doubts that it was of neo-fascist inspiration).

'Militant anti-fascism' was a strong driving force not only for BR but also for much of the Italian left, including a substantial sector of the Milanese intelligentsia, until the mid-1970s. By then, a number of extremist right-wing organizations had been banned and trials of right-wing terrorists had effectively removed the far right as a serious threat. Consequently the BR stopped referring to the state as *golpista* (favourable to a coup d'état), and instead used *gollista* (aiming at the installation of a presidential or Gaullist republic).

Not least important were the democratization and 'Westernization' of the Italian Communist Party (PCI), a process which led BR to accuse the PCI of betraying the proletariat and to portray itself as the true representative of the working classes. The PCI's 'historic compromise' with the Christian Democratic party (DC) between 1973 and 1978 led to the kidnapping of the DC leader, Aldo Moro, on the day the first 'government of national unity' was presented to parliament.

Lastly, its growth can be attributed to the unpreparedness of society generally, and of the state in particular, for this kind of onslaught. Indeed, at first there was a fashionable tendency in certain intellectual, cultural and 'drawing-room' circles to parade and defend what was called subversion. This was, in the view of Dr Nicolò Amato, Director General of the Italian Prison Service, particularly evident in the universities of Rome and Padua.[3] He maintains that had sufficient attention been paid to early warnings, or if there had been greater understanding of the direction in which events were moving, the degeneration into terrorism might have been avoided.

THE GOVERNMENT'S RESPONSE

Italian politicians are elected on the basis of proportional represent-ation, and since 1953 no one party has won an absolute majority. The DC has always enjoyed a relative majority and therefore the lion's share of government posts, while the PCI, always the second largest party, was denied posts in the government. This situation caused the DC to rely on the support of the smaller parties, whose influence was disproportionate to their size, but at the same time forced it to look over its shoulder at the PCI. Italy has had 44 governments since the Second World War, but only two non-DC Prime Ministers.

Terrorism has had a unifying rather than a dividing effect on Italian politics and, conversely, political unity has been a stimulus to terrorism. Although they disagree on many issues, the major political parties have taken an almost unanimous stand against terrorism. The most inclined to leniency has been the Socialist Party (PSI) which, in spite of an official refusal to negotiate, has tended to look towards mediation. The most intransigent has been the Communist Party which, for example, threatened during the Moro kidnap to bring down the government if there were negotiations.

All the major parties voted in favour of legislation against terrorism between 1978 and 1987, though crisis measures were largely an *ad hoc* response. As former Interior Minister Francesco Cossiga told the Parliamentary Commission set up to investigate terrorism in May 1980:

> A proper security policy against terrorism simply did not exist, not least because a security policy against terrorism demands a capacity for analysis that is not only technical but also political, social and cultural, which we only developed much later on .... And I have to say that in our country, unlike others, there has always been a great confusion between police activity and police policy....

Cossiga said he felt that in Britain and West Germany, where the functions are separate, better results were achieved. On a tactical level, the police learned that physical confrontation with crowds was counter-productive, and they had to learn how to respond to gunfire.

In an interview with *La Republica* in May 1977 Cossiga had said that it might have been better to dissolve the security services and to set up a totally new organization instead of trying to remove corrupt elements and practices. With hindsight, his remarks in this interview and comments to the effect that he believed the involvement of foreign intelligence services in Italian terrorism to be 'very likely', give a key to much of what went wrong in successive years.

Anti-terrorist forces

From 1977 the Prime Minister was given responsibility for the co-ordination of anti-terrorist programmes, though the Interior Ministry retained responsibility for maintaining public order. Constitutionally, the Prime Minister can declare a state of emergency and, through the Ministry of the Interior, delegate the powers to appoint prefects; to arrest or detain anyone believed to constitute a threat to public order; to seek the military's help in maintaining public order; and to over-ride existing laws in matters of public order and security. These powers were never invoked, in spite of calls for their use on the day of Moro's kidnap.

There are five national police forces in Italy:

- the state police, or public security force
- the *carabinieri*

- the finance police
- the confinement police, or prison wardens
- the forestry police.

The state police, under the Ministry of the Interior, hold overall responsibility for the maintenance of public order, while the *carabinieri* are under the Ministry of Defence. The finance police are responsible for fiscal duties, border controls etc., and come under the Ministry of Finance. The judiciary may direct elements of all three forces in the detection and prevention of crime; when this happens, they come under the Ministry of Justice and form the 'judicial police'.

There are 20 regions and 95 provinces in Italy. Each province has a prefect who is the central government representative subject to the Ministry of the Interior, and immediately subordinate to him is the provincial police chief or *questore*.

The Interministerial Committee for Security (CIS) is a consultative body whose task is to propose the general lines of national security policy. It is presided over by the Prime Minister, and includes the Ministers of the Interior, Foreign Affairs, Justice, Defence, Industry and Finance.

Italy has had various forms of intelligence service since the Second World War. The first was SIFAR (Armed Forces Information Service) from 1949 to 1965, followed by SID (Defence Information Service), from 1965 to 1977. The present organization was reformed by a law of October 1977, passed after revelations of corruption and allegations that some of its agents were involved in right-wing terrorism.

There are now two intelligence services, SISMI (Service for Military Intelligence and Security) and SISDE (Service for Intelligence and Democratic Security). SISMI is responsible for all intelligence and security functions relating to national defence, including counter-espionage; it comes under the Ministry of Defence. SISDE is responsible for intelligence and security functions relating to the preservation of democracy and the protection of institutions; it comes under the Ministry of the Interior. The two services are co-ordinated by the Executive Committee for the Intelligence and Security Services, (CESIS). CESIS is chaired by the prime minister, who decides its composition; the directors of the two services are permanent members. Each of the three armed forces also has its own intelligence-gathering section.

By law SISMI and SISDE are forbidden to employ members of parliament, regional or provincial councillors, members of the judiciary, clergymen or professional journalists. An all-party Committee of

Vigilance is given the task of monitoring the activities of the security services; and the Prime Minister must report to parliament twice a year.

In January 1978 the Central Office for General Investigations and Special Operations (UCIGOS) was set up within the Ministry of the Interior. Its function is to co-ordinate counter-terrorist operations within the state police. It has headquarters in each province, and where these are in major cities the offices are called DIGOS (Division for General Investigations and Special Operations). UCIGOS also controls small anti-terrorist units on instant alert known as NOCS (Central Operative Nuclei for Security).

UCIGOS has the following functions:

- collecting information on the general political, social, and economic situation of relevance to the operational needs of the Interior Ministry and the prefectures
- collecting information relevant to crime prevention and to the maintenance of civil order
- investigating means of preventing and suppressing crimes against public order, terrorism and crimes of a political nature against the security of the state or democratic institutions
- carrying out police and security duties and those of the judicial police at the request of, and in collaboration with, SISMI and SISDE.

The anti-terrorist units within the *carabinieri* are known as 'special anti-crime sections' and 'operative divisions'. Here too there are 'special intervention groups' (GIS) for use in emergencies, for example prison revolts.

The above is a summary of the state of affairs today. However, other anti-terrorist structures have been set up to meet particular emergencies from time to time. For example, on 1 June 1974, in the wake of the neo-fascist bomb which exploded in a crowded square in Brescia, a General Inspectorate for action against terrorism was set up within the state police under Emilio Santillo. This obtained excellent results against terrorism of both left and right, but was dissolved in January 1978 with the restructuring of the security services and the creation of UCIGOS.

The role of Dalla Chiesa

General Carlo Alberto Dalla Chiesa of the *carabinieri* was twice given an anti-terrorist mandate. First, after BR had kidnapped Genoese

Judge Mario Sossi in 1974, his mandate was to form a 'special nucleus' composed of 40 men. This unit had considerable success but was dissolved the following year. Dalla Chiesa was called on again in September 1978, in the wake of the Moro kidnap. The government decree that established his powers was kept secret for a year, and was highly controversial – it made Dalla Chiesa independent of parliamentary control, referring directly to the Minister of the Interior, and he was not obliged to brief the judiciary on his activities. He had control of 200 hand-picked men, operating throughout the country.

This was the first time that anti-terrorist direction had been entrusted to one source. Dalla Chiesa was also in charge of prison security at the time, and could place informers (prisoners or personnel) into the prisons and move them around accordingly. Because he had direct access to the Interior Ministry, he had both information and authority to act immediately. He enjoyed access to overseas contacts and intelligence; he could use the highest authority to encourage co-operation; he could obtain funds without bureaucratic delay or obstacle; and he could seize or release passports at will.

His operational methods were unorthodox and autocratic but were highly successful – the men in his team were specialists in making painstaking, methodical checks, in tailing and observing suspects, in telephone-tapping and in infiltration. The special unit was allocated a monthly sum for costs such as renting safe houses for logistic and operational purposes. Dalla Chiesa's special mandate was renewed in September 1979 at his own request without an expiry date, but in December 1979 he took over the command of the *carabinieri* in the whole of Northern Italy. He carried on his anti-terrorist work in Milan until 1982, when he was made prefect of Palermo.

Lack of co-ordination

The number and scope of the above-mentioned organizations show that there were too many forces undertaking similar tasks with no co-ordinated strategy. Other problems arose from rivalry between different police forces, especially between the state police and the *carabinieri*; from the low educational level of recruits; from outdated structures and training which were not overhauled until 1980; and from duplication of functions and lack of co-ordination between the forces of law and order. Pooling of information worked only if relations between the state police and *carabinieri* chiefs were good. Dalla Chiesa reported on at least one occasion that while his special forces were watching a house or tailing a suspect, checks on vehicles in the area proved that they belonged to other police forces. He aroused resentment within both the *carabinieri* and the state police by picking crack men to join his special squad. He also complained of political bias against him within the judiciary.

In 1990 police/*carabinieri* strength was around 200,000, but in 1978 the forces were undermanned. State police strength stood at 68,927, with 14,523 positions vacant. Of those employed, a little over 11,000 (16 per cent) were engaged in countering terrorism or organized crime. More than half of the total complement had no more than an elementary school education.

Traditionally police recruits come from the south, where recruitment and promotion are frequently gained by patronage rather than merit. It is true that those selected to work on terrorism were given special training, with particular emphasis being given to an understanding of ideology and motivation. Morale never plummeted – resignations were never due to fear. Even so, when Moro was kidnapped, in spite of warnings that should have kept his escort team alert, only one of the five in the team managed to draw his gun while the other four had theirs in the holsters with the safety catches on. The BR 'penitent' Patrizio Peci reported that the one weapon seized from the police on that occasion proved to be so rusted that it was thrown away. The politicians, however, supported the police, and their working conditions were improved. Under police auspices the public learned much from meetings in schools and town halls, and the police participated in radio and television debates and discussions. With this concentration of effort on political crime, relatively less attention was paid to the Mafia, whose activities expanded in the 1970s when organized crime was viewed with relative indifference by the politicians. The politicians began to sit up and take notice in the 1980s when the links between local politics and the Mafia came under scrutiny. During the 1970s the Mafia had ridden on the back of terrorism, whose practitioners learned from mafiosi imprisoned in the north. Contacts in prison, particularly between the BR and the *Camorra*, led to co-operation in the Naples area.

One problem in policing a capital city such as Rome is that of extraterritoriality – an estimate has it that, excluding the Vatican City, there are some 160 buildings in Rome which are 'off-limits' to the police, such as embassies and international organizations, as well as parliamentary buildings, government buildings, airports etc., all of which have their own security forces.

The deplorable inefficiency of the intelligence during the worst period of left-wing terrorism was largely due to the reorganization decreed by law in 1977. Military intelligence was not unduly affected, but domestic intelligence was totally reorganized. The one really effective counter-terrorist section in the state police, run by Santillo, was dismantled and its manpower and archives were dispersed. Generals Santovito and Grassini, respectively heads of SISMI and SISDE, did not see eye to eye, and there were frequent differences of opinion with the director of CESIS, to the extent that he felt compelled to resign in April 1978, at the height of the Moro kidnap. Grassini took over SISDE in January 1978 with a total staff of less than 100, and only five senior officials. Even by May 1978, when the restructured service was inaugurated, it had a staff of only 120 (compared to SISMI's 2,500) and its undermanning was not redressed until the end of 1980.

The situation in 1978 was so bad that for the duration of the Moro kidnap (16 March–9 May) there was not a single written contribution provided by either intelligence service, described by one official as being 'on vacation', and the police forces claimed to be 'without eyes and ears'. It later emerged that intelligence reports had existed but no one knew where to find them. The lack of analysis and of continuity within the anti-terrorist structures led to confusion; in the atmosphere of violent disorder created by the '77 Movement' – a generic name for the extra-parliamentary left – and the accompanying rise of terrorism, no clear distinction seems to have been made between extremism and terrorism. Members of the '77 Movement' were not clandestine but provided the 'sea' in which terrorists swam, though terrorist structures were not dependent upon this environment.

The P2 Lodge scandal

The period of maximum threat coincided with the minimum operational capacity of the security services, so much so that during the entire planning and executive phases of the Moro kidnap the domestic security service was virtually non-operational. At that time BR had not been penetrated. Some have tried to link this circumstance to the fact that both Generals Santovito and Grassini and the replacement director of CESIS, as well as innumerable other high-ranking officials, were all members of the secret Masonic Lodge 'Propaganda 2'. When the P2 Lodge scandal broke in March 1981 all were immediately relieved of their duties and the Ministry of Defence opened an internal enquiry into the SISMI P2 members (approximately 50 generals were members), but none ever came to court.

The relationship between the P2 Lodge and terrorism is still under enquiry, but there are strong indications that a parallel structure existed within the military security service whose aims included the subversion of democracy and whose tactics involved at the very least providing cover for terrorism, possibly even extending to its promotion. In July 1988 a Bologna court sentenced the former deputy director of SISMI and a colleague to ten years' imprisonment for having deflected the enquiries into the Bologna station bomb by laying a false trail of evidence. This verdict was upheld in the Court of Appeal. This, and other evidence, shows that in spite of the much-vaunted 'reform' of 1977, the Italian intelligence services have continued to harbour subversive elements at the highest level.

Problems of infiltration

Infiltration has probably been the major intelligence problem, although BR was twice successfully infiltrated in the early years, in 1972 and again in 1974. It is not clear whether the police informer Marco Pisetta, arrested in 1972 and then 'helped' into exile, was an informer before or after his arrest, but he was largely responsible for forcing the first generation of BR members underground. In 1974 Dalla Chiesa used a former priest with a reputation for revolutionary activities in South America to make contact with BR's 'historic leaders', and this 'Father Machine-gun' helped to round up some nine prominent BR members during the latter half of 1974. From then on BR introduced strict compartmentalization and clandestinity: in these new cicumstances anyone wishing to join the organization had to be well known first to sympathizers, and then to 'irregular' members, and would have to take part in a number of actions before becoming a clandestine 'regular'. BR also became virtually self-sufficient in terms of logistics – vehicle theft, document forgery and self-financing operations – and so gradually reduced its contacts with the ordinary criminal underworld, where the police had easier access.

One source of intelligence was the prison environment. Prison escapes had increased alarmingly during the early 1970s, and in 1976 they reached a total of 438. In 1977 (when there were 430 escapes) Dalla Chiesa was given charge of prison security. He set up eleven top security prisons where particularly high-risk prisoners were housed.

In 1978, the number of prison escapes dropped to 155. Dalla Chiesa also used prison guards and common criminals to collect information; this was astute since, throughout the 1970s, BR strategy was planned and directed from inside prison walls. BR inevitably got wise to this use of informers, and in time the amount of useful information that reached Dalla Chiesa diminished.

Another simple but important obstacle to intelligence collection was the sexual self-sufficiency of the terrorist organization and therefore the lack of recourse to prostitutes - normally a rich source of police information. As *carabinieri* commander Corsini said in his deposition to the Parliamentary Commission: 'Everyone knows Italians talk a lot in bed – if it's between themselves it goes no further, if they talk to prostitutes we get all the information we want'.

Until 1980 Italy lacked the computerized data bank that would obviously have helped greatly with intelligence collection. For example in 1978 the only firearms records were in the form of a card index in the Ministry of Interior. When a BR base was discovered with weapons, they could be traced only to the original purchaser, and even then only after long and exhaustive efforts.

In retrospect, there is a case for arguing that neither the Interminister-ial Committee (CIS) nor the co-ordinating committee (CESIS) has in practice ever functioned properly. The 1977 reform law gave the Prime Minister or his Under-Secretary specific responsibility for the security services. During the Spadolini and Craxi premierships, both men took total charge; under the De Mita government, an under-secretary was in control, but there was little outside consultation. As for financing, parliament is informed how much of the national budget goes to the security services but, apart from the transparent costs of wages etc., has no knowledge of nor control over how the money is spent.

It is not really possible to talk of 'continuity' of policy within the intelligence services, since the direction taken is always conditioned by internal struggles, either between different services or between politi-cal masters. For example, the 1970s were characterized by the political rivalry between Aldo Moro and Giulio Andreotti, a battle which was continued by service chief Miceli (Moro's man, pro-Arab) and Andreotti's man Maletti (pro-Israel). By the end of the decade, how-ever, Andreotti himself had moved to a pro-Arab position. The security services are predominantly made up of police and *carabinieri*, and so the old rivalry was a problem here as well.

Other countries' security services have helped to combat left-wing terrorism in Italy. The French were an exception until Chirac got into power; the Germans were more helpful. On the other hand, other services have at times helped Italian terrorists by giving sanctuary – Spain with the right-wing, France with the left.

The army was not used as an anti-terrorist force except at the time of the Moro kidnap, when 1000 men were asked to help to man roadblocks.

Crisis management

Italy had no crisis organization for dealing with terrorist, as opposed to civil, disorders. This led to particular confusion on the morning of Moro's kidnap when the head of UCIGOS mistakenly assumed that provinces had the same arrangements as had been formulated for Sardinia, where he had previously served as *questore*. Not surprisingly, police headquarters around the country were thrown into chaos as a result of this misunderstanding.

In the wake of the Moro kidnap two crisis committees took charge, one of which was the Interministerial Committee for Security (CIS) mentioned above, and the other a politico-technical committee responsible for co-ordinating the police, the security services, the judiciary and the Interior Ministry. It appears, however, that there is no record of any meetings after 3 April 1978.

Quite separately from these, Interior Minister Cossiga set up his own committee, members of which were schooled in psychiatry, psychology, graphology and terrorism; some were from overseas, including a US State Department secondment and a German who advised on the basis of the Schleyer kidnap (September 1977), which bore resemblances to the Moro case. Contact was also set up with the German police computer at Wiesbaden.

Apart from the day of Moro's kidnap, parliament debated the country's response to the terrorist attack only once in the course of the 55 days. All decisions were taken after internal party consultation by the secretaries of the major parties.

Afterwards, the measure that galvanized counter-terrorism was Dalla Chiesa's appointment in September 1978. Within a month Dalla Chiesa had located three major BR bases in Milan and had rounded up a dozen BR members, including two who were on the BR Executive Committee, which organized the Moro kidnap. Terrorism did not abate then – in fact it became even more ferocious in the following year – but Dalla Chiesa had set the scene for its control.

Criminal justice

In general the judiciary stood up to the strains put on it with courage and determination. Magistrates occupy a prominent public position in that they are in charge of investigating a crime. They cannot remain anonymous as they are involved from the beginning to the end of the legal process and are, consequently, in the limelight. They displayed a remarkable willingness to give press and television interviews, in spite of the 'armour-plated' existence forced on them. Undoubtedly some magistrates took early retirement, but the increasing work-load provided impressive career opportunities for the young and the dynamic. Together with the police forces, the judiciary was in the front line against terrorism; and as a result of the emergency legislation its powers were extended. Initially there was public and political criticism. In the opinion of Dr Nicolò Amato, Director General of the Italian Prison Services, the emergency was brought about by the unpreparedness of the state for the explosion of terrorism and its difficulty in responding. The excess of rigour was proof of weakness, not strength. The state delegated the fight against terrorism to the police, the *carabinieri* and to the judiciary, who paid a very high price. In the early days they operated in conditions of serious and painful solitude, amid the indifference if not the cynicism of many. Eventually, however, there emerged a solid unity between society and institutions through people's involvement, the trade union organizations for example, and this transformed the contest almost into a popular struggle. However, Dr Amato justified the severe measures because of the real and urgent requirement to change the circumstances in which escapes, revolts and murders imperilled order, security and legality inside prisons.

From 1974, with the kidnap of Genoese Judge Mario Sossi, the judiciary has been a prime target for the extreme left. Terrorists frequently tried to influence trials (and often succeeded). In June 1976 BR assassinated the chief prosecutor of Genoa, Francesco Coco, while the trial for the Sossi kidnap was in progress; in Turin the trial was postponed. In April 1977, before the trial could restart, BR shot dead Fulvio Croce, president of the Turin lawyers' association, whose responsibilities included the allocation of lawyers for the terrorists' defence. Once again the trial was postponed because it was impossible to assemble enough lawyers and jurors. The trial eventually came to court in March 1978 in Turin.

In spite of threats and intimidation, trials continued to be heard in public under more or less normal conditions: for example, the public

were allowed in after extensive bag and body searches. Specially reinforced 'bunker courts' were constructed, at great cost, to accommodate
terrorist trials, with defendants held in 'cages' constructed within the
courtroom. Because of the frequent interruptions from prisoners trying
to read out proclamations or shout defamatory remarks, from June
1978 prisoners who interrupted proceedings on a second occasion were
banned from court until the final day. Furthermore, the legal limitations
on the period of detention ceased to apply if the court was suspended
because of difficulties in forming a jury or the exercise of the defence.

Magistrates and lawyers at risk were given armoured cars and body-
guards – on a 24-hour basis if they were especially vulnerable; a number
still have them today. Jurors and witnesses were given armed escorts
to and from the courtroom, and if they were considered to be especially
at risk, guards were posted outside their homes during the trial.

THE 'EMERGENCY LAWS'

A series of laws were passed as a result of the terrorist threat. The
Public Order Law (*Reale*) No 152 of 22 May 1975 made no reference
to terrorism but was aimed at reducing criminality generally. However,
1974 had seen two neo-fascist 'massacres' (Brescia in June and the
Italicus train in August) and BR had carried out its first murders,
giving a strong impetus to new legislation to strengthen the arm of
the state.

The law reduced the power of a judge to grant provisional liberty
for specific charges; it extended police powers to stop and detain: police
could henceforth carry out on-the-spot searches of persons or vehicles
in search of arms or explosives; it restricted the punishability of police
in the exercise of their duties; and it forbade the public to take part
in demonstrations wearing helmets or with faces partly or totally hidden, in much the same way as attempts were made to outlaw symbolic
dress in Northern Ireland.

In 1977 Dalla Chiesa was given control of prison security and from
this time on prison regimes for high-risk inmates became extremely
harsh. For example, family visits were restricted to one a month, conversations took place through a glass screen via intercom and prisoners
were kept in total isolation for long periods. A series of projected
prison reforms did not take place, and problems of overcrowding,
drugs and violence grew.

The next law package, the law decree of 21 March 1978, converted into Law 191 of 18 May 1978, came in the aftermath of Aldo Moro's kidnap. This law:

- Extended the crime of kidnap to include the aggravating factor 'with the aim of terrorism and subversion of the democratic order'. This was punishable by up to 30 years' imprisonment, or by a life sentence if the hostage died.
- Reduced penalties for those who turned state's evidence, who ceased to act in a terrorist group and who helped with the release of a kidnap victim.
- Permitted magistrates to order telephone taps verbally, rather than by written instruction.
- Permitted arrested persons to be questioned in the absence of a defence lawyer in cases of 'extreme urgency', though the defence lawyer had to be summoned as soon as possible. Any evidence thus obtained could be used only for investigative purposes and was not valid in court.
- Permitted police to hold a terrorist suspect for up to 24 hours if they were not satisfied that he had given his true identity.
- Created new rules for the formation of juries.
- Permitted the police to ask a magistrate for copies of legal files. The magistrate concerned could, however, refuse on grounds of *segreto istruttorio* (the secrecy of the preliminary investigations).
- Made it obligatory to report to local authorities any rental/sales agreements regarding property. This was based on the correct assumption that BR depended on safe houses. In 1977 three women of the BR Rome column who had no criminal records each paid cash for an apartment in Rome.

The 'Cossiga Law'

Then came the law decree of 15 December 1979, converted into Law 15 of 6 February 1980 – known as the 'Cossiga Law'. This law:

- Introduced two new criminal concepts: 'association with the aim of terrorism and of subversion of the democratic order' and 'attack for subversive or terrorist purposes'. These were 'aggravating factors' which allowed prison sentences to be increased by half. For these charges arrest was obligatory, and if the crime was punishable with more than four years of prison no provisional liberty could be granted. For example, anyone who 'promotes, forms, organizes or directs associations which propose acts of violence with the aim of subversion of the democratic order' could face a prison sentence of seven to 15 years. Anyone 'participating' in such an association could get four to eight years.

- Increased by one third preventive detention for those held by police under these conditions; from this time until November 1984, when the clause was repealed, it was possible to spend up to 12 years in prison before a definitive court verdict was reached.
- Permitted the police to 'detain for reasons of security' and search both a suspect and the suspect's home (this clause was repealed after two years).
- Permitted the police to search individual houses or whole blocks of property without prior authority from a magistrate if someone wanted for terrorist crimes was 'reasonably believed' to be hiding there.
- Permitted the police to detain and question a suspect for up to 48 hours before informing the judiciary.
- Introduced compulsory identification for anyone depositing cash in excess of 20 million lire (approximately £9000).
- Reduced sentences for those collaborating with the authorities who made a decisive contribution to the reconstruction of facts and to the identification of participants. In such cases sentences could be reduced by between a third and a half, with life reduced to between 12 and 20 years (this clause was extended in 1980 to the common crime of kidnap for extortion, to great effect).

Two further laws, one at the end of 1979 and another in early 1980, were designed to facilitate the collection of intelligence on terrorism and to improve co-ordination between the police forces. The former instituted a Parliamentary Commission to investigate the Moro case in particular and terrorism in general; the latter provided for a computerized data bank to be set up within the Interior Ministry.

The penitence law

Law 304 of 29 May 1982 (expired 31 January 1983) is known as the 'penitence law'. This law was applicable to crimes of terrorism and referred to those who made a full confession of all crimes committed and who made an 'active contribution' to the cessation of terrorism.

For the *pentiti*, the law decreed that associative crimes were not punishable; arrest was not necessary for those who voluntarily gave themselves up (this to avoid prison retaliation); life imprisonment was reduced to 10 to 12 years; other sentences were reduced by half, and were not to exceed 10 years. If the contribution of the *pentito* was considered to be 'of exceptional relevance' the sentence could be further reduced by a third. This was applied for example in the case of Patrizio Peci, who was considered to have contributed to the dismantling of an entire terrorist structure. The *pentito* could be given conditional liberty once half the sentence had been served if his behaviour was such that his change of heart was not in doubt.

'Penitent' prisoners were given a differentiated prison regime, partly to protect them but also to help them to stay near their homes and to receive parcels and visits. The category of *pentito* was carefully differentiated from that of the *dissociato* or dissociated terrorist, who confessed personal responsibilities and contributed to the cessation of terrorism (without necessarily implicating others by name). For a *dissociato*, life imprisonment was reduced to between 15 and 21 years and all other crimes by a third, though these were not to exceed 15 years.

Law No 34 of 18 February 1987 – known as the 'dissociation law' – ran for one month only, and was applicable only to crimes committed before 31 December 1983. Dissociation from terrorism was defined as: the definitive abandonment of the terrorist group; admission of activities undertaken; the formal renunciation of the use of violence as a means of political struggle; and behaviour compatible with all of the above. Prison sentences were reduced from life to 30 years for the most serious categories of crime; sentences for crimes of association and various lesser offences were reduced by half; sentences for crimes of bloodshed other than those for which life sentences were imposed were reduced by a quarter and sentences for other crimes by a third; and prisoners serving sentences of less than 10 years were granted conditional liberty.

Public misgivings

Great controversy surrounded the so-called 'emergency laws', in particular those from 1979 onwards. Some feel the laws are not tough enough, others that the laws have overridden the boundaries of democracy and discriminate against those with extreme, though not necessarily terrorist, views. The two 'aggravating factors' introduced in 1979–80 (see the Cossiga Law above) were to a certain extent a 'catch-all' extension to the law and were used to arrest and imprison many youngsters who were on the fringes of terrorist violence – who perhaps had been used to drive cars or hide terrorists, vehicles, documents and cash, but who had little influence over or perhaps even understanding of the consequences of their actions.

Between 1979 and 1982 some 15,000 to 20,000 people were arrested for left-wing terrorist crimes, and about 4,000 were convicted. Five years' incarceration in the special prisons not only toughened and embittered some of them, but the forced contact with hardened bank-robbers, mafiosi and genuine terrorists tended to encourage continuing criminality rather than rehabilitation. As part of their sentences, many were banned for life from taking up work in the public sector and naturally found themselves discriminated against by prospective employers. Consequently, there developed a sizeable category of young, intelligent but 'marginalized' second-class citizens, whose frustrated energies were all too easily channelled against a state which seemed to offer no alternative to menial or black-market labour. Clearly the state had to punish law-breakers, but, through a combination of incomprehension, fear and public pressure to be seen to be acting firmly, a new complex of problems was created. The repercussions are still being felt.

The government has been severely criticized for the clause in the 1980 law which lengthened the maximum period of pre-trial detention by a third. The reason for the clause is obvious – the forcible detention of potentially dangerous members of society – but the measure ignored the real problem which was the excessive length of the judicial process. After 40 years of promising legal reform, Italy introduced a modified criminal trial system in October 1989; this is based on the Anglo-Saxon system, though until then the system operated on the 'Rocco code' of 1930. Trial is always preceded by the *istruttoria*, or preliminary questioning by an examining magistrate who then decides whether the charges justify sending the accused to court.

If the magistrate is convinced that the charges are justified, the defendant then goes through a three-trial system – Court of Assizes, Appeal Court and Cassation Court. Each court can throw out the judgement of the preceding one, causing the whole trial to be rerun. Only when a verdict is passed by the Cassation Court does it become definitive. Sometimes, therefore, terrorist suspects have spent several years in the severest prison conditions before being acquitted. This was what happened to some of the defendants in the notorious '7 April trial' which began in 1979, and did not reach the Cassation Court until October 1988.

The extension of the pre-trial detention period has been generally viewed as a short-sighted measure. If the government had allocated enough funds to make the judiciary more efficient in terms of manpower and resources, if it had reformed the penal code earlier and if it had recognized the inherent dangers of a patently unjust detention system, it would have avoided many problems. The judiciary did not (and still does not) have its own data bank; offices were overcrowded and often primitively equipped; documents were frequently written out laboriously by hand, or typed by the judges themselves. Once again, the Moro kidnap serves as an illuminating example: the magistrate in charge of co-ordinating all the investigations was not relieved of any of his other routine work, he was allocated no extra staff save a typist and, because his office had no telephone, he was obliged to make all his calls from a payphone in the corridor.

Of all the emergency laws, the 1982 'penitence law' has been criticized the most because of the utilitarian way in which it has been exercised: many believe that the morality of justice has been violated. Critics of the law are not confined to a political grouping but extend throughout the spectrum – former President Pertini was perhaps its most public opponent. To become a *pentito* there was no requirement to prove any genuine regret or change of heart, merely to provide information leading, for example, to the arrest of former companions or the discovery of bases. On this basis BR member Patrizio Peci, responsible for eight murders, and PL members Michele Viscardi (eight murders) and Roberto Sandalo (three) walked out of prison free men after a few token years of imprisonment. Meanwhile others such as BR founder member Renato Curcio, arrested in 1974 and guilty of no crime of bloodshed, are still in prison because they have not offered any form of collaboration to the authorities.

The benefits

There is a clear contradiction here, but the 1982 law was certainly of tremendous value. Peci, for example, revealed how the BR command structure worked, and his confessions served not only to capture between 85 and 100 terrorists, but also to clarify the role of those Milanese intellectuals previously thought of as the legal 'cover' for the Red Brigades. Although providing intellectual justification, they were not involved in strategic planning. There is no doubt that many people are alive today thanks to the law, even though proper protection was not afforded to the collaborators and their families, some of whom suffered death as a consequence.

The 'penitence law' has of course expired, but the provisions on collaboration in the 1980 law are applied to organized crime as well as to terrorism, and here the concept of 'penitence' has really fallen into disrepute. The reasons for a Mafioso to become a *pentito* differ radically from those of a young, ideologically naive member of BR.

The dissociation law was less controversial, though many believed that the simple renunciation of violence which the law required was just too easy. In the wording there was no requirement to help to stop terrorism. It was possible for a 'dissociate' BR member to admit to proof of contact in a murder enquiry, but to withhold further information.

Overall, emergency legislation was positive and effective. It enabled the authorities to overcome the internal compartmentalization that characterized the terrorist organization, and to understand its internal structure and mechanism. Terrorist groups were forced to recruit more carefully to avoid infiltration and betrayal, and this acted as a natural brake on the expansion of terrorist activity.

The legislation also encouraged the rehabilitation of many ex-terrorists who could look forward to a gradual return to society. There is a discernible movement from the utilitarian aspect to the rehabilitative aspect. The 1980 law benefited only those who actively collaborated; the 1982 law distinguished between 'penitence' and 'dissociation' but required the *dissociato* to make a positive contribution to the prevention of terrorism without necessarily implicating others; whereas the 1987 law rewarded those who merely renounced terrorism and admitted their own responsibilities.

The extension of pre-trial detention in 1980 was misguided and enabled the politicians to avoid facing up to the real problem. The delay in reforming the penal code, the poor resources at the disposal of the judiciary and the excessive length of the judicial process are essentially political problems for which the state is still paying a price. At least 50 per cent of the terrorist arrests between 1987 and 1989 were of those who had earlier been released from prison at the expiry of the maximum period of pre-trial detention and who preferred to flee the country or go underground rather than stay to await trial. Since then there have been few arrests. In short, some of the terrorist assassinations of the late 1980s might have been avoided under an efficient legal system.

PUBLIC RELATIONS

The government passed no special laws to control the freedom of the press with regard to terrorism. The only relevant restrictive law is that which protects the secrecy of the preliminary interrogation, the law on *segreto istruttorio*. This law has traditionally been applied flexibly, and there is nothing in Italy as restrictive as the concept of *sub judice* as applied in the United Kingdom. The press is free to write and speculate on court trials before they take place, and prosecuting magistrates have given interviews to the press in which they explained their accusations against the defendants in anticipation of the trials. The most serious violation of the *segreto istruttorio* occurred in 1980 when the deputy director of the domestic security service SISDE leaked the confessions of 'repentant' BR member Patrizio Peci to a journalist on the Rome paper *Il Messagero* which published them. Both the SISDE official and the journalist were arrested (to general public protest), but both were awarded light sentences.

The press certainly indulged in considerable speculation about terrorism, and to begin with much of it was ill-informed. A survey of Italian press coverage of political violence between 1977 and 1979 shows that 70 per cent of space was devoted to the simple recounting of facts and only 0.7 per cent to their analysis. During Moro's kidnap, the press published substantial chunks of the nine communications put out by the terrorists, as well as all of Moro's letters that it could get hold of. One paper published a survey of how editors would respond to a 'confession' from Moro to his captors in which he implicated his party in right-wing terrorism: six said they would publish with an accompanying caveat; three said they would not publish; and two said they would decide only after consultation with the others.

During the kidnap of Rome Judge D'Urso in December 1980–January 1981, a member of BR approached two journalists from the weekly magazine *L'Espresso* and offered them the opportunity to put questions to D'Urso's captors. There were two meetings: a series of written questions was provided, and answers were given both to the journalists' questions and to others invented by BR to illustrate its new strategy. In addition, BR provided an extract of its interrogation of D'Urso, and a propaganda document. *L'Espresso* published everything, with the exception of the names of prison and judicial officials mentioned by the prisoner. The journalists informed the judiciary, but only after the meetings had taken place; before the magazine came on the bookstalls, where it immediately sold out, they were arrested on charges

of reticence and favouring terrorism. They were kept in prison for
a month but were acquitted when the case finally came to court, eight
years later.

During the same kidnap, which was carried out largely to focus
attention on conditions in the top security or special prisons, 'action
committees of prisoners accused of terrorism' were formed in Trani
and Palmi special prisons. The BR kidnappers made D'Urso's release
conditional on the dissemination throughout the major organs of the
media of documents prepared by the action committees. If the action
committees pronounced themselves satisfied, D'Urso would be
released.

The lowest point

Parliament did not intervene. A number of newspapers had declared
a voluntary black-out on publishing terrorist pronouncements even
before the ultimatum, but others published anything and everything.
The ultimatum created a furore in the press, intensified by pleas from
D'Urso's wife to the Press Association to print the propaganda. The
Radical Party gave over its television time to the D'Urso family, who
appealed to individual editors to publish. Even D'Urso's 14-year-old
daughter appeared on the programme to read a section from a BR
document calling her father 'a swine who deserves to be condemned'.
Half a dozen papers gave in and printed the documents, which openly
boasted of the intention to requisition the Italian media and gave warning of more terrorist actions to come. Others refused and bitterly criticized their colleagues for publishing, but in particular attacked the
government and the prison service for their weakness in allowing terrorist prisoners to act as if they were judges in a court of law, 'leaving
private citizens to defend democracy'. The government had already
granted another of the terrorists' demands – the closing of the special
prison on the island of Asinara (defending the apparent weakness by
claiming that the prison was already scheduled for closure). So, with
its propaganda well-distributed throughout the press amid enormous
controversy, BR declared itself well satisfied and released D'Urso
unharmed. This was the lowest moment in terms of press–terrorist
relations, and one which naturally laid the media open to most criticism.

The government's weak stance against terrorism on this occasion
was largely conditioned by the battering taken by the judiciary in the
course of the year – five judges had been murdered by terrorists and
the government did not want to be seen to be too obviously obstructing

the liberation of another member of the judiciary kidnapped for carrying out his duties.

The Italian media have exaggerated the spectacular nature of terrorism and have at times been irresponsible in printing without proper reflection and analysis. Shock and disgust attended the attempt by reporters and television cameras to interview, in the hospital where they were taken immediately afterwards, the survivors of the terrorist bomb attack on a train on 23 December 1984.

Members of the security services do not give interviews, but police, carabinieri, politicians and members of the judiciary maintained constant relations with the press and generally made information available when asked. The principal reporters and accredited news agency staff would receive briefings at press conferences, and accredited foreign journalists would be given the same treatment. Government policy on terrorism was covered at great length by the three public television channels (controlled by the Christian Democrats, Socialists and Communists respectively) and the daily papers. Individual party policy had ample airing in the official party newspapers; each party had and has a spokesman responsible for 'problems of the state', whose views would be sought and freely given at a time of terrorist crisis.

ISOLATION OF HARD CORE TERRORISTS

'Disaffected elements' included marginalized youth, students, the unemployed and strongly politicized sectors of factory workers. For the first few years of left-wing terrorism, government, political parties, trade unions and factory management underestimated the degree of general disaffection, particularly in the industrial triangle of Genoa, Milan and Turin. After the first BR kidnaps in 1972–3, the Communist Party (PCI) denounced the crimes and refused to see the terrorists as part of 'the left'. Indeed, there was widespread confusion about the origins of BR. BR actions were tolerated and even gained a certain sympathy in the early years, in spite of repeated condemnations from all but the far left. The PCI and the trade union organizations probably made the most strenuous efforts to distance terrorism from the party and from the working-class image. Between 1969 and 1987 the PCI spent some £9 million on conferences, studies and information programmes against terrorism. The Christian Democrat party (DC) spent £6.67 million and the Socialist Party (PSI) £5.4 million in the same period.

The realization that sectors of Italian society were relatively indifferent to the kneecapping or wounding of industrialists, department heads and politicians hit home in November 1977 after the shooting (and death 13 days later) of the deputy editor of *La Stampa*, Carlo Casalegno. Impromptu interviews at the Fiat factory gates the day after the shooting showed a broad disregard for the fate of the victim, which was assumed to be indicative of the mood of the city of Turin and of the 'working class' as a whole.

> The PCI had to work very hard indeed to get its concept of left-wing culture across, especially in the factories. It's true that many saw BR as 'errant comrades', and the attitude probably lasted until after the Casalegno shooting. The unions organized a demonstration in the centre of Turin and the turnout was very low indeed. We realized then just what a struggle we had on our hands.[5]

Diego Novelli, mayor of Turin from 1975 to 1985, vividly describes the situation:

> After Casalegno's death, the charge of indifference, apathy and distance was immediately levelled at the city, and particularly against the Turinese working classes ... Despite that, I can say that the city did mobilize itself eventually. More than through individuals this came from political groups, trade union organizations and trade associations. After the first warnings, when I realized the dangerous cord that was beginning to tighten around the city and its people, I set in motion a long series of 'private' consultations with the various social, economic and cultural organizations. In all there were 93 meetings, all properly recorded and minuted, involving all the sectors of Turin – the professions, the self-employed, members of different trades or businesses, church dioceses, sports clubs. I even began to use the yellow pages to identify the main organizational centres to whom I wanted to get the same simple message across – 'This is a time when the city must not be allowed to close in on itself; the risk is that everyone thinks only of himself or at most about his own family; at nightfall the city must not become a desert, because then fear will triumph' .... In that kaleidoscope of representation there was everyone from the Jewish community to the local bowls club. Naturally the Turin bourgeoisie was also well represented. No one said no, no one gave up or drew back. It was necessary for everyone to be involved, it was the only way to count, and to influence the dramatic reality that we were all living through.[6]

The level of violence in the huge factories of the industrial triangle was constantly high in the late 1970s: in Fiat alone between 1975 and 1980 there were 58 vehicle arson attacks, 4 murders, 25 woundings, 18 arson attacks on factory premises, 5 attacks on the homes of employees and 26 other acts of violence to people and property. The high degree of violence had resulted from BR infiltration in the early 1970s, when members had influenced the more receptive workers towards adopting a stance of 'progressive militancy'. In the autumn of 1979 Fiat abruptly sacked 61 workers on the grounds of 'indiscipline and violence in the factory'. The unions protested, but agreed to provide legal defence only if the sacked workers signed a declaration deploring the use of violence. In the end some of the workers were taken back; some refused to sign, but eventually only five were actually tried and convicted of terrorist offences.

The role of the Communist Party (PCI)

Debates, meetings and conferences were held endlessly, and factory councils nominated vigilance committees to patrol factory premises at weekends and during holidays. The PCI put out a questionnaire in various districts of Turin (to be answered anonymously) asking what the inhabitants' view of terrorism was, what government or local administration could do to remove any social grievances and if the respondent could provide any information of use to the forces of law and order in fighting terrorism. The PCI was severely criticized for the question relating to the provision of information useful to the police, particularly by the Socialist Party. Overall the response to the questionnaire was low.

During 1976–9, the PCI maintained two successive DC-led governments in office without direct government representation. However, the party did have much more influence on industrial and economic policy during the period of 'national unity' than ever before or since. Industrial management and unions collaborated in restructuring and streamlining production, and this served to isolate the hard core of extremists. But the breakthrough – when industrial militancy really crumbled – can be pinpointed in September 1980 when Fiat announced 14,000 redundancies. The factory was occupied for 35 days, during which the PCI took a firm stand against the management's proposals. Fiat offered to convert the redundancies into 23,000 lay-offs with promises such as 90 per cent of pay for up to three years; PCI leader Berlinguer advised against acceptance but, after an unprecedented

'march of the 40,000' through Turin by employees of all grades demanding the reopening of the factory and the right to work, resistance crumbled and the lay-offs went ahead. There are innumerable accounts from
former terrorists who claim that this was a real turning-point, a moment
when they realized the battle for the souls of the working classes had
been lost, and when the realization of their own defeat began to sink
in.

Social factors

There is no evidence, either statistical or from accounts of former terrorists, to suggest that unemployment in itself was a particularly significant factor in stimulating terrorism, although, certainly after the oil
crisis in 1973 and the inflation that followed, many of the big car
works such as Fiat and Alfa-Romeo cut production drastically; the
redundancies that followed may have contributed to the climate of
indifference towards violence. The terrorist groups read the indifference
and general hostility to factory management as sympathy, even encouragement, for their actions. In fact, on the part of the man in the street
in Italy there has always been some hatred of power and of the ruling
classes, coupled with a feeling of frustration and discontent. In this
case, the man in the street's reaction was that those in authority had
had it coming to them, and he saw with a certain satisfaction that
they were getting their deserts. But this attitude was no more than
a non-committal expression of discontent. It did not amount to support
for BR.
    Social factors such as the neglect of the problems caused by rapid
industrial growth were influential, but were by no means the only cause
of terrorism. As for reforms, after the student rebellion in 1968 the
government passed a law permitting freer access to university – previously only those with a leaving certificate from the 'classical high
schools' could apply for university entry. This contributed to the politi-
cization of the universities, since after the new law in 1969 the universities were flooded with 'worker students', often mature students with
previous work and/or political experience. The social factors which
were very much a stimulus during the early years were much less in
evidence by the mid to late 1970s, as clandestinity increasingly isolated
BR from normal social groups.
    In 1980–1, the Milan 'Walter Alasia' column of BR broke away
and operated autonomously, concentrating specifically on factory/
social/labour issues. This group was about 150-strong and was almost

entirely composed of Milan factory workers. These workers saw themselves as the last line of resistance to factory restructuring and for
a time were encouraged by their fellow-workers, who were well aware
of their political position. But when rivalry with the 'official BR' had
twice pushed them into committing murder as acts of defiance of the
official BR line, they quickly lost what support they had had from
those who imagined they were genuinely fighting for the workers' cause.

There was no attempt by the government or local authorities to
finance or subsidize social services, housing or leisure facilities to try
to stem support for terrorist groups; nor did the government initiate
an education programme to counteract the attraction of political violence. However, local authorities, schools and political groups all organized meetings, debates and conferences. In the universities too there
were many meetings and debates, many of them rowdy and violent,
particularly in 1977, but here again there were no official counter-
terrorism education programmes.

The Church

Until the early 1980s the Church did not really involve itself in terrorist
issues, other than by condemning acts of violence and calling for peace.
Successive Popes have appealed for the release of kidnap victims (not
necessarily terrorist hostages), and in particular Pope Paul VI made
several appeals for the liberation of Aldo Moro. Pope Paul's involvement in the Moro kidnap is still not fully clear – Andreotti admitted
in a recent interview that the Vatican had organized the collection
of a large sum to be offered to BR in exchange for Moro. The Pope
may have done more than has been publicly revealed, in terms of facili-
tating a channel of communication in the Moro kidnap.

Since the early 1980s the Church has become deeply involved in
the rehabilitation of terrorists. Sacrifice and faith in 'the revolution'
are in some respects not so different from a devout religious conviction,
and many ex-terrorists have been converted from one 'religion' to the
other after sustained contacts with prison chaplains. The Church has
shown a remarkable capacity to help and encourage ex-terrorists, not
only in prison but also after their release, and many find their first
work in church-backed organizations. Apart from prison chaplains,
who have had a constant and continuing role in helping terrorists
to work through their guilt and responsibilities towards some hope
for the future, Archbishop Martini of Milan has been the most prominent national church figure in this respect. On one occasion after mak-

ing an open appeal for peace, he was rewarded when a consignment
of arms was deposited at his door.

The Church played a direct role as protagonist during a hunger-strike
by five BR prisoners (who had by then renounced terrorism) in 1983
in protest against the conditions in the special prisons. The chaplain
of Nuoro prison supported the strikers and helped them to have the
reasons for the protest published. In the days before Christmas the
chaplain consulted with his bishop and, with his backing, announced
that as a gesture of support for the hunger-strikers, he would not say
mass in the prison on Christmas Day. The bishop visited the strikers
and, in the presence of the prison director, agreed that prison conditions
had to change. The involvement of the Church on the side of the
prisoners, and their degenerating physical condition – all given much
attention by the national media – had the desired effect and most of
the strikers' demands were met.

FOREIGN LINKS

As far as limiting overseas aid to Italian terrorists is concerned, the
two main problem areas have been border controls and the lack of
legal harmonization among countries of refuge. The freedom with
which citizens from member states of the European Community can
move throughout the continent has facilitated contacts and in some
cases co-operation between national terrorist groups. The contacts
between *Prima Linea* (PL) and BR and the French group Armed Nuclei
for Popular Autonomy (NAPAP) were frequent, as were those between
BR and the German Red Army Faction until 1972, when it seems
that they were broken off for ideological reasons until 1978. The Executive Committee of BR was responsible for maintaining all foreign links
and at least from 1978 onwards had a base in Paris, where contacts
were made with the PLO and/or some of its breakaway groups. In
the early 1970s BR and other left-wing groups seem to have had no
difficulty in buying arms in Switzerland and bringing them into Italy.

Clearly, whatever border checks were in place were not particularly
thorough. Arms could be brought in on foot through the mountainous
territory separating Italy from its northern neighbours and, in any
case, given the constant flow of traffic over the borders by trucks,
private cars and trains, to prevent small quantities of arms entering
would have been an almost impossible task. In particular the border
with Switzerland seems to have presented no problems even for wanted

BR members. Only after 1978 did controls become more rigorous, and transport of arms across European borders became a more risky business. One 'repentant' PL member recalled that the offer of a large consignment of arms from southern France was turned down for that very reason.

In 1978 and again in 1979 consignments of arms reached the Italian left-wing terrorist groups from the Middle East. In both cases they were fetched by boat and brought back to Italy, where they were stored and then distributed. In 1978 a deal was done in Beirut by Maurizio Folini (close to PL) who distributed the arms throughout the Milan far-left groups (though few if any went to BR). In September 1979 BR took delivery of 150 Sterling machine-guns, 5 anti-tank rocket-launchers, 10 ground-to-air missiles, a number of Belgian Fal rifles and large quantities of the appropriate ammunition. According to the Venetian Judge Mastelloni, who has handled all the major illegal arms-trafficking cases in recent years, Yasser Arafat was at the very least 'aware' of the arms that went to BR in September 1979. Mastelloni originally issued an international arrest warrant for Arafat; this was annulled (on technical grounds), but in May 1987 the judge issued him with an 'order to appear in court' and issued arrest warrants for two of Arafat's men for illegal introduction of arms. The charges were subsequently thrown out of court. According to the BR–PLO agreement, part of the consignment was split between ETA and the IRA, part was for BR itself and the rest was for the use of the PLO when it wanted to operate in Europe. In fact, the Palestinians set up two arms deposits, one in Sardinia and the other in the Veneto region, both areas of strategic importance.

In 1979 Daniele Pifano, a member of another left-wing group, *Autonomia Operaia*, was arrested in possession of two Soviet Strela (SA-7) missile-launchers. After his arrest, the PFLP (led by George Habbash) sent a telegram to the court where Pifano's trial was taking place, claiming ownership of the missile-launchers and saying that they were merely 'in transit' through Italy.

Enquiries into exactly what was done to prevent such deals have been complicated by the investigations of Judge Mastelloni. For most of the 1970s the military security service (SISMI) chief in Beirut was Colonel Giovannone who maintained excellent relations with the Palestinians and with Libya. Mastelloni's investigations revealed suspicious conduct on the part of Giovannone, two successive heads of SISMI, the head of counter-espionage and the ex-head of SISDE. Various officials were arrested on charges relating to illegal arms traffic, includ-

ing the co-ordinator of the two security services Walter Pelosi (also
a member of P2), who was formally charged with favouring arms traffic
between BR and the PLO. Giovannone and some of the other suspects
are now dead, and in July 1988 an order from Prime Minister De
Mita called a halt to Mastelloni's investigations into the international
arms traffic and the 'triangulation' procedures by refusing him access
to SISMI documents for the period 1967–81 on the grounds that their
secrecy was 'indispensable to the defence of the delicate positions of
overseas countries'. If this attitude persists, it is unlikely that the truth
about what was done to prevent (or even encourage) overseas aid to
terrorists will be revealed.

International co-operation

For Italy, in spite of various multilateral and bilateral treaties, international co-operation in the arrest and extradition of terrorists seems
to have begun to operate successfully only in the last few years. In
cases such as Nicaragua, where some 30 Italian former left-wing terrorists are believed to have found sanctuary, no extradition treaty exists,
and so it has been a foregone conclusion that Italian terrorists would
not be returned to the Italian authorities.

Between 1980 and 1986 France gave refuge to as many as 150 wanted
left-wing Italian terrorists, as well as to some who left Italy before
arrest warrants were issued for them. Some of the wanted people had
been tried and found guilty of crimes of bloodshed and active participation, and had not merely been found guilty of associative crimes.

> The French authorities used three means of non-extradition. One
> was purely judicial, and alleged the non-coincidence between the
> charge advanced by the requesting country and the legal code of
> the country being requested; in other words, the non-inclusion of
> the crime in the bilateral treaty. The second was based on factual
> circumstances which could not be contested by the requesting auth-
> ority but which were held for various reasons not to be valid –
> for example, that the person concerned was not on French territory,
> was untraceable or that there was no proof of his residing in France.
> The third and simplest way was not to respond to the request at
> all.[7]

Of the 120 extradition requests made by the Italian government to
the French in 1985 none was granted. Spain, the United Kingdom
and Greece have all refused to extradite wanted Italian terrorists on

grounds of discrepancies in legal systems. It is not all one way, of course: Italy itself refused to hand over Abu Abbas, organizer of the *Achille Lauro* hijacking, to the United States. Since 1986, however, France and Spain have made significant contributions to the capture of wanted left-wing terrorists; pooled intelligence work and joint police operations led to the arrest of over 100 BR members in Paris, Barcelona and other European cities in 1987 and 1988.

With the completion of the European internal market in 1992, efforts to harmonize the various European legal systems, legal definitions of concepts such as 'political act', 'terrorist act' and 'probable cause', and differing means of acquiring and evaluating proof in the member states will have to be tackled seriously if effective judicial co-operation is ever to be realized. The situation is of course more complicated when non-allied countries are concerned, and foreign policy and trading interests have far more influence over international co-operation on terrorism than legal concerns. The exquisitely-balanced tightrope of allegiances that determined the outcome of the Achille Lauro affair is a prime example of this. Legal loopholes usually seem to be found when national interests are at stake.

COULD THIS CRISIS HAVE BEEN FORESEEN?

Italy has been unified for only a little over 100 years, and the present democracy is only 40 years old. Italy rushed from being a peasant nation into the forefront of industrial development without the political or institutional maturity to handle the transformation. The fascist legacy, bureaucratic stagnation and political immobility all impeded smooth progress to democracy. The average Italian not only does not identify himself with 'the state', he actually distrusts it. The indifference and suspicion with which Italians traditionally view their ruling classes left space for terrorism to incubate, and the early BR actions were certainly tolerated,though this was partly because no one, not even BR's companions on the extra-parliamentary left, really believed it capable of the violence that was to follow.

Documents from 1974 onwards gave a clear indication of what BR intended by its 'attack on the heart of the state', but, although BR had been wounding, kidnapping and killing for some years before it kidnapped Aldo Moro, there is no doubt that the level of that attack took everyone by surprise. The government and institutions would certainly have been more prepared and therefore better equipped to cope with terrorism if they had read and understood the numerous warning signals. The large, mobile protest movement of 1977 made identification of terrorists much more difficult, particularly as it coincided with a period of crisis which not only affected the Italian left in particular but also led to the redrawing of the entire political map of Italy.

The emergence of terrorism also coincided with the dissolution of many of the extra-parliamentary left groups which had formed around 1968, and therefore with the need for many thousands of 'ex-68ers' to find a new political identity. It coincided with the formidable bursting of feminism onto the political scene – a force that was not only anti-state but also opposed to the traditional dominance of the male working-class 'revolutionary' figure. As one former terrorist explains:

> The left in general (and the New Left was no exception) had paid scant attention to the ideology of women's liberation, consigning the task of resolving all the contradictions and evils generated by the society of profit to the cathartic flames of revolutionary fire. Women on the other hand, especially those within revolutionary groups and therefore the most politicized, rejected the tradition which placed them united to the proletariat in the struggle for communal emancipation with common interests against a common enemy, and claimed the right to their individuality as women with their own needs, ways of life and behaviour which were frequently incompatible with those of men, proletarian or not.[8]

Amid the whirlpool of social change, the expression of new needs and the various forms of anger which had given life to the groups of the 'New Left', it would have been impossible to follow the paths of all these individuals in 1975–6 to see who returned to conventional politics, who gave politics up altogether and who went into terrorism. No single package of reforms (social, political or judicial) would have prevented BR from emerging, or pursuing its course. When BR took the decision to kill Moro it was well aware that even its former companions on the far left were against the killing – a meeting in Rome University three days before Moro's death, attended by all the influential far-left ideologues, had come down in favour of his release – but BR nevertheless went ahead. Greater repression at the beginning might have stopped BR, but such repression might have set in motion an even greater counter-force, an eventuality for which BR was certainly prepared. Italian democracy could have defended itself better against terrorism in the 1970s, but it could not have avoided it altogether.

NOTES

1. For BR, clandestinity was primarily a strategic choice, whereas PL members usually only went underground from necessity.
2. The BR year for kidnapping was in fact 1981 when it took five victims. BR kidnapped once more in 1982 – the last time to date.
3. Interview with Dr Nicolò Amato, 2 December 1989.
4. Ibid.
5. Interview with PCI parliamentary deputy Luciano Violante, February 1988.
6. Diego Novelli and Nicola Tranfaglia, *Vite Sospese* (Garzanti, 1988).
7. Extract from talk given by Dr Rosario Priore at a conference on 'Legal Responses to the Terrorist Threat', Washington DC, 1987.
8. Taken from an appendix by Mario Massardi in Alison Jamieson, *The Heart Attacked* (London: Marion Boyars, 1989) p.262.

6 The Japanese Red Army

ORIGIN OF THE JAPANESE RED ARMY (NIHON SEKIGUN)

Birth and development of *Zengakuren* (General Federation of Japanese Students)

Student councils (*Jichikai*) were formed on university campuses in 1946, soon after the surrender of the Japanese government that had suppressed both labour unions and student activities. Some of the councils were democratic in spirit, while others adopted the Marxist philosophy that had been prohibited since long before the war. The new student movements had the support of the General Headquarters of the Allied Forces (GHQ), though they were led by the Japanese Communist Party.

There was social unrest everywhere in Japan. The economy had been destroyed and the cities were full of soldiers who had returned to their homeland with no hope and no jobs. There was an active possibility of revolution. The realities of international politics, particularly the antagonism between the free economies and the communist bloc, had a profound impact on radical social and student movements.

Plans to stage a general strike on 1 February 1947 were frustrated by the GHQ, which feared any further spur towards a communist revolution, and by the Japanese Communist Party, which judged the situation to be premature for revolution and asked students to return to their campuses for further deliberations. This shift in strategy antagonized students, who felt that the party had betrayed them. They subsequently met to establish their own national organization, *Zengakuren* (the General Federation of Japanese Students), so that they would be able to act in future.

The establishment of the People's Republic of China in 1949 and the outbreak of the Korean War in 1950 persuaded the GHQ to take more direct action, intervening in universities and trying to eliminate the influence of the Communist Party on students. This time the party reacted aggressively, and launched violent activities in the hope of starting a revolution. These activities not only produced new regulations against violence, but also earned the resentment of the public. As a result, the Communist Party, already unpopular because of the

Soviet seizure of Japanese territory, lost all its seats at the general election in 1952.

At that point the Communist Party began to move towards adopting a more modest and popular line. This change of strategy aroused further resentment among students and brought to a head the conflict between the party and *Zengakuren*, which wanted radical activities to continue.

The break with the Communist Party and the upsurge of radicalism

The aggressive activities of *Zengakuren* in the 1950s in connection with the anti-US base movement, the criticism of Stalin that began in 1958 and the movement of Soviet troops into Hungary in 1956 all helped to widen the gap between *Zengakuren* and the Communist Party. Finally, after competing for the leadership of the student movement, they broke apart in 1958.

A faction of students who were thrown out of the Communist Party at that time formed a new organization, *Bunto* (a nickname for *Kyosando*: the Federation of Communists), and this organization took a leading role in the student movement. Its ideological roots were in the reinstated Leninism that asserted the principles of international revolution and radical activities. In 1960, at the time of the renewal and signing of the Japan–US Security Treaty, *Zengakuren* speeded the introduction of a strategy inciting the public to block the treaty. The result was a general strike and violent conflicts with the police.

For a variety of political reasons, student power was divided into a number of factions. At the same time, however, the Japanese economy was heading for rapid growth and the people's interest was shifting from politics to the improvement of the standard of living. Against this background, an upsurge of student feeling in the mid-1960s, brought about by, among other things, the increase in tuition fees at a number of universities, gave impetus to the frustrated student movement and pushed it into radical and violent actions. The situation exploded when the Prime Minister set out to visit a number of Asian countries; on 8 October 1967, students who had gathered at Haneda Airport to hinder the trip were involved with police in a confrontation which caused several casualties. From that time on the student movement became extremely violent, and its members armed themselves with stones and iron bars and wore helmets in readiness for confrontations with the highly specialized police squad (*Kidotai*).

The late 1960s saw the student movement at its height. In addition to making political protests, students occupied the campuses, calling them liberated zones, and tried to enforce changes in the university system. They also fought against what they saw as international injustices such as the Vietnam war and nuclear arms. By this stage their movement was in fact part of a world-wide student movement, and similar radical protest was taking place in universities in many Western countries.

Birth of the Red Army Faction (*Sekigun-Ha*)

The turmoil the students were producing inevitably brought increasing confrontations with the police. In turn, mass arrests and the segregation of radical groups led to the gradual decline of radical student movements, whose members turned their attention towards politicizing indifferent colleagues.

As the police contained the national movements, small radical factions organized an even more aggressive armed combat force to resist police pressure. They took for their model the Red Army of the Bolshevik revolution, appeared publicly as *Sekigun-Ha* in 1969 and soon adopted a strategy of armed conflict, bombing and attacking police stations. However, because the police had tight control over the availability of arms, the students' only weapons were bars, stones and homemade bombs using conventional powder and steel pipe.

Showing neither realism nor any concept of strategy, *Sekigun-Ha* targeted the official residence of the Prime Minister, which they intended to occupy, and at the same time plotted a revolution. Police detected this naïve plan and 54 members of *Sekigun-Ha* faction were arrested as they gathered for training at Daibosatu-Toge in late 1969.

After this major set-back, the remaining members attempted to reorganize the group. However, they disagreed on the policy for promoting revolution. One faction planned to fly to foreign bases to establish international solidarity abroad. The other faction remained in Japan to build up the organization.

The United Red Army (*Rengo Sekigun*) and beyond

After the arrests of late 1969, and in the absence of the activists who had chosen to go abroad, the rank and file who stayed in Japan had to try to reconstruct their organization with limited resources in a climate of public indifference and fading student interest. In 1971, this Red Army conducted a series of attacks on banks and post offices to raise funds. At about the same time, members who had been expelled from the Communist Party formed a radical and militant faction, *Keihin Anpo Kyoto*. These activists – students and workers from the Keihin Industrial Zone – attacked a gun shop and, for the first time, took possession of firearms.

The two groups merged in July 1971, although they had little in common. The Red Army provided money and *Keihin Anpo Kyoto* provided arms, so giving birth to the United Red Army (*Rengo Sekigun*). To strengthen the organization and to train, they resorted to a mountain camp. There, lacking discipline, leadership and a common purpose, they fell to violent quarrelling in the most severe winter conditions. Their fanaticism drove them to purge and lynch the weaker members, 14 of whom died. In 1972 the surviving members were arrested after a televised gun-battle with police at a mountain cottage called Asama-Sanso, where the lynching was revealed. This incident had a profound impact on both the general public and students, whose already fading movement lost all credibility.

In the 1970s as Japan became a more mature and wealthy society, students in general lost interest in political protest and grew more individualistic and pragmatic, focusing primarily on their own material well-being. The student movement lost both resources and energy. Marxism, which had charmed young students in the 1960s, became outmoded and was largely abandoned. Moreover, developments in the communist world, such as the failure of the Cultural Revolution in the Peoples' Republic of China, the massacres in Kampuchea and the Soviet invasion of Afghanistan, increased public disillusionment with Marxism–Leninism.

It is true that, in addition to anarchist groups, the 1970s saw the birth of the East Asia Anti-Japan Armed Front, which conducted a series of bombings; one, at Mitsubishi Heavy Industry in 1974, killed eight people and injured 385. Only a small group, most of them professional activists, continue to agitate (on limited subjects only – such as the protest against Narita Airport) or to attack rival factions; but these activities were of no interest to students and were the last thing to win the applause and sympathy of the public.

The mountain debacle of the United Red Army was the real turning-point in the decline of the Japanese student movement. The public, which had once resented government activities and had sometimes supported the causes of student activists, withdrew its sympathy for radical behaviour. Even among the radical students themselves, the majority understood that there must be limitations on their activities.

Only some professional activists remain in the field. They have been supported by radical labour unions and sympathizers, but once again they have lost strong supporters, this time from the Japanese National Railways because of the privatization of the public sector. These activists are getting older, and it has become very difficult to recruit young successors from Japanese society.

The United Red Army itself is separated from any mass movement and from political parties. The members who are left adhere to old-fashioned ideological dogma and never cease their attacks on other factions. The best-known case is the fight between *Chukaku-Ha* (Core Faction) and *Kakumaru-Ha* (Revolutionary Marxists). This fruitless struggle has caused more than 80 casualties, and strife of this kind further increases the apathy of the average student and the general public. Today basically two factions, *Chukaku-Ha* and *Kakurokyo* (Federation of Revolutionary Unions), are still active in demonstrations and activities, but there are also a number of small independent groups, each with its unique political goal.

Attempts to block radical student movements

In addition to attempts by the police to find and suppress violent student groups, the universities and the Ministry of Education also tried to contain their activities. Most universities reinforced physical barriers, placed guards at entrances, established communication with police stations and restricted the use of university buildings for student activities.

Under guidelines set by the Ministry of Education it became difficult to increase the number of students on the original campuses so a number of universities sold their sites and moved outside Tokyo. These moves limited the possibilities for large student followings, since many students lived far away and isolated from one another and this prevented their gathering at any particular campus.

INTERNATIONAL DEVELOPMENT OF THE RED ARMY FACTION, AND THE BIRTH OF THE JAPANESE RED ARMY

International solidarity

The Red Army was formed at a time when there were many simultaneous radical movements, and consequent disturbances, in other countries. The Black Panthers and the anti-Vietnam war movement in the United States, student protests in France and West Germany, the Palestine issue and Cuba's export of revolution were all live issues. There was widespread sympathy with such international movements, and in addition a number of states such as North Korea, Vietnam and Cuba, as well as the Palestine Liberation Organization, were believed to be supporting radical activists fighting capitalist governments.

The Red Army's fundamental strategy was to take the first step of creating theatre revolutions in various parts of the world, and then to develop and integrate them into a world revolution. Accordingly, when the domestic situation ceased to favour the Red Army, it was easy to accept the solution of moving abroad, settling in one of the (seemingly) friendly nations and taking a step towards a world revolutionary war.

Ironically, it was during this same period that Japanese enterprises started the effective internationalization of their businesses.

The Yodo-Go hijacking and the North Korean Group

After the disaster at Daibosatu-Toge, what was left of the Red Army had to find some kind of international linkage to reinforce its organization and its efforts to achieve international revolution.

In January 1970, 14 executive members of the Red Army, including the future leader Fusako Shigenobu, met to try and reconstruct their group. They formulated a new strategy in which more than 250 members would escape from Japan to set up international support centres from which they might one day return to continue the revolution in their own country. This strategy was called Operation Phoenix in the belief that the Red Army would never die. The key planner was Takamaro Tamiya, one of the founders of the Red Army.

However, in 1970 even going abroad was an enormous and costly task for Japanese students, so hijacking was chosen as the means of escape. And once again, because they acted prematurely, the members committed basic mistakes. The list of potential candidates for the hijacking was far shorter than that detailed in the original plan. In the end, only nine eligible members were chosen, including an 18-year-old male high-school student.

These problems notwithstanding, Takamaro Tamiya and eight colleagues hijacked JAL flight Yodo-Go on 31 March 1970 and forced it to fly to North Korea. Apart from Takamaro Tamiya, the hijackers included Takahiro Konishi, Yoshizo Tanaka, Kimihiro Abe, Kintaro

Yoshida, Takeshi Okamoto (the elder brother of Kozo Okamoto – see **Lod Airport** below), Moriaki Wakabayashi, Shiro Akagi and Yasuhiro Shibata, a high-school student. They had intended to continue their activities in North Korea, but the North Korean government prohibited such operations and forced them to remain there until the late 1980s.

The Japanese Red Army in the Middle East

The police suppressed the Red Army after the Yodo-Go hijacking, and more than 200 members, including Shigenobu herself, had been arrested by July 1970. On her release from jail, Shigenobu judged that the situation in Japan did not favour revolution, and decided to escape abroad. At about the same time the Popular Front for the Liberation of Palestine (PFLP) in Beirut wrote, acknowledging the Red Army. In February 1971 Shigenobu married Tsuyoshi Okudaira (who later died at Lod Airport) and obtained a new registration which enabled her to apply for a passport to travel abroad. During the same month, she and her husband left separately for Beirut.

In addition to Red Army members, a number of student activists, responding to recruitment advertisements in activists' journals, left Japan and gathered in Beirut. At first they called themselves the Arab Red Army (as a branch of the world revolution) and tried to establish themselves as international points of strength under the auspices of the PFLP. In 1974 they changed the name to the Japanese Red Army to create the image of headquarters for the exiled Red Army; at the time no Red Army activities were taking place in Japan. But the name, crowned as it was with the word 'Japanese', was severely criticized by other radical groups in Japan who were at that time protesting against the Japanese government's suppression of other Asians.

Lod Airport

The first operation of the Arab Red Army was the attack at Israel's Lod Airport on 30 May 1972 by three commandos, Tsuyoshi Okudaira, Yasuyuki Yasuda and Kozo Okamoto (the younger brother of Takeshi Okamoto, who flew to North Korea). The purpose and plan of the operation are still unknown today. After, among other ideas, studying the possibility of hijacking an El Al flight, the three arrived via Air France at Lod Airport on 30 May. Taking machine-guns and grenades from suitcases, they fired on guards and passengers (many of them tourists from Puerto Rico) in the concourse and killed 24.

In the subsequent gun-battle Okudaira and Yasuda were either killed or committed suicide. Kozo Okamoto was arrested and the military court sentenced him to life imprisonment. However, he was released in 1985, together with 1150 Palestinian guerrillas, in exchange for three Israeli soldiers held by the PFLP General Command.

The Japanese Red Army after the Lod Airport Massacre

The Arab Red Army accelerated its activities after the Lod Airport massacre. On 21 July 1973, Osamu Maruoka and Palestinian guerrillas hijacked a Japan Airlines flight bound for Tokyo soon after it had taken off from Amsterdam. On 1 February 1974, Haruo Wako and Y. Yamada, with two Palestinian guerrillas, attacked a Shell oil refinery in Singapore and took hostage a number of crew members from a ferry. Simultaneously, five Palestinian guerrillas occupied the Japanese Embassy in Kuwait and demanded that the Japanese government should send them back to South Yemen; the Japanese government sent a special JAL flight, and the guerrillas were returned.

So far the members of the Red Army had referred to themselves as the Arab Red Army, but now they began to call themselves the Japanese Red Army and to act independently of the Palestinian guerrillas. Their first attack in this new guise was in The Hague. To rescue their comrade Yamada, who had been arrested in Paris, members of the Japanese Red Army successfully attacked the French Embassy there.

In 1975, after Junpei Nishikawa and Kazuo Tohira had been arrested in Sweden and sent back to Japan, the Japanese Red Army attacked the US Embassy in Malaysia and took a counsellor hostage. In response to their demands, the Japanese government released Nishikawa and Tohira, together with three other activists who had been held in jail in Japan. These included Kunio Bando (a former Red Army member) and Norio Sasaki (a member of the East Asia Anti-Japan Armed Front, which had conducted a series of bomb attacks against Japanese interests).

On 20 September 1977, in what became known as the Dacca hijack, Maruoka, Wako and Sasaki hijacked a JAL flight bound for Tokyo from Dacca and demanded from the Japanese government a ransom of $6 million plus the release of Okudaira, who had previously been arrested and returned to Japan. They also demanded the release from prison of three other radical activists – Tsutomu Shirosaki (a former Red Army member) and Ayako Daidoji and Yukiko Ekita (both of whom belonged to the East Asia Anti-Japan Armed Front). In addition, and to everyone's surprise, they demanded the release of two ordinary criminals, Hiroshi Sensui and Akira Nihei, who had both committed murder without any political motivation. In the end the Japanese government agreed to all their demands and delivered both the ransom and the prisoners.

This was the last Japanese Red Army operation to be identified and admitted by the members themselves. Since then the Japanese Red Army has not officially committed any acts of terrorism. In the 1980s it began to show more interest in public relations and published a number of declarations in left-wing newspapers. In 1981 it published an English journal, *Solidarity*, and used this to reinforce its efforts to explain itself.

Reaction of the Japanese Government

The Fukuda cabinet at that time gave priority to the lives of the hostages and bowed to nearly all of the terrorists' demands, saying 'Man's life is heavier than the Earth'. However, the easy concessions made by the government, the payment of ransom and the release of criminals caused criticism and great resentment among the Japanese public and the international community, particularly since the payments went to provide resources for the Japanese Red Army.

Some professional observers nevertheless sympathize with the Japanese government, since Japan lacks both the intelligence service and the operational troops to cope with terrorists outside Japan. In 1975 the Japanese police put five members (Shigenobu, Wako, Okudaira, Kazue Yoshimura and Maruoka) on the international wanted list, and asked Interpol to make a search. Today the number of members on the list has grown to 17 (including Kozo Okamoto), and the Japanese Police Agency recently asked a number of countries to find and arrest them.

Fusako Shigenobu

The JRA is unique in the Japanese radical student movement, and within the JRA the character of Shigenobu plays an important part. To understand the behaviour of the JRA, it is necessary to understand her background as well.

Fusako Shigenobu was born in September 1945: that is to say, she was born at the same time as post-war Japan. It is said that she was strongly influenced by her father, who was a radical right-wing nationalist before the war. He was said to have been connected with *Ketsumei-dan* (Blood Brotherhood), a radical nationalist group which assassinated politicians, business tycoons and government officials who were blamed for the economic disaster in the countryside and in farming communities. The group's motivation was at first the sort of grass-roots nationalism that has a long tradition and a fundamental base extending from the right to the left; however, it was soon exploited by military officers in search of power.

Shigenobu's father had been a science teacher. He had brains but, unlike many right-wing activists who became mediators between the government and business (for example Yoshio Kodama, who played a key role in the Lockheed scandal), he stayed poor because he went on trying to turn back the currents of society. He was sympathetic towards the Communist Party, and voted for it at each election.

Shigenobu grew up in the midst of contradictions: high intelligence in a poor family, democratic education in school and traditional education at home (the image of the samurai). After graduating from high school, she got a job with the Kikkoman company and at the same time studied at Meiji University at night, where she was involved in the student movement at its height. She soon resigned from the company and became involved in more radical and violent movements, though at university she continued to attend certain lectures and to dream of becoming a teacher.

The JRA's philosophy and targets

As well as modifying the ideas of Marx and Lenin on world revolution, the JRA's philosophy has some idiosyncratic features that have been developed as a result of Shigenobu's leadership. One of the most striking is a traditional, nationalistic (in a sense, patriotic) element.

Thus, although members support world revolution, their main focus has always been on social conditions in Japan. Moreover, they find positive values in the family (especially the father and mother) when many other radical factions see the family as a repressive institution. In one sense, JRA members are traditional radical activists who place more value on universal justice and self-sacrifice than modern terrorists tend to do; and it is beliefs like these that drive activists to desperate attacks regardless of any danger to their own lives.

The inner motivation of the Japanese Red Army is a mixture of *Yomeigaku* (a radical and revolutionary version of Confucianism) and the samurai spirit, which helped members to survive in the Middle East and to conduct the kamikaze attack at Lod Airport. It is important to note that the JRA is not entirely antagonistic to the Japanese Communist Party, unlike other radical factions of the student movement; indeed, some observers believe it is trying to gain access to the party.

Japanese embassies top the list of the JRA's targets; *Sogo-Shosha* (Japanese general trading companies) which co-operate with the Japanese government come second, followed by Japan Air Lines, which supplements the functions of the Japanese government, and Japanese corporations overseas.

THE SCENE CHANGES

The political environment

The Israeli invasion of Lebanon had a great impact on the JRA which, with its champion the PFLP and other PLO member groups, narrowly escaped from Beirut and had to find a base elsewhere. It soon regrouped in the Bekaa Valley, but there faced a situation which was far more severe than any it had known in the past. Before the members could make plans for world revolution, they had to protect themselves against Israeli troops and ethnic and religious groups such as the Falangists and Shia factions, while at the same time maintaining their political status within the PLO.

Since then the world has been changing, and with it the political stance of the PLO. By contrast with the upsurge of nationalism in the 1970s, the less developed world now tends to look for realistic solutions to its problems; and as Arafat and mainstream PLO factions have sought such solutions instead of practising terrorism, the activity of the JRA has had to be limited. More recently, the possibility of a restructured world order, exemplified by the new detente between the United States and the Soviet Union, is further limiting the space for radical groups, including the JRA.

Resources

The JRA's sources of money, supplies and weapons, as well as recruits, are drying up. The JRA has made every effort to recruit young members (even among high school students), but has had no success. One of the major factors operating against recruitment is no doubt the widespread knowledge of the lynching conducted by the United Red Army in 1972.

In the face of these difficulties the JRA has tried to strengthen its organization by employing a number of experienced radical activists regardless of their ideological backgrounds. At the time of the Dacca hijack described above, the JRA demanded the release of Daidoji and Ekita, who belonged to the East Asia Anti-Japan Armed Front which had been criticizing the JRA for its nationalist posture. The JRA has also gone so far as to recruit members with very little ideological background. Sensui and Nihei, whose release was demanded at the same time as that of Daidoji and Ekita, were no more than criminals who had committed murder, though they had fought against the authorities in jail.

Students today are reluctant to join radical groups such as the JRA which demand severe discipline and training. The younger generation understands the realities of the world better than the members of the JRA do, and does not entertain romantic dreams about the Middle East.

Illusion of world revolution

The Israeli invasion of Lebanon was significant for the JRA in three ways. First, it meant that the JRA lost operational bases. Secondly, it forced the JRA to see that the PLO was not only the organ of a suppressed Palestine but also an army of occupation, suppressing people in Lebanon. Thirdly, Lebanon had become the battlefield for a number of religious factions, engaged in conflicts which Marxist theory could not explain. The JRA found itself having to fight against such factions – a situation which undermined its beliefs in international solidarity and the world struggle for the oppressed and poor.

As a result of these problems and contradictions, apathy has spread even among the original JRA members. In February 1986 Yoshiaki Yamada, who played an important role in a number of operations, suddenly abandoned his post and returned to his native prefecture in Japan to see his parents; he was able to slip in through crowded immigration check-points and customs. In spite of his betrayal, the JRA has neither levied any sanctions nor retaliated against him.

Isolation

One aspect of the JRA's loss of resources is a shortage of funds for international operations. Another is lack of information. Shigenobu and other members do not know the current social situation in Japan and the world, even though they obtain Japanese newspapers, magazines, books and perhaps video cassettes and are familiar with the names and pictures of a great many political and social figures, as well as songs of popular young singers.

What is important is not so much the volume of information as the inability to analyse information realistically. For example, when the exiled activists come across a report that part-time workers are protesting to the government in an effort to improve their working conditions, they deduce that a massive workers' movement against the government and capitalists is emerging. In reality, these part-time workers (most of them housewives) are simply trying to better themselves, and negotiations result in compromise. Many examples in the JRA's propaganda demonstrate its inability to analyse contemporary Japan correctly.

NEW DEVELOPMENTS

Recent activities

After the Dacca hijack in 1977, the JRA seemed to be inactive for nearly a decade. In 1986, however, it resumed the armed struggle. In May of that year, as the economic summit was being held in Tokyo, the Japanese and US embassies in Jakarta were attacked with home-made rockets. A group calling itself 'The Anti-Imperialist International Brigade', believed to be a branch of the JRA, claimed responsibility for the attack, and the fingerprints of Tsutomu Shirosaki (released as a result of the Dacca hijack) were found in the hotel room from which the rockets were launched. During the summit, home-made mortars were launched at the government guest house in Tokyo, though it is not certain whether this attack was linked to the JRA.

In June 1987, during the economic summit in Venice, the British and US embassies in Rome were attacked with bombs and rockets, and according to Italian police, Shirosaki and Okudaira were responsible. The Japanese police became very sensitive to this issue since, in addition to the evidence of increased JRA activity, rumour had it that the JRA were planning to attack the Emperor.

ADF and the Yodo-Go group

In November 1987 one of the leaders of the JRA, Osamu Maruoka, was arrested in Tokyo. An examination of his possessions revealed that an organization called ADF (Anti-War Democratic Front) was being formed in the Philippines and in Japan. In 1988 Sensui, who had been released during the Dacca hijack, was arrested in the Philippines, where he had gone in 1983 after leaving the Middle East. He had set up a base there for the activities of ADF, and had penetrated the local community in the guise of a Japanese businessman. A great deal of evidence uncovered with the arrest of Sensui revealed that other JRA members, such as Tohira Kazuo, Norio Sasaki and Kunio Bando, were carrying out activities in Manila. There was a possibility that some of them had returned to Japan.

To the surprise of the police Yasuhiro Shibata, who as a 16-year-old high school student had been the youngest member of the Yodo-Go hijack group and who was believed to have been kept in Pyongyang, was arrested in May 1988. He had been in Japan since the spring of 1986, working as a part-time volunteer with handicapped people.

In April 1988 Yu Kikumura, who is believed to be a sympathizer or peripheral co-operator with the JRA, was arrested on the New Jersey Turnpike in the United States for carrying explosives. Kikumura was once arrested in the Netherlands for carrying bombs but was soon released.

These arrests showed that JRA members who were reportedly in the Bekaa Valley, and members of the Yodo-Go group who had been restricted to North Korea, were freely travelling the world, visiting Switzerland, Yugoslavia, Thailand, Hong Kong, the Philippines and China, and were in contact with each other. The arrests revealed a common organization, which provided forged passports for the JRA and the Yodo-Go group.

Another revelation for the Japanese police came when the Italian police declared that Okudaira and Shigenobu had been responsible for the bombing of the American Club in Naples in April 1988.

GOVERNMENT RESPONSE

Japan is the only major advanced nation that does not have any established intelligence office or agency to detect international terrorism. However, shortly after the Jakarta incident in 1986, the Japanese government established a new inter-ministry intelligence group composed of representatives from the Prime Minister's Office, the Foreign Ministry, the National Police Agency, the Public Agency, the Public Security Agency and the Defence Agency. These representatives are reported to hold monthly meetings and make recommendations. In 1987 Japan modified its criminal code, making it possible to arrest (in Japan) Japanese terrorists who have committed crimes such as hijackings overseas.

Facing the threat of mounting international terrorism, the National Police Agency requested 5.6 billion yen in the fiscal year 1989 to establish a new office (the International Terrorism Countermeasure Division) within the agency to cope with international terrorism. This new division will have a staff of 32, who will gather information on the activities of international terrorists and co-operate with police investigations in Japan.

7 Some Social and Psychological Aspects of Terrorists and Terrorism

INTRODUCTION

In the preceding chapters we have looked closely at six examples of politically inspired terrorism. It is important to remember that terrorism has not been restricted to any time or place. The factors which in recent decades have made it much more efficient and dangerous are, first, the enhanced facilities available to the terrorist, combined with society's vulnerability to terrorist damage; and second, the enormous impact of the media. Now we consider why people become terrorists in the first place, and what it is that keeps them on that course. Most writers on this subject describe the origins of terrorism in very general terms, rooted in the problems of politics, housing, employment, education, the suppression of minorities and so on, but we believe that there must be something more that turns a man or woman into a terrorist.

For the purposes of this study we define political terrorism as the use of terrorism for political aims by a body other than a state (institutionalized terrorism carried out by states is something else, and not our concern here); and we define a terrorist as someone who is capable of cold-blooded acts of violence against innocent people. It would be an over-simplification to say that all such terrorists are mentally disturbed in the psychiatric sense, but we strongly believe that a thorough study of their psychology and their relationship with society must be made if we are to come to terms with them and what they do.

It is impossible to overlook the facts that, in spite of the offer of generous settlements, hard-line resistance still continues in, for example, the Spanish Basque separatist movement; and that, for some, terrorism seems to have become a way of life – a situation that would be impossible if something in the personalities of those involved did not demand it. Equally, it is widely accepted that every organization that employs violence will generate opportunities for those who are prone to terrorist behaviour as a result of psychopathic tendencies

185

or other character disorders, or perhaps through a combination of personality and societal circumstances of the kind described below. On the other hand, none of this means that the terrorist organization as a whole must necessarily be seen in the same light.

In this chapter, therefore, we are trying to draw a picture of unusual people whose exploits have so far attracted more attention than their personalities. How much weight we give to any one factor in the make-up of a terrorist will depend on character and political, economic, social or cultural circumstances. In so-called 'ideologically motivated' terrorism, the psychological profile of the perpetrator will be more dominant, while the attitude of terrorists in liberation movements is determined more by social, political and economic factors.

The terrorist will always have problems with aggression and power, but only rarely will recognition of such problems lead to his coping with them positively. The fact that he will often go on behaving in a terroristic fashion even when political and social circumstances have changed so as to modify or remove his own original justification for resorting to terrorism shows that the tendency is largely rooted in his personality: it will persist as long as his internal conflicts remain unresolved, or until they are diverted to more productive ends. If his personality is pathological in the medical/psychiatric sense, he may combine the use of power with sadism – though this is not the general rule. In such cases it may be appropriate to try to transform his behaviour into more socially acceptable patterns.

WHAT MAKES A TERRORIST?

Society consists of people – sometimes with common ideals, thoughts, feelings and energies, and sometimes not. Notwithstanding strong feelings of individuality, people depend on each other socially and cannot detach themselves from the broader community. Everyone needs society, though everyone has problems with it, and sometimes these problems take the form of aggression.

Aggression is an intrinsic part of man's personality which drives his self-development; aggressiveness results when aggression becomes directed against other persons or things. In some societies it is possible to externalize aggression, but in First World societies, over-population, urbanization, industrialization and over-regulation make this more difficult. At every stage in the development of every society there will always be people who row against the stream of development, as well as others for whom the rate of development is too slow, and such people will suffer from frustration. When this frustration is internally directed it can cause physical or psychic illness. When it is directed outwards, it can lead to the breaking of social conventions and self-imposed restrictions, through, for example, the abuse of alcohol or other drugs, gambling or sexual licence. In the past, the resulting tensions – primarily caused by society's resistance to irregular behaviour – could be resolved by emigration, pioneering and adventurous activity. Today there are fewer and fewer unexplored frontiers: it is harder than it was to escape.

In every society there is a potential for disagreement and discord, giving rise to the desire to 'do something about it'. In particular, when an intelligent, though perhaps young and inexperienced, person thinks analytically, and starts to promote concepts of change, his ideas and theories may attract others with the same feelings and result in the formation of small groups of dissatisfied people, or nuclei, who then embark on action. This can produce a feeling of satisfaction in the leader, and by reducing his frustration lead to the possibility of his reincorporation in society. But when these ideas or patterns of behaviour do not take root, and especially when they are met with a clear rebuff, the members of a nucleus will find themselves faced with a choice: to continue or to stop. Most will give up, which may result in great frustration and/or physical illness. Some, however, will choose to work even more zealously for reform, and their frustration and disappointment will be translated into still greater efforts and still more zeal. They will make harder and harder demands both on themselves and on others in their efforts to reach their goal.

In this process, personality and environment work together with the centripetal force of isolation. These forces are largely the result of early childhood experience and environmental education. In nearly every terrorist they produce risk-seeking behaviour and, allied to that, tendencies towards suicide (which can often be regarded as introverted homicide), feelings of insecurity, problems with authority (including parental), lack of social integration and, most importantly, a very narcissistic and immature ego-development. When this happens, all the conditions required for the possible final development of a terrorist are present. The presence of any of these groups of factors does not guarantee that a person will become a terrorist, but this combination of personality, environment and development is a common feature of terrorists. This appears most clearly in terrorists of the kind found in the German Red Army Faction; it also appears, with modifications, in terrorists representing sizeable ethnic or nationalist groups.

The influence of peer approval will grow when concepts of glory, honour, friendship and martyr-veneration come into play. So, too, will hatred of the oppressor or supposed oppressor, and feelings of hatred or hostility towards the father can be transposed into hostility towards the authorities or the state. Early childhood experiences can be responsible for leaving an adult with a feeling that society rejects him. This produces depression which, even when it is masked by heroism, grandiloquence and role-playing, can result in risk-taking behaviour which is an expression of suicidal tendencies. The fact that 'traitors' in terrorist groups are hated even more than the targeted enemy can be explained by the shock the terrorist feels when he finds that what he holds most dear can be rejected, undermining the rationale for his own self-created image. This increases insecurity and doubt and brings a disturbing confrontation between his ego-inflation and what lies deepest in himself. One of the reasons why terrorist groups, or the terrorist nuclei within movements, can never be numerous is that the development of an inflated ego-image will not leave room for many rivals.

Among other elements thought to be intrinsic to the mind of the terrorist is an incapacity for enjoyment – the so-called anhedonic personality. A terrorist's relationships with other people are always disturbed, and so he finds it easier to treat his fellow-humans brutally – a prerequisite for terrorism. He will, of course, try to convince himself and others that this is not so, and will argue that he is striving for high ideals. The fear of failing to achieve these ideals makes it difficult for him to establish lasting relationships, and often produces a two-fold reaction. On the conscious level the terrorist will try to overcome this fear by striving to achieve high goals. Subconsciously, he is forced to set his goals too high because his subconsciousness wills him to fail, in this way he reinforces his existing feelings of failure and his negative view of himself. Imprisonment reinforces the depression by imposing further physical and social isolation which, combined with the belief that martyrdom is all that is left to him, leads easily to suicide.

Because of these psychological characteristics the individual terrorist is particularly affected by the break-up or disintegration of the group, and this break-up may well lead to panic reactions and aggressiveness, including murder. It is essential to bear this in mind when considering how to respond, particularly during terrorist actions. On the other hand, the personality characteristics commonly found in terrorists could equally have produced, for example, mountaineers, actors or politicians – all callings in which the ambition to rise above others, literally or figuratively, can be present. It follows that reorientation is possible, and there are many such examples.

As women come more and more to the fore in Western society we can assume that they will play an increased role in terrorism, though their behaviour will be different from that of males. The female does not require the same degree of ego-inflation as the male and, being therefore more rooted in society, she is less vulnerable. She withstands more, copes better with stress and is less inclined to give in. Her attitude during negotiations and subsequent trial and detention demonstrates remarkably more resistance than that normally shown by men.

Bonding and treachery

To help to ensure that a terrorist does not withdraw from the group, he is systematically encouraged to kill, even when the murder has no other purpose. Once he has killed, it will be difficult for him to turn back. Subsequently, in order to maintain this bond, the leader encourages further killings, giving the killer the satisfaction of feeling close to the group. By this time his ego, identity and consciousness are submerged in those of the group.

Those who have given up will be labelled as traitors who abandoned 'the fight', and these concepts of 'traitor' and 'fight', introduced so early in the terrorists' thinking, will run like a thread through their lives. When their frustration is translated into aggressiveness, their appeals to society degenerate into a fight against it. After a latent period – often necessary before widespread reaction and resistance are provoked – society begins to react and to create what will finally be an unbridgeable gap between the two sides. On the one hand are a small group of activists and on the other the great mass of people – by then no longer passive but overtly critical and, finally, as the fight develops into subversion, disgusted. The activists have completed their social alienation. It is not uncommon at this stage for someone to leave the group and so to qualify for the description of Judas, and from then on those who remain lean increasingly and reactively on each other, seeking mutual support, approval and justification. This process protects each member of the group from outside political influence and, as in criminal gangs, it is accompanied by clear and coercive rules which are mercilessly enforced.

Thus, as mutual revulsion develops between society and the group, and as the group consolidates and is bound together by terror, attitudes that began as criticism of society are transformed into a state of homogeneity in which the group members support each other in everything. Collective behaviour is manifested, for example, in the adoption of certain gestures, modes of dress and ways of thinking and speaking, coupled with a narrowing of the group's aspirations and rationale, leading to endless reiteration. Because society is therefore unable to exert any corrective influence, the group tends to overestimate its own power. It imposes increasingly severe limits on members' freedom, and becomes a self-chosen elite. There is no longer any communication with the external world, though members live within it, and the time is ripe for the development of Messianic ideas and behaviour. The group's cohesion is further strengthened, though at a later stage harmony may suffer as a result of differences in members' education, language, social status, nationality and gender, especially when they come to set tactical and strategic goals.

This ever-increasing feeling of not being understood, and the chronic frustration resulting from it, finally develop into severe aggression against society, as the combination of isolation and frustration always does. Increasing isolation also produces a marked reduction in critical faculties, so that even extreme and unreal goals are felt to be attainable.

The crucial move into active terrorism comes with an increase in suspicion, which is typical of disturbed communications. Members of terrorist groups are in a way hard of hearing, in mental, psychic and social terms. Their feeling of not being understood can start to control the functioning of the mind to such a degree that reactions are rooted in something more than extreme suspicion – a sort of paranoia – and while the condition can proceed nearly unnoticed it will narrow thought processes and actions. A further consequence is that there will be a tendency for the egos of individuals in the group and of the group as a whole to be strengthened by the development of a 'superiority complex': an attitude which the outside world sees as arrogance. The 'chosen few' begin to feel that they are greatly superior to their 'stupid', 'ignorant', 'cowardly', 'bourgeois' fellow-men. The ultimate step of disposing of such inferiors, who may impede the pursuit of the group's goals, needs only a certain justification and some organization.

Although we assume that in principle most of the terrorists cannot be said to be ill in a psychiatric sense, this process of isolation and disturbed communications leads them to function close to or within the borders of abnormality. Indeed not a few of them can be regarded as borderline personalities of which the most significant symptom is an ego that is extremely immature, infantile and therefore narcissistic.

Ideology and isolation

However, one last element is needed to make them commit terrorist acts of violence against people. It is ideology – philosophical, political, religious or nationalistic – that provides the guilt-reducing factor. This factor is crucial, because it reduces or eliminates normal inhibitions from practising violence as the terrorist's conscience is taken over and becomes dependent on the collective conscience. The individual has delivered himself to another world of ideas and norms, having been driven there subconsciously by his need to indulge his urge towards aggressiveness.

By contrast with the motivation of, for example, the followers of the late Ayatollah Khomeini, urban terrorist violence is directed not against an external enemy but against the terrorist's own society. In particular, when religion and nationalism are combined, a situation will be created where banners and slogans become the conscience of those who do not have sufficient individuality or whose individuality has been gradually impaired or dissolved.

While all this is happening, and especially in a small group, tensions are ever-present. It is much easier to find oneself carried along in a mass movement based on an ideology, even if it is vague, than to be a member of a small extremist group in which the members depend strongly on each other. Individual differences and antagonisms will gradually emerge. They may be expressed initially as differences in radical or ideological interpretation, but the real differences come to light when theories have to be turned into decision-making. In addition, the poverty of the terrorist's psychic life is often accompanied by an absurd tendency towards austerity and self-punishment, which in some ways resembles the purifying rites associated with certain religions.

The general process of alienation, isolation, deprivation and diminished conscience occurs not only in individuals. It may also occur in small or large groups or even in whole communities and nationalities. The fewer people involved, the stronger the alienation, and it is at its most powerful in the lonely individual, in whom it can produce psychosis and an inability to co-ordinate the functions of the mind. Where there is open dialogue, and therefore an element of correction, the process of alienation will be blocked. But where there is isolation, the process accelerates because group members rely more and more on each other; isolation increases self-preoccupation and this in turn makes possible the development of a Messianic attitude. If this process continues to be reinforced and accelerated, suicide is the logical result, though the response may take the form of extreme risk-taking behaviour.

Ritualization promotes alienation, particularly if compulsive behaviour develops. This applies especially to recent immigrants who have moved from their own culture to an entirely strange environment where climate, social customs, religion and language are different. In this identity-destroying environment they have only their memories, and their children do not even have those. Not only are they frustrated in their collective identity, but they are also involved in what is to them a new and unbearably regularized system. The main symptoms, evident for example among the Moluccans in the Netherlands, are uncertainty and a lack of confidence in themselves and in others – leading to apathy and depression and, particularly for the younger ones, to an aggressive attitude towards society.

The 'fatherless society'

The 'fatherless society' has developed with the loss of authority in the home, at school and at work, and with increasing disregard for institutions. This has meant that hierarchical systems have been replaced by horizontal relationships, which tend to produce conflict between groups rather than between classes. Society has not yet learnt how to handle these properly. The tendency is often accompanied by concern for far-away problems and, in the young particularly, a disposition to cry out in the name of the world, humanity, the deprived and the underprivileged. To cope with these attitudes, technical solutions are now preferred to more thoughtful, human approaches, and quick results are expected in areas where change can be brought about only over time. There has been an enormous growth in the development and use of devices aimed at speeding all kinds of social, individual and physical processes.

The circumstances and processes described above can interact in various ways to develop a terrorist mentality. In spite of the differences between the terrorist groups chosen for study in this book, these patterns will in one way or another be found in all of them.

A Moluccan education, for example, traditionally follows strong authoritarian patterns: the authority of the parents (and leaders and teachers in general) has always been unassailable. Transgressors were punished harshly. Moluccans in the Netherlands lived an extremely isolated life, and perpetuated their own closed group. Unable to communicate with their environment they developed a mythical orientation towards their 'fatherland' in Indonesia. The *adat* – habits that are embedded in culture but unwritten – laid particular social and political stress on the 'we' approach to life. This ethnic group was suddenly transposed to the Dutch polder country, and to a community which functions on a strong 'I-You' basis; in retrospect, it is easy to see that harmony could never have come about. What happened was that the strong and deep frustration the Moluccans felt towards the host (dominant) country imperceptibly developed into isolation and finally slipped into terrorism – in spite of the material and cultural support that demonstrated the goodwill of the Dutch population and authorities. With the best will in the world democratic societies, convinced of their superiority, cannot prescribe materialistic measures for ethnic groups which do not share a common background.

So, and this is crucial to the study – communication was never established even though in practically all material and educational aspects the Moluccan minority lacked for nothing. Communication depends on a thorough understanding of the fundamental differences and it is the immediate neighbourhood, not authorities or politicians, that confers recognition or, in withholding it, sows the seeds of isolation. There are differing views on how far reinforcing the identity of the minority group will help to get it accepted.

An active nationalist group without a fatherland, or no longer having a rapport with its fatherland, presents special difficulties. As time goes on the breach widens, leaving the group isolated and prone to antisocial behaviour, sometimes even to terrorism. This is because an uprooted ethnic group is deprived of the corrective influences of the original society as well as those of the adopted society.

Terrorists from the German Red Army Faction, the Italian Red Brigades and the Japanese Red Army depend on their ideology as a justification for staying together and acting as they do. This justification has no geographical or historical basis and so it lacks roots; cohesion suffers as time goes on, and disintegration begins. Nevertheless the circumstances that gave rise to the terrorism remain, and new groups emerge; this means that anti-terrorist measures alone are not enough because they can never be the basis for permanent success.

THE ROLE OF SOCIETY

The complexity of present-day society, whether democratic or not, produces pressures which can lead to personality limitations and to a failure of the individual to integrate. Many leading thinkers have considered the relationship between aggression and the structure of society – among them Adorno, Habermas, Huizinga, Elias, Kolakowski, Freyer, Luhmann, Rousseau, Kidder and Horkheimer.

An ability to behave aggressively is part of man's natural make-up, but aggression can be non-violent and can be seen symbolically in parades and tournaments. Today there are fewer opportunities than there were for symbolic forms of behaviour. The primary function of aggression is to defend life and possessions especially dear to their owner. The more a man learns about his environment and his peers, the greater is his ability to calculate his chances of realizing his expectations and the chances of his becoming socially isolated are reduced. By contrast, the more an individual finds that he has no control over his environment and that he cannot influence the course of events, the more insecure he becomes and the more critical becomes his need to control his environment. In this situation his only options when he perceives danger are to fight or to flee. In the short term, this results in aggressive behaviour.

So far we have considered what is known as the 'primary' system – man's immediate circumstances. By contrast the 'secondary' system (the terminology is Freyer's) influencing man is made up of institutional forces, for example the state administration. Both systems have factors that promote aggression to a greater or lesser degree. The secondary system has to do with people's functions in society, and so diminishes their attributes within the primary system. In this way, humanity can be devalued, a home can become merely somewhere to live, personality can be submerged in uniformity, and inclinations and abilities can become no more than a 'job'.

The relationship between the two systems has changed over the centuries. As early as 1893 Adolph Wagner predicted the increasing importance of the role of the administration in his *Gesetz der wachsenden Ausdehnung der Staatstätigkeiten* (Law of the Extension of State Interference), and it is perhaps symbolic that in a number of countries (for example, the United States) the state authority is known as the administration: a word which is associated with, and therefore suggests, functions such as management, bookkeeping, and accountancy. The secondary system reveals itself in democratic countries very clearly in the concept of the Welfare State, though in this concept there are many possibilities for feeling defrauded because needs are, in essence, unlimited and insatiable.

In general, growing bureaucracy and computerization have led to civil authorities becoming increasingly abstract, while the erosion of religious frameworks and norms, and the difficulties of life in densely populated countries all combine to promote an inability to express the natural, healthy and productive aggression in man's personality. (As Huizinga has put it: 'Modern man has lost the possibility of creating an intensive meaning of life'. Similarly, Kidder notes that: '"La Machine" [the state] has its own laws and reasons, but these are not intended to take account of individual human beings'.) The resulting psychological condition is regression caused by increasing feelings of powerlessness. Such feelings of insecurity and powerlessness (often not perceived by individuals themselves) can go unnoticed or be misunderstood by the majority of society's decision-makers, and this in turn gives rise to the strong but largely concealed feelings of suppressed aggression, waiting for a 'cause' to bring them to the surface, as discussed above.

Clearly one way to reduce the high level of latent and unperceived aggression in modern Western society would be to reduce the influence of the secondary system rather than – as is sometimes proposed – strengthening it.

Uniquely among animals, man is able to consider the future and to influence his surroundings, and in so doing contribute to the shaping of his own identity. He can also satisfy his need to influence the future, even after death, by writing, building and creating works of art. Even those who are unable to do these things leave possessions or property of some sort and may hand down ideas and spiritual values – threats to which will provoke the same physical reactions as will danger to life, loved ones and valued material possessions. When the secondary system erodes this primary system, the result is uncertainty which itself produces aggression.

Apart from this submergence of one system in another, it is alarming that the state seems to lose contact with social developments, enforcing rules and regulations that ignore social reality. The enforcement of such rules creates an intolerable situation for those for whose benefit the rules were originally drawn up. On the other hand, a shift towards individualism in society implies not only the relaxation of group rules and values but also a lack of feelings of recognition and mutual support, particularly in an unfamiliar neighbourhood. When a primary system develops from inner pressures, social cohesion is largely lost.

From a philosophical point of view there are some striking parallels. During the 1950s, modernism, with its belief in progress, 'the tradition of the new', was extremely influential. Modernism dehumanized society and believed that science would bring man closer to truth; that technology would enhance welfare and well-being; and that freedom, justice and solidarity were attainable ideals. They proved not to be and disillusion set in; ideologies have lost their appeal; norms are suffering from a legitimacy crisis; 'progress' is thwarted by environmental problems; individualism has undermined social cohesion; and social poverty hides behind the restored facades in our cities. We are now living in the era of post-modernism. Lyotard, one of the most interesting thinkers in the post-modernist era, has repeatedly claimed that this modernist way of thinking is to blame for today's level of violence. He even defines 'terror' as the attempt by one person or movement to decide what has to be reality for another. This leads to the important thought that future terrorist groups based on ideology in First-World democracies will peter out quickly.

This accords with our increasing conviction that in Western democracy the most serious and long-lasting of the types of terrorism that have been described is that stemming from ethnic and immigrant problems. Occasional outbursts of ideological terrorism can only be short-lived.

8 Conclusions

The diverse nature of the case studies in the preceding chapters illuminates the truism that terrorist outbreaks, like all individual or collective manifestations, are conditioned by the political culture, history and economic circumstances of the society in which they occur. Nevertheless a surprising number of common factors are discernible. The 'ethnic' (South Tyrol and Canada), the 'post-colonial immigrants' (South Moluccans) and the 'ideological' (Italian Red Brigades, German Red Army Faction and Japanese Red Army) outbreaks were all influenced to a greater or lesser extent by the international climate of national independence, self-determination and 'anti-imperialism'. In some cases, the wave of student radicalism which originated in the United States of America, the activists of the Algerian and Cuban revolutions, particularly Che Guevara, as well as the ideological terrorists of South America, the *Montoneros* of Argentina and the *Tupamaros* of Uruguay were also influential. All these influences were least apparent in the case of the South Tyrol, and most marked in the three 'ideological' instances.

There are other common factors. On all occasions governments were taken by surprise although, where the South Tyrol was concerned, there were clear, prior indications that frustration was likely to turn into violence. Having failed to pre-empt violence by political and/or security means, the authorities fell back on improvisation, frequently chaotic and less than successful at the outset, but they remained secure in the thought that they could manage events. Again in all cases, governments were assisted in their efforts by the fact that, in each of the highly distinctive societies under review, public sympathy and support for the terrorists, whether from ethnic communities or intellectual constituencies, ebbed away rapidly once the terrorists resorted to violence against the person in the form of killing, maiming or hostage-taking. It is this factor, amongst others, which differentiates our case studies from the intractable problems of Northern Ireland and the Spanish Basques in both of which the defeat of terrorism has been hampered by the collusion of important sections of the public, both within and outside the territories, with those who are committed to violent means.

To put the picture into focus, the fatal casualties incurred as a result of the outbreaks recorded in the six cases were very small, below one hundred (compared to three thousand in Northern Ireland between 1969 and 1989), less than the deaths inflicted in one bad afternoon in Beirut of the 1980s, minuscule when related to the casualties in one day of the Sudan Civil War. And yet, at the time, they precipitated reactions in the countries concerned close to national emergencies and were given public prominence out of all proportion to their seriousness in terms of a threat to the security or integrity of states or of the societies as a whole.

There are many questions implicit in these general observations. Could governments have been more perceptive in anticipating terrorism and taken steps to defuse it before it developed? Did governments, albeit taken by surprise, eventually put in place adequate security structures to deal with the movements themselves and with specific incidents? Were appropriate practical measures adopted to allay genuine grievances? To what extent was the unfettered nature of public media in open societies the cause of the over-dramatization of incidents which were intrinsically only marginally threatening to overall security? Were the public media on balance unintentionally helpful to the terrorist, or was publicity a conscious or unconscious aid to the authorities? Can it ever be said that a terrorist problem has been finally liquidated or are there people whose psychological make-up requires recourse to continued violence even when the cause has demonstrably failed or been accommodated? By analysing the individual case studies and by drawing on Chapter 7, we hope to find the answer to at least some of these questions.

THE ETHNIC PROBLEMS

The South Tyrol

By the early 1950s Italian political leaders should have realized that the situation in the South Tyrol was ripe for political violence. The German-speaking Tyrolese had never accepted their incorporation into Italy in 1919, which was enacted without a plebiscite or any other form of consultation of popular opinion. The ruthless Fascist policy of Italianization which was designed to eradicate their language and cultural heritage, combined with the encouragement of Italian settlers (who also took their jobs), further alienated them and reduced the ratio of Austrians to Italians from 86:8 to 64:36. Hopes that the Allies in the Second World War would grant self-determination (i.e. reunification with Austria) when peace came were dashed. The Autonomy Agreement of 1946 negotiated between Italy and Austria was limited, slowly implemented and diluted by the regional amalgamation of the South Tyrol with Trento which left the Italians in the majority. The best jobs, as well as the best economic and social prospects, were dominated by Italians in the cities and towns while the indigenous inhabitants were relegated to rural poverty. In 1954, the single political party, the *Südtiroler Volkspartei* (SVP), addressed a detailed memorandum to the central government setting out their complaints about the fulfilment of the autonomy statute arising out of the autonomy agreement of 1946. Rome ignored the memorandum, the only response to it being an attack on the South Tyrolese in the province's leading Italian newspaper.

Against this background, it is remarkable that the Italian government was taken entirely by surprise when the first bombing attacks against electric pylons and railway lines were launched in 1956. Frustration at the inability to make themselves heard had prompted activists to turn from legitimate protest to violence.

Although the Italian police succeeded in arresting the perpetrators of the first wave of bombings, the problem thereafter developed on lines familiar to any British observer. Austria became involved in support of their kith and kin in what had once been Austria, and the question was internationalized – in 1960 an item was inscribed on the agenda of the UN General Assembly and a pro-Austrian resolution adopted. Extremist splinter groups opposed the relatively moderate policies of the mainstream SVP. In 1959 the South Tyrolese withdrew from the regional government, ending power sharing, and the bombing of installations – monuments and Italian-occupied public housing – was resumed. In 1961 a lucky break enabled the Italian police to arrest virtually all the South Tyrolese leaders involved in the violence. However, this had the effect of transferring leadership to North Tyrolean extremists and cross-border terrorism was initiated, this time directed against people rather than installations. Targets were no longer confined to South Tyrol. Between 1962 and 1967 bombs were also placed in railway stations elsewhere in Northern Italy, members of the security forces were attacked and there were several fatal casualties.

The consequences of these developments were crucial to defusing the problem. The early violence paid off in that, in 1961, the Italian government established a Commission of Nineteen (including seven South Tyrolese) to study the problems of South Tyrol. The report of this Commission led directly to negotiations between the Italian and Austrian governments which culminated in the Package Agreement of 1969 (implemented in stages since 1972) which transformed the question and effectively satisfied the South Tyrolean 'moderates', i.e. those seeking genuine autonomy in their region rather than continuing to press for the politically unrealistic goal of reunion with Austria.

Meanwhile the sympathy of the bulk of the population evaporated as terrorism directed against people replaced attacks on installations. Not only was there no tradition of political violence in the South Tyrol but terrorism was adversely affecting the growing tourist industry, thus threatening incipient prosperity. Moreover, by the mid-1960s, the Austrian government, alarmed at a crisis in Austro-Italian relations, began to clamp down firmly on terrorists operating from the Austrian North Tyrol.

Hence terrorism was scotched if not eliminated. Although the prosperity of the tourism-led South Tyrolean rural economy grew rapidly in the 1970s and 1980s, even creating something of an Italian local backlash, sporadic bombings were resumed in 1986, demonstrating that a few implacable terrorists who will settle for nothing short of reunion with Austria are at large and able to operate.

However, all in all, the handling of the problem of the South Tyrol between the 1950s and the 1970s must be counted as a success story. Luck played its part – the arrest of the bulk of the South Tyrolean violent leadership through information gained from a single informer – and the Italian government, with its chaotic multiplicity of security agencies, never had to face a large-scale insurrection. Blind though Italian politicians were to the mounting frustration in the South Tyrol, once they grasped the nettle, the policies of successive governments were soundly directed down several tracks. These included co-operation with Austria, combined with firmness against indications of Austrian collusion with, or turning a blind eye to, the activities of the terrorists based on Austrian soil; a determination to maintain the integrity of the Italian state including South Tyrol, thus eliminating the uncertainty which breeds extremism; and a willingness to alleviate genuine grievances, thus cutting the ground from under the terrorists and other extremists. But it also has to be said that if the South Tyrolese had not turned to violence (short of terrorism against people), it is unlikely that their voice would have been heard and that they would have secured the mastery in their own house which they enjoy today.

Canada: the Quebec Liberation Front (FLQ)

Although it was not without its tragic consequences, the terrorist campaign of the FLQ had something almost ludicrous about it: the bungling amateurishness of the perpetrators, the failures of intelligence and policing by the authorities and the massive over-estimation of the threat by the Canadian government. It is somewhat symbolic of the affair that one of the few deaths, inflicted when bus company security guards opened fire on a mob in 1969, should have been that of an undercover policeman; also that the terrorists who eventually murdered the Minister of Labour in the Quebec government, Pierre Laporte, should have had to borrow money from their victim in order to buy food. However, at the time, the kidnapping of the British diplomat, James Cross, and the kidnapping and murder of Laporte, together with the prospects of French support, detonated a national emergency of major proportions. Yet, it must be said, the invocation of the War Measures Act inflicted no long-term harm, even though some have argued subsequently that the authorities used a sledge-hammer to crack a nut.

There are superficial similarities between the anxieties which led to political violence and terrorism in Quebec in the 1960s and 1970s and the situation in the South Tyrol. Both movements have deep historical roots. As with the South Tyrol, the linguistic division reflected demographic division, the greater part of the 80 per cent French-speaking majority in Quebec being concentrated in rural areas while the English-speaking minority was located in the urban areas whence they controlled the economy and the better paid-jobs. Fears of linguistic and cultural assimilation loomed large amongst the majority.

The so called 'Quiet Revolution' pursued by the newly elected provincial government of 1960, as a result of which more economic aid and social power was vested in French Canadians, seems to have encouraged separatist sentiment, particularly amongst very young students and labour groups. This was combined with revolutionary anti-capitalism inspired by Algeria and the Cuban Revolution, while General de Gaulle's clarion call of *'Vive le Québec Libre'* during his 1967 visit further energized the separatist cause.

By that time the FLQ had been carrying out sporadic bombings against targets symbolic of the federal government for four years (fatal casualties: one nightwatchman), but widespread arrests (the Canadian government created a Montreal-based Combined Anti-Terrorist Squad [CATS], in 1964) had led to the reorganization of the FLQ into a relatively uncoordinated patchwork of tightly knit cells with no central leadership or structure. By 1968–69 the bombing attacks had taken on more of an anti-capitalist than anti-federal complexion although separation still lay at the heart of the matter. And, in 1970, the failure, as a result of the first past the post system, of the separatist *Parti Québécqois* (PQ) to win seats in the provincial election proportional to their share of the vote, fuelled the anger of the separatist movement, even though, in 1969, the Trudeau government had adopted the Official Languages Act making Canada formally bilingual. Bombings resumed.

In response, the federal government established a Strategic Operations Centre (SOC) in addition to the CATS, as an intelligence-gathering and analysis unit. Hence, by the autumn of 1970, after seven years of the sporadic bombing campaign and widespread thefts of explosives, the government had in place a co-ordinated anti-terrorist structure which had seriously disrupted the FLQ and had gathered a mass of intelligence. This makes the subsequent failure to anticipate the kidnapping, particularly after two bungled attempts against an Israeli and an American diplomat had been exposed for what they were, and the gross over-estimation of the numbers and capabilities of the FLQ, all the more extraordinary. There were also remarkable failures in policework: on occasions the right culprits were identified and the right premises were searched, but those hiding there were not discovered.

The kidnappers of James Cross and Pierre Laporte were quick to make use of the public media to air their demands – for instance the broadcasting of the FLQ manifesto, the release of 'political prisoners', and safe conduct to Algeria or Cuba. By sending copies of their communiqués to several media outlets simultaneously, they were able to outflank the attempts by the authorities to suppress the publicity they were gaining. In this context, there is no doubt that the FLQ terrorists came out on top: the widespread publicity excited public sympathy for their aspirations, created pressure on the authorities to make concessions and gave the impression that the FLQ (active terrorists probably never amounted to more than about 30 people) was a far more widespread organization than it in fact was.

Although the government had a co-ordinated security structure in place, its performance still suffered from jurisdictional disputes and information lacunae between the various agencies. For example, it seems almost unbelievable that the representatives of the Department of External Affairs on the joint action committee set up to deal with the Cross kidnapping did not even know of the existence of the SOC.

This chaotic situation must have contributed to the blunders and intelligence failures.

The decision of the authorities to play the Cross kidnappings in a low key, although frustrated by the terrorists' use of the media, was sensible although they were prepared to make concessions – broadcasting of the FLQ manifesto and safe conduct for the terrorists – in order to achieve Cross's release. In the international atmosphere of 1970 this attitude was not untoward.

However, Canadian domestic policies precipitated a more dramatic reaction to the subsequent – and uncoordinated with the Cross affair – kidnapping of the politician Laporte. The War Measures Act was invoked, thousands of troops were deployed and there were mass arrests of FLQ sympathizers. On the other side there were public demonstrations in support of the FLQ. It was in this atmosphere of national emergency that governmental estimates of 3000 terrorists in Quebec with thousands of weapons were made (even the RCMP estimates were seriously exaggerated).

It was the (probably accidental) killing of Laporte which turned the tide in the government's favour. The group which had been holding him were left in limbo and public opinion swung sharply and massively against the FLQ. The people of Quebec were not prepared to support their aspirations once killing became a means of achieving them. This change of heart gave the authorities a free hand to continue the search for Cross whose release (in return for the safe conduct of his captors to Cuba) was brought about at the beginning of December. Thereafter, with no fear of adverse public reaction, the RCMP was in a position to mount a major and successful campaign of penetration and disruption of the FLQ.

As in the South Tyrol, the fact that the saga of the FLQ between 1963 and 1970 culminated in a success story for the constituted authorities owed more to luck, the essentially pacific nature of the population and the willingness of the government to address French Canadian grievances, than to the skill of the Canadian security forces; much also to the amateurishness of the terrorists. Throughout there were very few fatal casualties, all of them accidental, except the death of the minister which had a decisive effect on public opinion. There was also a growing recognition that both terrorist violence and excessive insistence on the use of the French language was causing a flight of business, particularly American business, from Montreal to Toronto. Moreover there was never any question that the legitimate, democratic road to reform was open; although the violence may have had an accelerating effect on the government, the people of French Canada demonstrably preferred the democratic road and, in essence, got what they wanted within the framework of a united Canada. However, for all their general incompetence, the terrorists succeeded in manipulating the public media to some effect, thus providing an object lesson for future such movements. The question must also be asked: if their kidnap victims had been people of less prominence, would the governmental reaction have been comparable?

A post-colonial problem: South Moluccans in the Netherlands

It would be unjustifiable to criticize the Dutch authorities for failing to anticipate that groups of young people in the Moluccan community would resort to terrorism, or for failing to pre-empt the seven major Mollucan terrorist incidents which erupted between 1970 and 1978, that is, the occupation of the Indonesian Embassy (1970), the attack on the Hague Peace Palace (1974), the two hijackings of trains (1975 and 1977), the hostage-taking at the Indonesian Consulate (1975), at a school (1977) and at a provincial centre (1978).

It is true that this particular episode in the process of Dutch decolonization was bungled. The Moluccan community of about 15,000 people were all soldiers of the Dutch Army of the East Indies who, with their families, had been brought to the Netherlands for demobilization and, as they perceived it, thereafter to fight, presumably with Dutch support, for an independent state in their original homeland. Hence, unlike other immigrants from the former Dutch Empire, they rejected all encouragement to assimilate and their impossible dream assumed the nature of a promised land, binding the community together. The Dutch authorities were originally aware of, and may initially have encouraged, this unrealistic aspiration but had no reason to suppose that it would be sublimated in terrorism, first against Indonesian targets in the Netherlands then against Dutch targets and finally against the traditional leadership of the Moluccan community. Moreover, advance intelligence was virtually impossible to secure from a closely knit and deeply traditional community from an exotic culture. It also emerged that the individual terrorist attacks were spontaneous and virtually unprepared.

The South Moluccan terrorists gained nothing by their actions, neither a change in Dutch–Indonesian relations, any vestige of Dutch support for their aspiration of an independent state, nor even the narrower demands such as the release of prisoners, money and safe-conducts out of the Netherlands. Furthermore, as their actions became more murderous and directly affected a wider spectrum of the population, they forfeited the sympathy and support of their own community and aroused the lasting hostility of the Dutch people as a whole.

However, although fatal casualties over the whole period amounted to only 15, including six terrorists, and although there have been no further incidents since 1978, the Dutch government cannot regard the episode as a complete success story. The Moluccan community still refuses to assimilate or to disperse among the rest of the population. Their morale, particularly that of the younger generation, is low, and drug-taking is widespread. Further outbreaks of terrorism, as spontaneous and unexpected as the first round, cannot be excluded. The community, its isolation compounded by the hostility of the Dutch people, remains an alien element, held together by tradition and by the unrealizable dream of eventual independence.

The Moluccan terrorists failed to achieve their objectives but they briefly succeeded in generating widespread international publicity for their actions. Hijacking trains full of innocent people and holding innocent people hostage were more dramatic and newsworthy events even than the kidnapping of a government minister (as in Canada), far more so than blowing up electric pylons and military lines or attacking members of the security forces (as in the South Tyrol). The performance of the public media throughout highlighted the insoluble dilemma inherent in the handling of a terrorist incident in a free and open society – namely that, as stated in the case study, 'The public's right to know conflicts with the hostages' right to survive and the terrorists desire to succeed'. The conclusion is unavoidable that the widespread publicity was helpful to the terrorist aim of drawing attention to their cause and that the more detail publicized about each incident, the greater the danger to the lives of the victims.

In the 1970s the Netherlands experienced a large number of terrorist incidents apart from those perpetrated by the South Moluccans. Although taken by surprise at the outset, the government fashioned an effective chain of command for dealing with such incidents, coordinating the legal, security, foreign policy and military aspects. While recognizing that all incidents are different and that appropriate structures will vary according to the different constitutions of individual states, the detail on pp. 95–8 provides valuable guidelines for any government in a similar situation. The same is true of the detailed description on pp. 98–101 of the operational organization evolved by the Dutch government to deal with the South Moluccan terrorist incidents.

IDEOLOGICAL TERRORISM

Since the establishment of modern nation states, important differences distinguish violence based on political ideology from violence arising out of 'ethnic' or 'nationalist' causes. Ideologies such as communism, fascism, anarchism or other extreme forms of radicalism tend to ebb and flow with changes in intellectual fashion or economic, social or political circumstances. Ethnic causes are, generally speaking, less mutable and more deeply rooted in history. Such aspirations may lie dormant for long periods but they do not die. It is understandable that, in the 20th century world of strong nation states dependent on the notion of self-determination and independence of peoples, they should have surfaced, when coupled with a strong sense of grievance, across the world.

In this sense, such problems are intrinsically more intractable than ideological movements, especially in cases where, for various reasons, aspirations cannot be even moderately satisfied (as they were in in the South Tyrol and Canada). Ireland, the Spanish Basques and Corsica are outstanding contemporary cases.

The three ideological groups examined in the case studies were all part of the New Left thinking current in the Western world, particularly in the United States, in the 1960s. They were chosen for study because the countermeasures were relatively successful. Although they all emerged in the former Axis powers in the Second World War, they sprang from a movement that was widely present in Europe and the United States and which also existed in Japan. They also possessed the common factor, absent from 'nationalist' movements, that all three regarded 'the system' as being corrupt and designed to maintain in power a capitalistic structure and/or a military–industrial complex which, under the cloak of democratic freedom, was unchangeable except by 'armed struggle'. This exemplified the extreme utopian or anarchist belief that existing political structures had to be dismantled by violence in order to be rebuilt in an ideal form.

The German Red Army Faction (RAF)

Between 1972 and 1990 the RAF carried out 35 terrorist attacks, including bombings, kidnappings, assassinations and assassination attempts in cities and other urban areas including West Berlin. The targets were members of, or institutions identified with, the German 'establishment' or the American military presence in the Federal Republic of Germany or with 'NATO imperialism'. As the case study states, a small hard-core RAF membership still exists and, for the immediate future, Germany will have to live with sporadic attacks. However, the scale of the terrorism has been contained and the danger of escalation has declined as the RAF has become increasingly isolated.

There are some interesting parallels between the actions of, and reactions to the RAF on the one hand and the FLQ and South Moluccans on the other. First, the resort to murder alienated the RAF's constituency of New Left intellectuals and other sympathizers in the same way as killing had alienated the ethnic sympathizers of the FLQ and the South Moluccans. These two are more closely analogous to the RAF than the South Tyrolese as they engaged in kidnapping and hostage-holding; the South Moluccans, like the RAF, also occupied Embassy premises.

However, the German authorities, in spite of adopting a tough 'no concessions' policy in all but one instance, were for recent historical reasons more inhibited than their Dutch and Canadian counterparts. National consciousness of the violent and repressive nature of German fascism sensitized the population to the danger of over-reaction by the state, a factor on which the terrorists played cleverly in their public campaign. Terrorist suicides in prison, force-feeding and surveillance were presented as state counter-violence, creating sympathy for the RAF and hostility towards the authorities. In the early days of bank robberies to fund the movement, the terrorists were pictured as Robin Hood figures being hunted down by the massive resources of the state.

Nevertheless, as kidnappings and murders progressively drained away sympathy for the terrorists, and the RAF was reduced to a hard core of people dedicated to violence, the authorities were able progressively to tighten the law, increase penalties for terrorist offences and spread the intelligence-gathering network more widely. The masses, on whose behalf the middle-class, intellectual RAF was allegedly functioning, did not rally to their cause and, by the 1980s, any danger there might have been of the RAF escalating to a movement commanding support outside its limited membership, had been neutralized. Its isolation was substantially due to the RAF's own uncompromising elitism, which alienated a wide body of political support that found expression in less rigorous forms of terrorism.

The Italian Red Brigades (BR)

Although there was similarity of aim – the violent overthrow of the state and the substitution of a society loosely based on Marxist–Leninist ideas – between the Red Army Faction and the Red Brigades (with its associates the Armed Proletarian Nuclei (NAP) and the Front Line (PL)), the Red Brigades were far more numerous and broadly based and inflicted much greater damage and casualties than any, or indeed all, of the other ideological and ethnic terrorist groups considered in this study. Between 1970 and 1980 BR carried out some 439 attacks involving 55 murders, 68 woundings and 11 kidnappings. In its peak year of 1978, it carried out 106 attacks. The reasons why Italy has suffered so much more seriously than other First World democracies from ideological terrorism can be found in Italian history and the nature of Italian society.

Italy and Germany (up to 1945) had both been unified states for roughly the same period (less than 100 years) but, whereas the Germans (and the Japanese) traditionally respected 'the state', Italians distrusted it. Germans (and Japanese) respected their ruling class; Italians regarded theirs with indifference and suspicion. The transformation from an agricultural into an industrial society had also been particularly abrupt in Italy and thus disruptive of traditional society. During the Second World War there was little or no organized internal resistance to German National Socialism (or Japanese militarism) whereas, from 1943 onwards, after the Allied landings, Italian partisans, particularly communists, were fighting actively against fascism and the German occupation. Moreover, the mass amnesty of fascists in 1946 (many of them returning to state employment including the police and armed forces) plus the emergence in the immediate post-war decades of neo-fascists and other extreme right-wing thuggery and terrorism, created genuine alarm on the left. Furthermore the proportional representation system ensured a succession of centrist governments excluding the extremes of left and right from a share of power.

It is therefore not all that surprising that the extreme left spawned groups devoted to violence (in the partisan tradition); that these groups were not confined to young intellectuals (as in Germany) but included numbers of factory workers; and that, in the beginning, they were even funded by rich left-wing intellectuals including a millionaire publisher. At its strongest, BR had about 500 members, more than the Japanese Red Army, and probably more than the South Tyrolese, FLQ and South Moluccan activists put together. However, to put the whole question of Italian terrorism into proportion it is important to state that casualties inflicted in five bombing incidents by right-wing groups have far outnumbered those sustained as a result of BR terrorism.

In this general climate of political violence, which had continued virtually without a break from the fascist era, it is remarkable that the Italian authorities were taken by surprise by the outbreak of left-wing terrorism. Equally, they appear to have learnt nothing from the South Tyrol experience of the 1950s and 1960s regarding the necessity for a co-ordinated response by the security forces. It was not until 1977 that the Prime Minister was given responsibility for the co-ordination of anti-terrorist programmes; throughout, performance was bedevilled by the multiplicity of competing police forces and intelligence agencies and by the lack of capability to analyse intelligence. Only in 1978 was a Central Office established in the Ministry of the Interior to co-ordinate counter-terrorist operations within the state police. The most effective campaign was conducted not as a result of the creation of fresh structures, but by the autocratic and unorthodox methods of an individual *carabinieri* general. Crisis management was never organized on a continuing basis: even the most serious incidents, such as the kidnapping of Aldo Moro, were dealt with *ad hoc*. Up to the time of writing, such organizations as have been created are inhibited by internal competition and personality clashes.

There is however much on the credit side to balance these operational inadequacies. Terrorism unified the divided Italian political scene: the major political parties stood firmly against it. This was true particularly of the Communist Party which saw left-wing terrorism as a threat to their 'parliamentary road to socialism', a policy they had been pursuing with some success. Their tough stance, seen as a betrayal by the radical left, acted as a stimulus to the terrorists; the formation of a government of national unity, supported by a pact with the Communist Party, was the trigger for the kidnapping (and subsequent murder) of Aldo Moro. By the same token, the judiciary withstood the challenge in spite of kidnappings and assassinations of judges and lawyers. Trials continued to be held in public with maximum security precautions and prosecutors did not seclude themselves from public scrutiny.

Emergency legislation played an important role in reducing the scale of terrorism. Three principal packages of laws were adopted in 1978, 1979 and 1982 bearing on such matters as the time of detention before charge, reduced penalties for state's evidence, extension of preventive detention, and relaxation of constraints on search. The most effective was the 1982 'penitence law' which granted major concessions including substantial reduction of sentences to those who fully confessed to crimes and who made 'an active contribution' to the cessation of terrorism. This law, as well as the 1987 law of 'dissociation' (reduction of sentences for those who abandoned terrorism, admitted activities previously undertaken and formally renounced violence as a means of political struggle) were publicly controversial but there is no question that the information acquired from *pentiti* led to the break-up of major terrorist groups and the saving of many lives. This has to be set against the release from prison as *pentiti* of three multiple murderers, while others who have committed no crime of bloodshed remain incarcerated. The catch-all nature of the 1979 laws, which led to the arrest of between 15,000 and 20,000 people and the conviction of 4,000, also excited criticism. The question remains. Did this measure save lives by disrupting the terrorist cells to a greater extent than it criminalized, through prolonged incarceration, young people who had never ventured beyond the fringes of political violence? The reduction in terrorist murders since 1981 suggests that it did, though the number of embittered young prisoners driven into a Mafia-style life of crime cannot be assessed.

It is also to the credit of Italian governments that no attempt was made to impose special restrictions on the public media which regularly sensationalized terrorist incidents and gave gratuitous publicity to terrorist pronouncements and demands. It is not so easy as it was in the previous cases discussed to categorize exactly the reasons why BR (and other terrorist groups) declined from their peak in the late 1970s to their present status as a virtually neutralized and isolated hard core. Italian governments undertook no social, economic or political reforms designed to appease their less extreme aspirations. Possibly hardened by Mafia violence, people as a whole did not recoil from killings in the same way as they had when, for example, terrorists in Canada, South Tyrol and Germany resorted to such measures. The security authorities responded chaotically at the beginning and never co-ordinated their action. Even the influential Roman Catholic Church focused its attention more on the rehabilitation of former terrorists than on discouraging terrorism itself.

There were, it seems, many contributory causes. The realization that, for all their efforts, the movement was not attracting cumulative momentum and that the structure of the Italian democratic state was holding firm was a major discouragement to the terrorists as the years passed. Improved management–worker relations in the large factories, dating from the 1980s, severed or at least weakened the links between

BR and the industrial proletariat. The attraction world-wide of the philosophies of the New Left declined with the evanescence of the power of the radical student movement in the 1970s and 1980s. Meanwhile the performance of the Italian security system was improving and the new legislation, particularly the laws of penitence and dissociation, had a profound influence. Today, as is the case with the RAF in Germany, further outbreaks of BR violence can be expected but any serious threat, particularly one involving widespread escalation, appears to have evaporated.

The Japanese Red Army (JRA)

The JRA has been in many ways the most bizarre as well as the most ruthlessly lethal of the 'ideological' terrorist groups. Japanese students participated enthusiastically in the world-wide protest outbreak of the 1960s, occupying campuses and protesting against the Vietnam War and nuclear weapons. But the tough response of the police crushed the mass protests, stimulating an extreme minority to resort to armed violence. Many of the activists combined the ideological drive for world revolution with the samurai spirit, and Japanese nationalism with anti-Americanism.

At that point, similarities with the other groups end. The JRA and its Japanese analogues excited no sympathy amongst a population in the process of carrying out an 'economic miracle'. The factions split and murdered each other, thus doing the work of the security forces for them. Many were arrested. Despairing of striking a chord of response in Japan, some hijacked a plane to North Korea, others headed for the Middle East where they teamed up with extremist Palestinian groups in the Lebanon. In 1972 three members of the JRA carried out the movement's bloodiest attack, the machine-gunning of passengers at Lod Airport, killing 24 people. This was the only occasion on which the JRA inflicted fatal casualties.

Between 1973 and 1977 the JRA carried out several terrorist attacks, some in conjunction with Palestinians, including aircraft hijacks, assaults on foreign embassies and hostage-taking. None originated in Japan although two JAL aircraft were hijacked. On all these occasions the Japanese government acceded to the terrorists' demands, whether for ransom payments or for the release of prisoners. This policy, heavily frowned upon by other vulnerable governments, was adopted partly for humanitarian reasons, partly because Japan lacked both the intelligence resources and the special forces to deal with terrorism outside Japan. It has to be said that the policy did not appear to encourage the terrorists to launch further attacks. Although the last incident in 1977 netted the terrorists a ransom of six million dollars and the release of seven prisoners including two murderers with no political motivation, there were no further operations attributable to the JRA until 1986 when Japanese terrorists began to launch home-made rocket attacks against selected targets – the Japanese and American Embassies in Jakarta, and the Tokyo and Venice Economic Summits being examples.

It seems that the JRA is now reduced to a hard core handful who are still able to move freely around the world and who maintain a small base in the Bekaa Valley in Lebanon. Hence there will continue to be a threat of further incidents either on their own behalf or on behalf of other terrorist groups.

It was irresponsible of the Japanese government to fail to establish an intelligence agency to track down their nationals engaged in terrorism outside Japan or to co-ordinate measures with other governments to capture them. It was not until 1986 that the Japanese (mainly out of fear for Japanese industry overseas) created an inter-ministerial intelligence group (following the attack on the Japanese Embassy in Jakarta) and, in 1989, budgetary provision was requested for the creation of a small International Terrorism Countermeasures Division within the national police force: better late than never particularly since hardened Japanese terrorists are still at large.

COMBATING TERRORISM IN THE MODERN STATE

This book has set out to examine those terrorist outbreaks in First World democracies which have been reduced to manageable or even negligible proportions, in other words success stories. However, the analyses in the earlier part of this chapter demonstrate that the phrase 'success stories' is misleading. Even though the terrorist movements in question have lost public support and no longer pose a serious threat, they cannot be said to have disappeared. In every case a hard core has remained, comprising people implacably devoted to violent means. Original grievances may have been satisfied and ideological causes may have withered, but the threat of outrages remains; indeed they may be even more unexpected and brutal than before as the hard-core becomes more tightly knit and impenetrable and its members more exclusively possessed by the psychological characteristics described in Chapter 7. To such people terrorism has become a way of life in a world in which harmless means of sublimating natural aggression are limited, and in which authority has become a remote and mechanistic abstraction no longer commanding the obedience natural in the intimacy of more primitive societies. Radical ideologies can satisfy the terrorist's aggression. It is also regrettably true that the means of terror will always be at hand. The world is awash with weapons and explosives: First World countries are also awash with money which can be extorted or robbed by intelligent, reckless and determined people. In a nutshell, political terrorism is, in absolute terms, almost as ineradicable as violent crime and incorrigible terrorists as persistent as incorrigible criminals.

Rehabilitation of such terrorists to normal participation in society is of course sometimes possible by psychological, psychiatric or educational means as is the case with the common criminal equivalent. There are successful examples from the German RAF and the Italian BR. But these remedies will never be comprehensive and the process of self-recruitment will continue. At this point it is important to make clear that the Group does not take the view that the mentally disturbed as described in chapter 7 are confined to 'terrorists', or indeed that all terrorists possess these tendencies. They can and do exist in regular armed forces, police and security forces in even the most law-abiding of democracies. However, in state organizations they are a liability to be discouraged by careful recruitment and subsequent discipline, whereas in terrorist organizations they are an asset, the characteristics of the spearhead of the group. Moreover this book is concerned with organizations committed to hostility to states for a multiplicity of reasons, not with 'state terrorism' nor with terroristic actions carried out by personnel in the services of democratic governments.

Terrorism is as old as the human race but, for a number of reasons, it has become a pressing problem in the First World in the decades since the end of the Second World War. In the first place, the respectability of opposition to the Axis occupation of Europe between 1940 and 1945 conferred validity on the notion of armed resistance to conquerors and occupiers. The international community itself subsequently enthusiastically subscribed, in the Charter of the United Nations, to the principle of the self-determination of peoples leading to the sovereign independence of states, thus again conferring respectability on resort to 'armed struggle' when other means of achieving the goal had failed. Secondly, the passing of wartime social constraints and disciplines, followed by a widening 'generation gap', fostered student radicalism, which transmuted in a number of cases into ideologically based terrorism. Thirdly, greater ease of travel and communication facilitated the movement of people, thus contributing to what is known as 'imported terrorism', that is, the projection of regional disputes such as the Palestine problem into other countries including First World democracies. Finally, the revolution in information technology disseminated to a far wider Western audience than hitherto vivid details of far-off crises – the Vietnam War and South African oppression of the black majority being leading examples – thus inspiring politically aware Western Europeans and North Americans to take up the cudgels on behalf of causes remote from their own lives and national concerns.

Hence, the authorities in most of the case studies examined above were not only having to confront the indigenous terrorist movements discussed, but were also simultaneously having to cope with outrages committed, for example, by Palestinians, Libyans, Iranians and others in pursuance of disputes which had nothing to do with Germany, Italy or the Netherlands. At the same time, Western democracies not discussed in earlier chapters were in the same boat – Britain wrestling with the Provisional IRA and with various forms of 'imported terrorism' mainly of Middle Eastern origin, France confronted with Corsican terrorism (ethnic), *Action Directe* (ideological) as well as with Palestinian and Iranian inspired bombings, assassinations and hostage-taking. Hijackings of aircraft (a favourite Palestinian and lately Shia' Moslem *modus operandi*) has transcended frontiers and involved nationals of several countries simultaneously. There are many other examples.

Against this background, although the governments concerned were all taken by surprise by the outbreaks of political violence discussed in Chapters 1–6, and had to improvise political and operational reactions, the widespread experience of the past three decades has led to the creation of elaborate international and national structures to combat terrorism. The subject is on the UN Agenda and a number of UN conventions on specific aspects of terrorism (hijacking, hostage-taking etc.) have been adopted. It figures prominently at Seven Nation Economic Summits and at the deliberations of the European Community, and a European Convention on the Suppression of Terrorism was adopted by the Council of Europe in 1977. There is no shortage of international conventions and more limited multilateral instruments. Appropriate national legislation has been adopted in most Western countries exposed to the threat. Special military units have been created as well as counter-terrorist and bomb squads in police forces. Intelligence organizations have been sharpened and, in all senses, national and international co-ordination of anti-terrorist measures has improved. Outside governments, the study of terrorism has become an academic discipline; seminars, books (including this one), and articles have proliferated and private agencies concerned with security against terrorism and other forms of violence have become a new feature of the landscape. In brief, although all the structures fall short of perfection, and although the various international instruments contain loopholes which, for various political reasons, are likely to remain unplugged (limitations on extradition agreements and a definition of terrorism being conspicuous examples), it is improved performance and extension of existing machinery, rather than additional mechanisms, which is now at issue. An opportunity could well exist to extend this co-operation to Eastern Europe and the USSR.

First and foremost is the question of anticipation and pre-emption, the application of the doctrine that prevention is better than cure. It is clear that the Italian government could have anticipated that in the 1950s South Tyrolean frustration, if unallayed, would turn to violence. If they had granted in the 1950s the measures of autonomy which were adopted from 1969 onwards, there might well have been no political violence or terrorism in the South Tyrol. Even in the climate of the time, it is not unreasonable to suggest that Italian governments, had they been more alert and far-seeing, could well have done so without creating unacceptable political problems for themselves.

In the other cases, the answer is less clear cut. However, in all except that of the South Moluccans, there was a period of some years before violence escalated to terrorism directed against people. During this phase of demonstrations, strikes, sit-ins and attacks on installations and buildings, it is surely arguable that the various authorities, had they been as well prepared as they now are, should have been able to identify most of the small number of people who ultimately turned to assassination and kidnapping. It is ironic in this context that the Japanese police, though succeeding in crushing mass student protest, actually encouraged individuals with classical terrorist characteristics to resort to terrorism outside Japan.

Nevertheless, this whole question of pre-emption raises an important issue of principle, regarding the fight against terrorism in a democratic society. In seeking to undermine a democratic system, the terrorist is aiming to provoke over-reaction, leading to undemocratic, police state behaviour on the part of the authorities. In Joseph Conrad's novel, *The Secret Agent*, published in 1907, the Professor 'the perfect anarchist' puts it well:

> To break up the superstition and worship of legality should be our aim. Nothing would please me more than to see the police take to shooting us down in broad daylight with the approval of the public. Half our battle would be won then; the disintegration of the old morality would have set in, in its very temple.

This rubric is relevant to all aspects of counter-terrorism. Totalitarian regimes have long since crossed the dividing line between legitimate intelligence-gathering and mass surveillance, between skilful dispersal of protesting crowds and gratuitous counter-violence, between the apprehension of known terrorists and punitive mass arrests, between interrogation under the law and torture, between appropriate penalties for properly convicted offenders and collective punishment, between attempts to persuade the public media to exercise restraint and state censorship, and so on.

In the cases under study, Japanese police action against student protesters, notwithstanding the violence of the latter, and the mass arrests of BR suspects and associates by the Italian authorities are the most obvious instances which aroused criticism at the time. Subsequently much of the equipment and some of the tactics were more widely introduced elsewhere. On the whole all the governments concerned emerge with merit for withstanding terrorist pressure to cross the invisible frontier.

This is not to downgrade the importance of the right to life and liberty of the victims of terrorism. As already noted, elaborate operational and legislative structures have been created in First World democracies to reduce the dangers. But they must be used with discretion, with the eyes of those involved firmly fixed on the necessity to avoid corruption of the principles which democratic societies exist to defend, and which the terrorists are resolved to destroy. Even if it means a less than ideal response, there must be no resort to illegality – where law has been transgressed, as for instance in Franco's Spain, the authorities have lived to regret it because it compounded the problem.

Did the handling of any of the terrorist outbreaks described above carry lessons for combating the terrorist movements in Western Europe which have yet to be brought under control, namely Northern Ireland and the Spanish Basques? It is tempting to draw parallels with the South Tyrol in these cases – ethnic minorities resorting to armed struggle to free themselves from political, economic and cultural domination by an unsympathetic and alien majority, a friendly community across the border to provide safe haven and the opportunity for cross-border operations. But the analogies with Northern Ireland are incomplete and therefore not generally helpful. Firstly, there was no religious sectarian divide between the South Tyrolese and the Italians nor between the Basques and the Spanish population as there is between the Catholic and Protestant communities in Northern Ireland, and religious differences are known to have been one of the most intractable sources of conflict for millenia. Furthermore, there was no income disparity, as exists in Northern Ireland. Thirdly, there is a long tradition of political violence and armed resistance amounting to myth in Ireland, a feature totally lacking in the South Tyrol. Fourthly, the mix of extreme left-wing political ideology and nationalism in Basque terrorism was absent from the leadership in the South Tyrol including those who took up arms. Fifthly, in spite of attrition and fascism the South Tyrolese and the Basques constitute majorities in their respective sub-regions. This enhances the likelihood of their being satisfied with the principle of local autonomy which makes them democratically masters, albeit within the framework of a larger state, in their own houses. In Northern Ireland the reverse is the case. The community which is dissatisfied with the *status quo* is in a local minority. No amount of proportional representation arising out of devolution would affect the balance favouring the Protestant majority so long as politics are conducted on sectarian, rather than British national, lines.

So far as the Spanish Basque region is concerned, government policy has moved a long way since General Franco's authoritarian intransigence was replaced by democratic structures with political parties representing the various strands of nationalist feeling. As in the South Tyrol region, co-operation between governments exists, in this case between Madrid and Paris. In addition, a remarkable degree of national consensus has been reached in devising and implementing a counter-terrorist strategy, which includes the development of a locally recruited police force accountable to regionally elected democratic authorities. Terrorism persists, but the lessons of European experience, where relevant to Spanish circumstances, have been drawn and contribute to the fundamental guidelines of present policy.

All in all, successive Italian governments had a far less complex and less deeply rooted problem to deal with, additionally facilitated by the general acceptance by the majority of the South Tyrolese of the certainty that their future lay, willy-nilly, within the Italian state;

the international environment of post-1945 Europe removed any doubts there may have been on that score. Union with Austria was not an option. The fight was about degrees of autonomy and the preservation of their own language and culture.

Looking to the future, there is a suggestion in Chapter 7 that new radical terrorist movements based on ideology will either not get started or will peter out quickly, that is to say that the thinking of the New Left which animated the German RAF, the Italian BR and the Japanese Red Army have had their day. This theory is based on the conclusion that world-wide change is taking place away from modernism or utopianism towards individualism. The belief has been exploded that science will reveal Truth, that technology will solve all material problems, and that freedom and justice are attainable through the search, if deemed necessary by violent means, for an ideal political and social system. It is arguable that 'ideological' terrorism was the cutting edge of this utopianism and had been since the days of the nineteenth-century European anarchists. Certainly it is the case that the world, including the Communist and Third Worlds, is rapidly moving away from collectivism with its ideals of universal perfectability towards the free market with its accent on the rights of the individual. If, and it is a very big if, such a climate persists, it is true that movements based on radical political ideologies – either of the left or of the neo-fascist corporatist right – are unlikely to prosper and thus to attract fresh recruits to what could become terrorist organizations. Against this, the emergence in neo-capitalist societies of a permanently deprived and disillusioned underclass is likely to produce forcing beds for violence of which terrorists could easily take advantage.

This does not mean that there will cease to be fashionable causes which will attract people dedicated to violence in complex and multi-faceted modern societies. In Britain and elsewhere the cause of animal liberation has already generated terrorist-type action. This may continue. There are also environmental issues – the use of nuclear energy, of pesticides and herbicides and CFCs being examples – which have fostered strong emotions from protest groups which could breed factions committed to violence. Those people with the psychological characteristics described in Chapter 7 will always find movements in which they can exercise their proclivities for leadership, conspiracy and violence.

However, as previously suggested, such ideologies, like the 'New Left', tend to be transient and to flow and ebb with changes in economic, social and political pre-occupations. It is also suggested in

Chapter 7 that the most serious and long-lasting types of terrorism are those stemming from ethnic and immigrant problems. History certainly validates this theory. Such problems have deep roots: passions and aspirations are transmitted from generation to generation. Neither the hopelessness of a cause nor the passage of time seem to extinguish the flames, while even the partial attainment of a goal fails to satisfy extremists. Illustrations of these three points are the South Moluccan outbreak (the hopeless cause), the revenge killings of Turkish diplomats by Armenian terrorists (the failure of time to heal wounds) and the persistance of ETA terrorism after the autonomy of the Spanish Basque region (the inadequacy of partial fulfilment of aspirations).

By the same token, so long as basic Palestinian aspirations for an independent homeland are frustrated, Palestinian terrorism will continue, directed not only against Israeli targets but against Palestinian moderates in or out of the region and those whom the terrorists regard as Israel's champions, mainly the United States. Even if the Palestinians achieved the limited objective of a mini-state in the West Bank and Gaza Strip embodied in a peace treaty with Israel, the 'all or nothing' groups would be likely to continue the struggle albeit on a reduced scale.

There are other ethnic groups which have so far confined their 'liberation struggles' to their regions, but who might be driven in desperation to international terrorism against the 'champions of their oppressors', today mainly the West but tomorrow the East as well, if their aspirations continue to fail to be satisfied. The Kurds in Iraq and Turkey, the Armenians, and the Sikhs in India are cases in point.

Then there is the terrorism stimulated by the Iranian revolution and other extreme forms of Islamic revivalism. It too has an 'ethnic' or 'national' coloration, being rooted in the history of Iranian and Lebanese Shia' Islam as well as in Moslem support for the Palestinian and other 'anti-imperialist' causes (Libyan terrorism falls into this category). The Western world may well be bedevilled by outrages arising from these phenomena for years to come, certainly until the Iranian revolution has settled down (as all revolutions eventually do) and until some kind of authority is restored in the Lebanon.

As regards immigrant communities in Western democracies, the potential for terrorism has expanded as nationals of Third World countries choose to come to the West in increasing numbers for a variety of reasons, including economic betterment, flight from totalitarian oppression or civil conflict, or as a result of revolutions leaving substantial numbers in danger of their lives in their homelands. Britain for example must by now have well over two million people answering to these descriptions resident in this country, the majority being from the Caribbean and the mainland of the Indian sub-continent but including also significant numbers of Iranian and Iraqi exiles, Sri Lankans, Libyans, Palestinians and others. There are three potential or actual springs of terrorism inherent in these communities.

First, and hitherto most serious, is the use of Western territory as a base for the conduct of international terrorist operations, that is to say operations against innocent nationals of host countries or against international airlines. The destruction of the Pan Am aircraft over Lockerbie in December 1988 and the failed attempt by Hindawi to smuggle a bomb on to an El Al flight from Heathrow in 1987 are lurid examples. Many such outrages have originated in Western Europe in recent years, demonstrating the ease with which terrorists have been able to mingle with blameless compatriots already settled here. In the United Kingdom, the mainland activities of the Provisional IRA have been a classic case in point.

Secondly, there is the danger of domestic disputes in the countries of origin being projected into communities settled into the West. For example the majority of recent Libyan terrorist activities in Europe, assassinations and bombings, have been carried out by supporters of Colonel Qaddafi against the exiled opponents of his regime. Several 'moderate' Palestinians have been gunned down by Palestinian extremists in European cities. Iranians have murdered Iranians, Iraqis have murdered Iraqis and so on. This infection could spread to the larger communities, Sikhs against other Indians, Sri Lankan Tamils against Sinhalese. Citizens of host countries are by no means immune from this type of terrorism, for instance the murder of WPC Yvonne Fletcher outside the Libyan Embassy in London in 1986, caught in the crossfire between anti-Qaddafi protesters and Libyan gunmen inside their Embassy. In the Netherlands-based community from the former Dutch East Indies, the South Moluccan outbreak fell broadly into this category, Dutch civilians being terrorized and dying in a quarrel not of their making.

There is a third, and in the long term, perhaps more difficult problem. Larger numbers in immigrant communities are now of the second, even third generation and have grown up and received their full education in host countries. Some would wish to assimilate with the indigenous culture of a host country, others, particularly in the Moslem communities, are resolved to cherish their social, cultural and religious heritages. All have suffered, or perceive themselves as having suffered, social and economic discrimination and they have been exposed to monstrous racist thuggery. Asians have been the chief victims, including women and children. It is surprising that, so far, inter-racial violence has not escalated to terrorism as the younger generation become readier than the first generation immigrants to retaliate against their tormentors. In Britain the first glimpse of terrorist tactics came in 1988–1989 with the powerful reaction of the Moslem community to the publication of Salman Rushdie's novel *The Satanic Verses*. Bombs in bookshops and other attempts to intimidate publishers and booksellers against producing or stocking the book are a long stride beyond peaceful protest or even less than peaceful protest such as publicly burning copies of the book. In this instance, the international reaction has stoked the fires in the British Moslem community: the late Ayatollah Khomeini's death sentence on Mr Rushdie has unquestionably raised the temperature and encouraged recourse to intemperate statements and illegal actions which are part of, and promoted by, conflict for leadership in the Islamic world between Iranians and Saudis, and the corresponding cliques among London Moslems (as distinct from Moslems in Bradford).

As the twentieth century draws to a close, there is thus no respite in prospect from the threat of terrorism to First World democracies. The remaining indigenous ethnic problems, such as Northern Ireland, seem intractable, and 'imported international terrorism' will persist for so long as there are no peaceful solutions to problems, such as the Middle East crisis, over which Western, or indeed East European, governments, can exercise little control. Some of these problems may take years, even generations, before they are either settled or begin to subside. It also seems that what are described in Chapter 7 as 'secondary systems' – the complex, urbanized, bureaucratic and impersonal nature of the authorities in the First World – tend to encourage those individuals and small groups of psychologically disturbed people in the direction of alienation and rejection and to radical causes on to which they graft the ingredient of terrorism. Such 'systems' and the societies which they represent have also yet to learn how satisfactorily to accommodate immigrant communities. The United States of America, a society almost entirely composed of immigrants, has at least been relatively successful. Even relative success, however, was due to factors that make close comparison with other countries practically impossible. Most immigrants were filled with positive expectations combined with a confidence that their future lay in their own hands in a huge, thinly populated, immensely rich country with enormous potential for expansion. Furthermore, they were imbued with a common desire for freedom and therefore met with no resistance from a previously forged society with different norms, nor were they confined in crowded conditions that could give rise to environmental aggression. Moreover, the introduction of strong and effective race legislation encouraged an upwardly mobile society in which black as well as white citizens could and do aspire to and attain the highest positions, including that of the Chairman of the Joint Chiefs of Staff. However in the United States, too, violence and terrorism are very much on the increase, in part related to the very serious drug problem. There is also concern about the growing disaffection for the present polity displayed by significant sections of the black and Hispanic communities. The Hispanic community in particular has been seeking increased recognition of its separate cultural identity, and a failure to address the social problems which are disproportionately felt by these minorities may well lead to increased violence in the future.

On the credit side, the democracies have learnt much from the experience of the past few decades of which the six case studies above are a part. International and national co-operation and co-ordination in the fight against terrorism have vastly improved, appropriate legislation and operational structures have been created in virtually all states – Japan still lags behind – which should ensure better advance intelligence and more efficient handling of terrorist incidents. All this has been achieved without any serious departures from the norms and principles of democracy and the rule of law, the main targets of the 'ideological' terrorist.

Finally, although this may seem to be a statement of the obvious, it is no use expecting governments alone to anticipate or even to combat indigenous terrorism, and it should not be forgotten that the vigilance of the public plays an important part in scotching the imported variety. Many of the ills lie within society and it would be fanciful, and undemocratic, to expect the authorities to create a permanent organization to monitor all sections of the populace for signs of trouble. The remedies lie in the hands of those who shape all aspects of our destinies, including parents, educators, community leaders, employers, trade unionists and the public media. To borrow a phrase, *la lotta continua* at all levels.

Index